Bertolt Brecht

Cahiers du Cinéma
and Contemporary Film Theory

Studies in Cinema, No. 13

Diane M. Kirkpatrick, Series Editor

Associate Professor, History of Art
The University of Michigan

Other Titles in This Series

Bertolt Brecht

Cahiers du Cinéma
and Contemporary Film Theory

by
George Lellis

UMI RESEARCH PRESS
Ann Arbor, Michigan

Produced and distributed by
UMI Research Press
an imprint of
University Microfilms International
Ann Arbor, Michigan 48106

Library of Congress Cataloging in Publication Data

Lellis, George.
Bertolt Brecht, *Cahiers du cinéma.*

(Studies in Cinema ; no. 13)
Revision of thesis (Ph.D.)–University of Texas at
Austin, 1976.
Bibliography: p.
Includes index.
1. Moving-picture criticism–France. 2. Cahiers du
cinéma. 3. Brecht, Bertolt, 1898-1956–Knowledge–
Performing arts. 4. Brecht, Bertolt, 1898-1956–
Aesthetics. I. Title. II. Series: Studies in cinema ;
no. 13.
PN1995.L424 1982   791.43'05   82-2051
ISBN 0-8357-1300-8   AACR2

To my parents

Contents

Acknowledgments

I am most grateful to Dr. George Wead for his special confidence and guidance in this project, to Dr. Robert Brooks for much practical help in getting it completed, and to Dr. Stanley Donner, Dr. R.J. Policy and Dr. Donald Weismann for their various forms of aid and support. Thanks are due to the following people, each of whom helped give the study shape in its earliest conceptual stages: Jacques Aumont, Pierre Baudry, Michel Ciment, Serge Daney, Bernard Dort, Pascal Kané, Thierry Kuntzel, Michel Marie, and Jean-Paul Török.

I very much appreciate the enthusiasm and encouragement of the UMI Research Press Studies in Cinema Series Editor, Dr. Diane Kirkpatrick.

I would also like to thank Isabelle Potts and Dr. Jean H. Puyet for their help with French translations; Manson Marshall of the Coker College Library for her help with interlibrary loans; Greg Beal, Kim Chalmers, and Dr. Edward Lowry for their help in proofreading; Carolyn Perkins, Nick and Kathleen Barbaro, Jon Shannon, Annette Wint and most especially Karen Kington for their work in the preparation of the manuscript. Drs. Lois and Jerry Gibson also provided valuable help with certain library research.

I would like to acknowledge the cooperation of Martin Weaver of Farrar, Straus & Giroux in getting me permission to quote from John Willet's translations of Brecht's writings.

Above all, thanks go to my wife Susan, who has been an honest, perceptive and loving critic, and to my daughters, Julie and Martine, who were gracious enough to spend hours at the baby sitter's so I could have a quiet house to work in.

Part I

Introduction

1

Introduction

This study will be constructed around a central argument or thesis: that Bertolt Brecht's theories of theater are a primary influence in the development and evolution of the French film magazine *Cahiers du Cinéma*. The Marxist, materialist ideas espoused by the *Cahiers* of the 1970's are at first glance almost diametrically opposed to those of the same magazine at its founding in the early 1950's. While there are many explanations for this change of position, one primary reason is the increasing infiltration of Brechtian theory into the magazine. The goal of this study will be to trace the process of this change, to see the way in which the magazine adopts the principles of the German dramatist, adapts them to the cinema, and in the 1970's expands them to become a part of an elaborate theoretical system aimed at the almost total revision of existing film theory.

The importance of Bertolt Brecht as a major twentieth century dramatist is well known and needs little elaborate justification. Plays such as *The Threepenny Opera, Mother Courage, The Caucasian Chalk Circle,* and *The Resistible Rise of Arturo Ui* may for various reasons be discussed somewhat more than they are performed, but they are generally regarded to be landmark works in the twentieth-century theater. As a dramatic theorist, Brecht remains somewhat less well known. Many of his important writings, for example, are not yet translated into English. Nonetheless, since Brecht was a playwright whose work arose rather directly out of a certain set of theoretical preoccupations, his central concerns, such as the notion of Brechtian "distancing" or the use of types to allow for a didactic message in a play, have become increasingly well known and practiced.

Brecht's activities in film were limited, though certainly important, as were his writings about the medium. In general, it has been only since the 1960's that any systematic effort to apply Brechtian principles to film has even been attempted, but such attempts, by directors like Jean-Luc Godard, Jean-Marie Straub, Nagisa Oshima, Rainer Werner Fassbinder, and others, have met with much critical discussion and interest, and even some popular success. In intellectual circles, at least, Brechtian thought is now a serious part of international filmmaking. In 1975, for example, a symposium on Brecht and the cinema was held as a part of the Edinburgh Film Festival, for which screenings of twelve recent films were assembled.[1] It is too early to tell if this current interest is merely a fashion or will be incorporated into the mainstream of thought about film, but it is certainly significant as a phenomenon of the 1970's and 1980's.

The importance of *Cahiers du Cinéma* in the area of film is unquestionable. In the 1950's and 1960's, *Cahiers* all but single-handedly revised intellectual attitudes toward film with the introduction of the celebrated *auteur* theory of directors, whereby previously overlooked figures in the American cinema, such as Howard Hawks and Alfred Hitchcock, and later others like Otto Preminger, Raoul Walsh, and Jerry Lewis, received serious treatment as film artists. A good part of the magazine's fame may be attributed to the fact that three of its critics, François Truffaut, Claude Chabrol, and Jean-Luc Godard, became highly successful film directors, key names in the French New Wave of the 1960's.

Much of *Cahiers du Cinéma's* reputation now rests on its pre-1968 period. In the early 1970's the magazine experienced a decline in circulation and lost a good part of its popular readership. Truffaut remarked in 1970 that the magazine was now being written for university graduates.[2] The 1976 *International Film Guide* dismissed the magazine with the sentence, "Now not even a pale shadow of its former self, this monthly is bare, polemical and of limited appeal."[3] In its shift to the left, *Cahiers* became a leader in the development of contemporary Marxist thought about film, partially by reflecting changes on the French intellectual scene, partially by having been able to capitalize on its former reputation in advocating and publicizing its new Marxist line. One might well argue that much of the 1970's, politicized writing in English language journals like *Film Quarterly, Screen* or *Jump Cut* was directly influenced by changes in *Cahiers du Cinéma.*[4]

By the late 1970's the magazine was able to shed somewhat its extremist image. The 1982 *International Film Guide* announces that the magazine "has recovered something of its old zest."[5] But *Cahiers du Cinéma* in the early 1980's is hardly the monolithic force it was in the late 1950's or early 1960's.

This book was originally a doctoral dissertation written in 1976. At the time of its writing it was, at least to this author's knowledge, the only work in English—with one exception—covering the magazine's transition into the 1970's. The exception was an article by Maureen Turim in *The Velvet Light Trap.* While Turim's survey is well-considered and comprehensive within its five-page range, she does not particularly emphasize the contribution of Brecht's thought to the magazine, reducing his influence on the magazine more or less to his influence on Jean-Luc Godard.[6]

Since Turim's article and this study's first appearance, several other works have covered similar ground. A major monograph is *Cahiers du Cinéma,* edited by T.L. French, which includes an invaluable interview with Serge Daney, a major writer and editor of *Cahiers du Cinéma* since 1964.[7] Daney's comments provide for a kind of self-evaluation of the magazine during the period 1968 to 1977. A second comprehensive study is Sylvia Harvey's *May '68 and Film Culture.* Harvey provides excellent historical background on the changes in French film production and criticism following the events of May 1968 and also offers an excellent analysis of how Brecht's theories, applied to film, extend those of the Russian formalists of the 1920's.[8] William Guynn's "The Political Program of *Cahiers du Cinéma,* 1969-77" describes the specifically political influences on the magazine, finding its editors inconsistent and vacillating in their attempts to engage in a specifically political critical practice.[9] The serious scholar should consult all of these sources for a balanced view of the post-1968 *Cahiers du Cinéma.*[10]

None of these studies puts particular emphasis on Brecht, and this work in no way seeks to deny other influences and preoccupations that are also important to the *Cahiers* critics. At the same time, a Brechtian approach to thinking about the film medium is evident in *Cahiers du Cinéma* in ways that go far beyond the obvious applications of Godard cited by Turim. Before 1968, the magazine is particularly pluralistic in the range of opinions one may find in it, so that its Brechtian direction is only one of many to be found in the magazine. After 1968, while there would most likely be unanimity on the part of *Cahiers'* authors in their appreciation for the German playwright and theorist, he is only one preoccupation among several primary ones. For both periods, however, this writer will examine not only those writings which refer to Brecht directly but also those that show affinities to his thought, those writings that betray attitudes that are either contemporary to those of Brecht or which are tangential to his positions in a particularly interesting way.

Thus, the method to be employed in this book is one of a selective reading of *Cahiers.* If one selects the right articles, one can trace a direct line between the earliest mentions of Brecht and *Cahiers'* earliest modes of theorization, and some of the most recent articles to appear in the magazine. Several steps may separate the two levels, but the connections do exist and are of significant interest to the scholar of the contemporary film and its accompanying theory.

This study will be divided into three main parts. The first, introductory section, consisting of the first three chapters, will give background material both for Brecht (in a short summary of his theories) and of *Cahiers* (in a discussion of the formalist tradition of the magazine which leads directly into its more politicized tendencies). The second section will treat the influence of Brecht in *Cahiers* before 1968. This will include a short, historical treatment of Brecht in France in general, a discussion of some of the reasons why *Cahiers* becomes interested in Brecht, and a survey of both film criticism from the magazine that would apply directly to Brecht and related writings that suggest patterns of thought close to him. The final section will deal with, successively, *Cahiers'* post-1968 politicization, the magazine's attempts to provide alternative theories of film, and finally significant recent film criticism practiced in the magazine, particularly those articles which come out of the journal's Brecht-influenced line.

Obviously, the principle sources to be used will be the articles in *Cahiers du Cinéma* itself. This study is in no way intended to be a comprehensive treatment of the magazine as a whole; rather, it will seek to trace the development of certain ideas about film and its relationship to its audience, and how these ideas become reflected in the criticism practiced by the magazine. In short, let us propose the following thesis: the ideas first suggested by Brecht about the theater become central concerns of *Cahiers du Cinéma* in its treatment of film, first on a purely aesthetic level, in a concern for the relationship between the film and its audience; second, and subsequently, on a directly political level, in which the Marxist goals of Brecht are adopted by *Cahiers* as an orthodoxy, as a political and aesthetic line to be held as one of the magazine's main premises.

There are eleven chapters to this book. Part I includes the first introductory chapter, a short chapter summarizing the theatrical theories of Brecht (Chapter 2), and a survey of the philosophical principles underlying film criticism in *Cahiers* during its early formalist period (Chapter 3). Part II will treat Brechtian criticism in *Cahiers du Cinéma* before 1968, with one chapter treating certain roots and precedents for such criticism (Chapter 4), another discussing key texts on Brecht and theorizing related to him (Chapter 5). Part III, which takes for its subject *Cahiers* after 1968, is divided into five chapters. The first two are about film theory (Chapter 6 on *Cahiers'* post-1968 politicization; Chapter 7 on the magazine's reworking of conventional film theory). The next two are about practical criticism of particular films as they relate to certain sets of issues (Chapter 8), and in general application of *Cahiers's* new politicized principles (Chapter 9). Chapter 10 discusses how *Cahiers du Cinéma's* extreme positions from the early 1970's soften a bit by the end of the decade, when the magazine seeks a kind of synthesis between its earlier, apolitical formalism and the Brechtian approach. Chapter 11 offers a summary and conclusions.

The greater part of the texts cited in this book were originally published in French. In some cases, published English translations are available and have been used; in most instances, the translations are the author's.

2

A Short Summary of Brecht's Theories

The following chapter is intended to have a purely functional, preliminary purpose of outlining the theories of Bertolt Brecht to establish the main points of interest relevant to the discussion which will follow. It may therefore be skimmed or skipped over by those who have a close familiarity with the subject. The author's intentions in it are not to present any new material but rather simply to review Brecht's primary preoccupations.

These preoccupations fall into three main areas: the notion that the form of a work of art is as important to its political meaning as its content; the use of typed actors and characters to produce a genuinely political discourse; the *Verfremdung* effect. These three areas of interest are surely related, but let us consider them one by one to establish what exactly were the goals of the theorist's writings.

Form and Content

Brecht was a Marxist, and, as such, he believed that historical events were determined by economic and political forces. Thus, he saw the society that produced a theater as affecting directly what that theater would say. In his "A Short Organum for the Theater," Brecht compares ancient Greece to the court of Louis XIV, noting, "The theater was required to deliver different representations of men's life together: not just representations of a different life, but also representations of a different sort." He explains:

> According to the sort of entertainment which was possible and necessary under the given conditions of men's life together the characters had to be given varying proportions, the situations to be constructed according to varying points of view. Stories have to be narrated in various ways, so that these particular Greeks may be able to amuse themselves with the inevitability of divine laws where ignorance never mitigates the punishment; these French with the graceful self-discipline demanded of the great ones of this earth by a courtly code of duty; the Englishmen of the Elizabethan age with the self-awareness of the new individual personality which was then uncontrollably bursting out.[1]

Brecht then discusses the way in which recent science has begun to take control of the lives of men, noting, however, that this process of scientific analysis has not extended to the sphere of human relations on the economic level. For Brecht, as for Marx, history and economic relations between men are a science and subject to the same kinds of laws as the natural sciences. "The reason why the new way of thinking and feeling has not yet penetrated the great mass of men is that the sciences, for all their success in exploiting and dominating nature, have been stopped by the class which they brought to power—the bourgeoisie—from operating in another field where darkness still reigns, namely that of the relations which people have to one another during the exploiting and dominating process."[2] In other words, the power structure of capitalism seeks to avoid thinking of human relationships in a scientific, Marxist way.

It is not surprising, therefore, that the culture produced by this same society should seek to inhibit a recognition of the social forces at work in it. "The theatre as we know it shows the structure of society (represented on the stage) as incapable of being influenced by society (in the auditorium)."[3] The culprit, in Brecht's eyes, is realism, for realism, he argues, tells us nothing about the underlying social relationships between men; to reproduce the externals of men's lives tells us nothing about the processes of cause and effect that make them the way they are. Rather, he argues, realism (and other forms of bourgeois drama) seek to convert the material forces of reality to universals.

Thus, in another essay, Brecht writes:

> The bourgeois theatre emphasized the timelessness of its objects. Its representation of people is bound by the alleged "eternally human." Its story is arranged in such a way as to create "universal" situations that allow Man with a capital M to express himself: man of every period and every colour. All its incidents are just one enormous cue, and this cue is followed by the "eternal" response: the inevitable, usual, natural, purely human response.[4]

This approach rejects the notion, so crucial to Marxist thought, of history as a predictable social process. The treatment of so-called universal truths avoids consideration of specific social forces. At the same time, by presenting a particular instance of a situation, the realistic theater treats that situation as though the circumstances are applicable only to that one particular instance and not to a society in general. In this way, realistic theater promotes the status quo because it allows for generalization only to humanist or spiritualist universalities and not to scientific laws of economic determinism.

Brecht's rejection of realism is, in effect, a rejection of empiricism as well. A good dramatic presentation will show, he asserts, the contradictions of a given situation, a notion which goes back directly to dialectical materialism, and one which is directly antithetical to realism. The realistic drama invariably resolves the contradictions presented within the dramatic framework; in Brechtian thought, the resolution must come from the audience.

Thus, for Brecht, the form of a dramatic work is always political. If the approach of the work is scientific, if it presents social relations in an analytical way, which treats them as historical, as specifically dependent on economic and social circumstances, the work stands a chance at being genuinely revolutionary. If, on the other hand, it seeks to treat universals or presents what are purportedly the externals of reality without any analysis, the work supports an ideology which seeks to keep people mystified about the real nature of their relations with one another. Brecht's primary contribution is that he makes form in a work of art a political issue, because he sees the forms of a work of art as being, like everything else, determined by the society in which they appear.

The Social Gest

To achieve the analytical, politicized, scientific theater that is his goal, Brecht advocates a new use of the actor and a new concept of characterization. He favors the use of what he calls the "social gest," which he defines as "the mimetic and gestural expression of the social relationships prevailing between people of a given period."[5] Brecht goes into more detail in another discussion:

> Not all gests are social gests. The attitude of chasing away a fly is not yet a social gest, though the attitude of chasing away a dog may be one, for instance if it comes to represent a badly dressed man's continual battle against watchdogs. One's efforts to keep one's balance on a slippery surface result in a social gest as soon as falling down would mean "losing face"; in other words, losing one's market value. The gest of working is definitely a social gest, because all human activity directed towards the mastery of nature is a social undertaking, an undertaking between men. On the other hand a gest of pain, as long as it is kept so abstract and generalized that it does not rise above a purely animal category, is not yet a social one. But this is precisely the common tendency of art: to remove the social element in any gest.... The social gest is the gest relevant to society, the gest that allows conclusions to be drawn about the social circumstances.[6]

In other words, Brecht believes that the actor should work from the external signs of social behavior and that these signs should be molded into a discourse about the operations of a society. This notion of the social gest, one may see, offers one attractive point of comparison with film, in that it emphasizes externalized, visual aspects of human behavior. (This is a quality of the film medium very much prized, as we shall see, by *Cahiers'* pre-Brechtian critics, and we may see here an important affinity between the two lines of thought.)

The social gest is not necessarily a realistic one, in the traditional sense; Brecht favored the use of typed characters who could be seen as representative of their particular historical class. As a matter of fact, Brecht has written in favor of the cinema for its use of typed characters:

For theater, the position of the cinema with regard to the characters of the action, for example, is equally interesting. To give life to its characters, who intervene only by virtue of their functions, it uses ready made types, appearing in particular situations and adopting particular attitudes. All characterizing motivation is excluded, the interior life of the characters is never given as the fundamental rationale for the actor, and it is only rarely the principle result: the character is seen from the exterior.[7]

In other words, the intelligent use of types allows for intelligent discourse on a greater level of generality. (Again, there are some striking similarities between this point of view and some auteurist criticism, in which the use of typed characters is seen as being not at all a drawback by the critic.)

The Verfremdung Effect

What is perhaps the central idea in Brecht, however, is his notion of the *Verfremdung* effect, frequently translated in English as the Alienation effect and known, on occasion, as both the V-effect and the A-effect. By this, Brecht means that the playwright and stage director must make the event strange, must wrench it out of a credible, naturalistic context and produce an effect of heightened theatricality whereby the audience remains constantly aware of the theatrical illusions being presented before it. The purpose of this is, for Brecht, to produce observation and criticism of the social processes that the audience might take for granted. Brecht links this to a scientific approach:

Characters and incidents from ordinary life, from our immediate surroundings, being familiar, strike us as more or less natural. Alienating them helps to make them seem remarkable to us. Science has carefully developed a technique of getting irritated with the everyday, "self-evident," universally accepted occurrence, and there is no reason why this infinitely useful attitude should not be taken over by art.[8]

The techniques that Brecht advocated were many. The actor, he thought, should not attempt to identify with the character he plays but should always remain present as an actor, both demonstrating and commenting on that character's actions. "In this way his performance becomes a discussion (about social conditions) with the audience he is addressing. He prompts the spectator to justify or abolish these conditions according to what class he belongs to."[9] Other methods promoted by the German theorist to produce this effect are the use of placards and verbal headings to announce the purpose of a given scene, the use of music in contrast to the text, as commentary on it rather than supplement to it, or the use of non-naturalistic, geometric groupings of actors on stage.

The purpose of alienation effects in the theater is, to Brecht, to struggle against the passivity of the spectator. In the "epic" theater, which Brecht opposes to the older "dramatic" forms, "The spectator was no longer in any way allowed to submit to an experience uncritically (and without practical consequences) by means of simple empathy with the characters in a play."[10] Brecht sums up the change in the role of the audience:

> The dramatic theatre's spectator says: Yes, I have felt like that too—Just like me—It's only natural—It'll never change—The sufferings of this man appall me, because they are inescapable—That's great art; it all seems the most obvious thing in the world—I weep when they weep, I laugh when they laugh.
> The epic theatre's spectator says: I'd never have thought it—That's not the way—That's extraordinary, hardly believable—It's got to stop—The sufferings of this man appall me, because they are unnecessary—That's great art: nothing obvious in it—I laugh when they weep, I weep when they laugh.[11]

This notion can be applied to film as well; it implies that it is necessary for a change of relationship between the audience and the work of art. The necessity for the movie to move the audience emotionally in an empathic relationship with the characters is secondary to the rationality and intellectual quality of the discourse presented by it. Brecht's theater aims at developing perceptions and intellectual understanding more than feelings and emotions for their own sake.

There are two texts by Brecht which are specifically and particularly important in connection with *Cahiers du Cinéma.* The first is the essay produced following Brecht's loss of the lawsuit he had over the film version of *The Threepenny Opera,* which he felt the producers had spoiled in their adaptation; they ignored the fact that they had allowed Brecht approval of the script in his contract. Much of the essay, sometimes known as "The Threepenny Lawsuit," deals with Brecht's thoughts about the way in which the courts of a capitalist society serve to protect the existing economic system and not the rights of the individual. Yet there are several sections of the article which are particularly relevant to later *Cahiers* theory. The first version of the text to appear in French was in *Cahiers'* special Brecht issue, in December of 1960,[12] and it is additionally important because it is one of the few texts in which Brecht discusses film at any great length. Brecht divides his essay into what he calls thirteen "bourgeois propositions." Let us consider, for our purposes here, only four of them:

1. "The cinema cannot do without art." Brecht sees the need for "art" in the cinema as questionable and the use of "art" as a smokescreen to hide the merchandise quality of the product. He writes, "Since films are sold only under the form of luxury products, they have had from the very beginning the same market as art, and the current representation according to which it is necessary to embellish luxury products, making that the task of art, which is itself the most refined of all luxury products, has assured the regular engagement of artists by the cinema."[13] Brecht's conclusion is that what is needed is not so much art in the cinema but a new concept of art.

2. "A film is a merchandise." Brecht separates this into two sub-propositions: a) "the quality of the cinematographic work which is saleable ('bad') is cancelled, overcome by art"; b) "the artistic quality of other artistic genres is not affected by this (bad) process which affects the cinema."[14] In other words, Brecht repeats again that film is indeed a product, a commodity or merchandise, and that to deny this is to misunderstand it fundamentally. These two propositions are particularly important because the notion of treating film as an object for economic exchange becomes very significant in the post-1968 *Cahiers*.

3. "A film must have some 'human interest.'" In this section, Brecht attacks the humanist psychology of the bourgeois theater and novel which becomes transferred to the cinema. He argues that the emphasis on metaphysical and moral values in bourgeois ideology inhibits an understanding of material realities. He finds vulgar, commercial cinema preferable, writing:

> What the film really demands is external action and not introspective psychology.... Capitalism operates in this way by taking given needs on a massive scale, exorcizing them, organizing them and mechanizing them so as to revolutionize everything. Great areas of ideology are destroyed when capitalism concentrates on external action, dissolves everything into processes, abandons the hero as a vehicle for everything and mankind as the measure, and thereby smashes the introspective psychology of the bourgeois novel. The external viewpoint suits the film and gives it importance. For the film the principles of non-aristotelian drama (a type of drama not depending on empathy, mimesis) are immediately acceptable.[15]

Brecht links this attitude to behavioral psychology, which he finds progressive and revolutionary. What is important is external behavior in men, not internal morality. This attitude is remarkably similar to the one found in *Cahiers*, coming admittedly from entirely different roots, which sees film as an art form based on the presentation of external human behavior.

4. "A film can be progressive in its content and retrograde in its form." "Here, the form is the presentation of the merchandise."[16] The form of a work of art is basic to its nature; it determines the way it is bought and sold. The buying and selling is the film's material nature, and therefore its primary one. This simple assertion is perhaps the most important one linking Brecht to *Cahiers du Cinéma*. Particularly after 1968, *Cahiers* will engage in constant criticism of works which are progressive in content and, to them, reactionary in form. This is the constant message of the new *Cahiers:* a revolutionary film must be revolutionary in form as well as content. Implicit throughout the "Threepenny Lawsuit" is the thesis that the economic system under which a film is made affects that film's content.

The other text of primary importance is "The Modern Theatre is the Epic Theatre," Brecht's notes to his opera, *The Rise and Fall of the City of*

Mahagony. In it, Brecht calls for a revolutionizing (not just a renovation) of the opera, to eliminate the passivity of the audience. Brecht's ideas on this are easily summarized, for he himself summarizes them in the following table:

Dramatic Theatre	Epic Theatre
plot	narrative
implicates the spectator in a stage situation	turns the spectator into an observer, but
wears down his capacity for action	arouses his capacity for action
provides him with sensations	forces him to make decisions
experience	picture of the world
the spectator is involved in something	he is made to face something
suggestion	argument
instinctive feelings are preserved	brought to the point of recognition
the spectator is in the thick of it, shares the experience	the spectator stands outside, studies
the human being is taken for granted	the human being is the object of the inquiry
he is unalterable	he is alterable and able to alter
eyes on the finish	eyes on the course
one scene makes another	each scene for itself
growth	montage
linear development	in curves
evolutionary determinism	jumps
man as a fixed point	man as a process
thought determines being	social being determines thought
feeling	reason[17]

The above is as concise a demonstration of Brecht's ideals as is anything. It is a text which, again, is published in French in *Cahiers du Cinéma.*[18] It is particularly important in that Jean-Luc Godard refers to it in his film, TOUT VA BIEN (1972), as being the model from which he made the film, a film which is of prime importance for *Cahiers* and the development of its new ideas.

3

Formalism: *Cahiers'* First Heritage

In a sense, *Cahiers du Cinéma* comes to Brecht backwards. Brecht began with political and philosophical considerations and sought to develop new theatrical structures out of them. Implicit throughout his theorizing is the assumption that form is as much a political issue in the work of art as content is (if indeed one can make the artificial distinction), and that one therefore cannot make a politically advanced work without it also being a formally advanced one.

By contrast, up until 1968, the *Cahiers'* critics are relatively apolitical or in some quarters even considered right wing. Their early interest in Brecht is likewise apolitical (and is therefore, one might argue, a distortion of Brecht): they see aspects of Brechtian philosophy and its accompanying techniques as providing a provocative approach to questions of form in film, but they are little interested in their directly political ramifications. Yet this apolitical Brechtian approach very much sets the stage for the committed writing that is to follow it. While one may easily attribute the changes in *Cahiers* to shifts in its editorial staff, what remains particularly interesting is the relative continuity that may still be found in the magazine. *Cahiers* does move increasingly to the left, and today much of its writing may be seen as a repudiation of positions held some fifteen or twenty years earlier. Nonetheless, the process is far more orderly and logical than would appear at first glance. The seeds of the revolution to follow are firmly planted in the early, "right wing" *Cahiers.*

Let us consider, therefore, *Cahiers'* formalist period and in doing so discuss three main areas of interest: the philosophical roots of *Cahiers'* formalism; the use of geometric metaphors in some of the critics' writing about film; and the conception of film as an art dealing with the physical relationships among the actors presented on the screen.

The Philosophical Roots of *Cahiers'* Formalism

One may trace the formalism of *Cahiers* in the 1950's and '60's back to three main sources: a philosophic tradition more Platonist than Aristotelian, the importance of painting in the French cultural tradition, and the popularity of phenomenology in French thought at that time. Let us consider each area in turn.

A Platonist Tradition

Several of the key figures in the founding of *Cahiers du Cinéma,* and in particular André Bazin, are associated with Catholic intellectual thought in France at the time. This bias brings to *Cahiers* the whole of a classical, humanist tradition, one which attaches to it the idealist notion of pure forms that is behind the greater part of classical aesthetics. Perhaps the greatest proponent of such a classical, Platonist approach is Eric Rohmer, whose highly articulate, theoretical writings exhibit a constant awareness of the tradition out of which he comes. Although Rohmer represents an extreme branch of thought at *Cahiers,* it is nonetheless a very important one, for he shows no hesitation about asserting the idealist notion of essences. In one of his earliest *Cahiers'* essays, under the pen name of Maurice Schérer, he writes, "So the first end of art is to reproduce, not the object, without doubt, but its beauty; what one calls realism is only a more scrupulous search for this beauty."[1] There is, Rohmer implies, a beauty in nature that can be separated from its material existence.

Rohmer's philosophy of film is summarized in a series of articles in which he compares film to the four *beaux arts:* painting, poetry, music, and architecture. It is not surprising, therefore, that Rohmer should be particularly impressed with the affinities of film to music, which Plato prized above the other arts. Rohmer writes, for example, of the relationships between film and the pure forms of music:

> It is, above all, because it expresses itself in time that the cinema attains artistic dignity. I say indeed time and not movement. What the screen knows to offer to our eyes is not the pure luster of appearances, the mechanical abstraction of I don't know what cosmic ballet: the material filmed is on the contrary so much more permeable to our senses that it lets itself be difficultly closed up in the system of a physics of movement. It is not by the door of determinism that we enter into the temporal dimension, but by that of liberty: the flesh is here ceaselessly marked with the seal of the spirit which animates it: we move up immediately to this "inferiority" to which Hegel privileged music. Man, returning to himself, liberates himself from the organic magma in which contemporary art tries to dissolve him: no other form of art has known how to give us such a high idea of what we look like, to make shine in full fire the original nobility of the human face, gesture and comportment.[2]

Thus, Rohmer treats film on an almost spiritual level. Later in the essay, for example, he notes that, although music and film could be placed at opposite ends of a spectrum of the arts, the former being at the highest level of abstraction, the latter dealing most concretely with material reality, the effect of the two art forms is remarkably similar; they have the ability "to stir up directly, intensely, our senses, our spirit, to draw them away from themselves, like the most effective and refined of drugs."[3]

Rohmer makes an important contribution to the philosophical framework that the *Cahiers* formalists are to adopt, one which emphasizes the purity of geometry and forms. Rohmer writes, for example:

> All original poetic expression rests on an abstract line, of a quasi-mathematical rigor, an emphasis of the mysterious, sacred power of the number. With some of my colleagues, the term of *mathematician* is a reproach in addressing Hitchcock, but would turn to praise with regard to Virgil or Edgar Poe. . . . When the author of REAR WINDOW gives in to the same fascination, it is only a formal exercise. In the same way that one cannot conceive of a poet insensitive to rhyme, one finds constantly in all great cinematographic works the presence of a certain geometrical rigor not added on, surely, like a useless ornament, but absolutely consubstantial with it. It seems that each gesture, each look, whatever may be its momentary function, must insert itself in a system of carefully worked out structural lines.[4]

In these various ways, film, for Rohmer, approaches certain ideal, spiritual forms. Rohmer's writings are the most explicit articulation of the philosophical assumptions behind much of *Cahiers'* formalism, although Rohmer is not, to be sure, the only critic to espouse such a line. In the schema that he sets up, Rohmer converts geometry to morality, thereby establishing a valuable precedent in *Cahiers* for the examination of the forms of works of art for their implicitly ethical signification.

The Importance of Painting

The connection between *Cahiers* and a cultural tradition more of painting than of literature has been made by Richard Roud, who in 1960 discussed the differences between the French approach and an Anglo one. Roud links *Cahiers'* formalism to Maurice Denis' nineteenth-century notion of a painting as "a certain arrangement of lines and colors."[5] Thus, the *Cahiers'* critics would be prone to emphasize the formal aspects of films, the visual rather than the literary, because of the privileged position of painting in the cultural tradition. The tendency is to treat film as an object, to be interested less in what it represents than in what it is. The dominant thrust of twentieth-century art, from post-Impressionism through Paul Cézanne and cubism and beyond, has been in this direction. The *Cahiers* critics merely extend this tradition to film.

This idea is again articulated by Rohmer, who uses it to defend the notion of Hitchcock as a formalist. He writes:

> I readily concede to the detractors of Hitchcock that our author is very much a formalist. Yet it becomes a question of knowing if this label is as pejorative as they indeed wish to make it. What is, for example, a formalist painting: a painting without a soul, purely decorative, where the play of lines and colors seems imposed by a preconceived design of the artist rather

than born of the very vision of things? Or would one say on the contrary that a painting has no other way to express than by the intermediary of spatial relationships? I see nothing in this enterprise that is incompatible with the very essence of art, certainly a difficult task, that the greatest alone know how to carry out, the most superficial on the contrary expressing their emotion by means foreign to plastic means. In this sense, a *cinéaste* can never be too formalist.[6]

Similarly, it is instructive to consider an article by Jacques Rivette on Roberto Rossellini. In it, Rivette somewhat hesitatingly compares Rossellini to Matisse, in a manner that makes clear the connection between the involvement with painting and a Platonist preoccupation with underlying forms. He writes of VOYAGE IN ITALY (1953):

> It is enough first to see: throughout the first part, verify the taste for large white surfaces, barely but precisely underlined, an almost decorative detail; if the house is new and comparatively modern, it is certainly because Rossellini is attracted first to contemporary things, to the most recent forms of our surroundings and our manners; it is also a simple visual delectation. Why, good God, can that be surprising coming from a realist (even a neorealist)? Matisse is also a realist, I know: the economy of an agile material, the appeal of the white page with only one sign, the virgin beach open to the invention of the precise line, all this seems to me a more genuine realism than the overloading, the grimaces, the pseudo-Russian conventionality of MIRACLE IN MILAN.[7]

Rivette is clearly aware of the Platonist implications of what he writes. Later in the essay, after describing Rossellini as having an "ability to see through beings and things to the souls and ideas they convey, this privilege of reaching by appearances the double which creates them," he asks, "Would Rossellini be a Platonist?" He answers, "Why not? He had indeed thought of filming *Socrates.*"[8]

The coupling of this Platonism with a cultural involvement with painting leads, in turn, to two other notions. One is the attempt to see films in terms of an underlying geometry or rhythm. Rohmer thus continues in his article on Hitchcock:

> Just as a certain rhythm is conceived for a poem by its author even before he has discovered the right words to fill it in with, I bet that a film by Hitchcock is organized not only beginning with a preconceived rhythm, but with a whole secret system: a magnetic fluid sweeps over the screen, polarizes it, gives to space which up to that point had been dull and amorphous an orientation, a flavor, I dare say, at each point different, where each displacement will be, by the fact of its existence, charged with meaning.[9]

The second is a justification for the *auteur* theory, in spite of the fact that Hitchcock never wrote any of his own scripts. The underlying visual and geometric style, the formal properties of the film, are, argues Rohmer, what make it a Hitchcock film: "Pressed into the mold of Hitchcock's *mise en scène,* all stories, good and bad, immediately take on another allure, the accent is put on what may have escaped the author of the script, the detail becomes the essential."[10] Formalism becomes the way of justifying what otherwise seem the eccentric or frivolous tastes of the *auteur* critics.

Phenomenology

Phenomenology is doubtless the dominant contemporary philosophy of the early days of *Cahiers* and continues to be represented in its writings until about the mid-1960's. In this respect, *Cahiers* reflects many of the central philosophical concerns popular in France at that time. The phenomenological approach, whereby consciousness itself is considered the first object of study for the philosopher, may be found in post-war France in such diversely opposed philosophers as, for example, Jean-Paul Sartre, who popularized existentialism, and Gabriel Marcel, who used phenomenological methods to argue for Christianity and the existence of God. In both of these extremes, however, the emphasis is on a perceived reality (rather than an objectified one) and individual consciousness.

André Bazin was very much influenced by the phenomenological school of thought, and much of the writing in the early *Cahiers,* particularly on neo-realism and the Italian film, sees the cinema as a kind of mediator between the world and the perceiver. Although the philosophical bases for some of this writing are not identical to those of Platonist thought, their similarities are important. Much of the relevant criticism sees the film art, in effect, as a way of picking out what might be called essential forms from a reality of richly varied surfaces and phenomena. (That is, a film selects from and understands reality in much the same way individual perception does.) For the phenomenological critics, film objectifies and clarifies perceptual reality and man's place in it.

A most radical use of phenomenology in *Cahiers* may be noted in Amedée Ayfre's 1952 article, "Néo-réalisme et Phénoménologie," in which he argues that the neo-realist movement is essentially one of "phenomenological realism." Ayfre sees neo-realism as falling between the completely objective documentary and the verism of the naturalist theater. He writes:

The documentary aspect here, specifically in Rossellini, has no pretenses to a certain passive "objectivity"; the "neutral" presentation never wishes to indicate coldness and impersonality. There is conscience, subjectivity, even if there is not Reason and a formal thesis. There is social polemic even if there is not propaganda. But above all, all these elements—objective, subjective, social, etc. ... are never analyzed as such; they are taken in a situational block, with all its inextricable swarming, a block of duration as well as volume, which spares no second of time, nor any gesture. Thus before this All the attitude of the spectator must radically change. To look becomes an act; because all is in question here, one must respond, one must act. It is a call to liberty.[11]

Ayfre's rejection of rational analysis is of course the very antithesis of Marxism, but his moral approach is very compatible with Brecht's. Every film has moral consequences.

To return to Ayfre's thesis, however, it is this mixture of conceptual elements with a phenomenal representation that make neo-realism "phenomenological realism." To the phenomenologists, such as Merleau-Ponty, one must take experience as a whole; the objective world can never be wholly separated from so-called subjective perception. This lack of separation, such as one finds in neo-realism, is what links it to phenomenology. Ayfre continues:

> It is this finality [exemplifed in the "thesis play"], even subtly understood, that phenomenological realism is opposed to by its will not to meddle with events, not to put into them artificially ideas or passions. But this globality of the event allows at the same time a relation between its spatio-temporal reality and the human consciousness which forms part of its very nature and which is its "signification," its "meaning." And this "meaning," because it can only be deciphered by a consciousness and because it is never a rigid finality, can always be interpreted and colored by the consciousness, according to its own norms, theories, its *Weltanschaung,* exactly as happens in the real universe. The result is a fundamental ambiguity.[12]

Ayfre ultimately links this phenomenological approach to religion, and specifically Catholicism. He calls for faith to give sense to the ambiguity, arguing that through the consciousness of man one can distinguish the presence of God behind the ambiguities of appearances.

Ayfre's ideas, like Rohmer's, can be found reflected once again in the writings of Rivette. Rivette makes the following observation in one of his reviews from the early 1960's:

> To make a film is thus to show certain things, and *at the same time,* and by the same operation, to show them with a certain bias; these two acts being rigorously indivisible. Just as one cannot have the absolute in *mise en scène,* for there is no *mise en scène* in the absolute, so the cinema will never be a "language": the relationships of the sign to the signified have no operation here.... Any approach to the cinematographic fact which attempts to substitute addition for synthesis, analysis for unity, will bring us back soon enough to a rhetoric of images which has as little to do with the cinematographic fact as an industrial diagram has to do with the pictorial fact; why does this rhetoric remain so dear to those who entitle themselves "critics of the left"?[13]

If Marxists would dismiss Ayfre for his religiosity, Rivette puts his ideas in language which, while it says essentially the same thing about film, is far more materialist in style. Rivette's articulation of the problem is, indeed, surprisingly close to the scientific rhetoric of Christian Metz, and even makes use of some semiological terms.[14]

We will argue shortly that Rivette is a key transitional figure in *Cahiers'* development, but one may see already in the above quotation how a critic like him, who comes out of the magazine's phenomenological roots, can demonstrate the affinities between the journal's early and later positions. Later *Cahiers* critics would no doubt take issue with Rivette's statement, objecting to his acceptance of the assumption that cinematic representation has a direct relation to reality. But the changes that arise in *Cahiers* are far more easily explained when one sees that the precedent for analytical, philosophical writing is well established in the magazine.

Serge Daney has spoken of the article cited above, Rivette's review of Gillo Pontecorvo's 1961 film KAPO, as one that had a profound influence on him.[15] For Jean-Louis Comolli, who was to become a leader in the post-1968, Marxist *Cahiers,* phenomenology serves also as a point of departure. In one of Comolli's first theoretical essays, for example, he argues for film as a mediator between the spirit of man and the truths of the world around him.[16] Phenomenology is a prime philosophical ground against which many of the changes in *Cahiers* are made.

The above three influences, a Platonist tradition, painting, and phenomenology, are clearly all related in their role in molding *Cahiers'* formalism. Its phenomenology may be viewed as a somewhat more sophisticated expression of Platonist principles, while the notion of dealing with forms, as abstractions from reality, comes directly out of Platonist theory and painterly practice. In this manner, *Cahiers* defines itself in opposition to the other main forces in French thought of the time—the orthodox leftism of the French Communist Party, the avant-garde, surrealist-influenced left (which was to become represented by *Positif*), the existentialism of Sartre. The vitality of these ideas in *Cahiers* at the time is in part a function of their vitality outside of it; as the Catholic wing was to become a less dominant influence in French intellectual thought, its influence in *Cahiers* was to decline also. But it does represent the starting point of theorization at the magazine, a not fully developed tree trunk onto which a branch of Brechtian thought will very shortly be grafted.

The Use of Geometric Metaphors

One of the more provocative aspects of some *Cahiers* criticism during the magazine's formalist period is the use of geometry and geometric metaphors to talk about and describe films. Some of this goes back to the Platonist preoccupation with pure forms described earlier by Rohmer, some of this criticism uses such language to discuss *mise en scène* more precisely, while still other articles seek to discuss a director's work in general in geometric terms.

Perhaps the most advanced and revealing essay to equate film with geometry is Jean-Luc Godard's critique of Alexandre Astruc's UNE VIE (1957). Godard sees a film as comparable to a geometrical locus, an arrangement of points which possess the same property in relation to a fixed element (the scenario). Thus, Godard writes:

Astruc has set up his dramatic and visual coordinates over this vast invisible area. Between the abscissa and the ordinate there is no curve that might reveal some secret progression in the film. The only curve is either the abscissa or the ordinate—which in fact adds up to two kinds of progression, one horizontal, the other vertical. The whole *mise en scène* of UNE VIE has this basic principle as its axis. Maria Schell and Pascale Petit's dash down to the shore is horizontal. Marquand bending down to help his partner onto the jetty of the port is vertical. The exit of the married couple after the wedding feast is horizontal. The stroke of the knife that rips open the bodice is vertical. Again, the movement of Jeanne and Julien rolling in corn is horizontal; that of Marquand's hand seizing Antonella Lualdi's wrist is vertical. And so on. For Astruc, the *mise en scène* of UNE VIE lay quite simply in emphasizing one of these two movements, horizontal or vertical, in every scene or shot that had its own dramatic unity, and in doing so in an *abrupt* way, so that all that did not form part of this abrupt movement sank into the background before or after it.[17]

Godard's piece implicitly praises Astruc for having made a film so easily convertible into geometrical terms: he sees the film art, the art of *mise en scène*, as one of conveying ideas through geometry. The fact that it is a film by Astruc may well be significant. Astruc, himself a film critic and inventor of the notion of the *"caméra-stylo,"* whereby he called for film authors to use the camera for personal expression in much the same way that the writer uses a pen, is considered something of a father figure for the New Wave. Consider, therefore, Jacques Rivette's reaction to another film by Astruc, LES MAU-VAISES RENCONTRES (1955):

What is Astruc's procedure? That, so say the nasty tongues, of a formalist. I note on the contrary that it is that of someone who has something close to his heart to say, who wishes to be understood, and wants to be sure above all that all the elements of the work are submitted to his purpose. His efforts all converge in a single direction. And without doubt it is exactly this absence of ambiguity which bothers the "impressionistic" critics, always more at ease with an absence of avowed ambitions. . . . The beauty is in the exactitude: Astruc's whole ambition, let us repeat, was to make an exacting film.[18]

Both Godard and Rivette admire the formal precision of Astruc's work and the unity of form with narrative. This prizing of a clear discourse is certainly something held in common with Brecht, as is the suspicion of ambiguity. All would agree that form becomes a function of the underlying purposes of the work; the only essential difference in Brecht is that he postulates that those purposes should be political.

Similarly, Rohmer later develops and applies his ideas about underlying form in Hitchcock in his review of VERTIGO (1958). Rohmer sees the spiral shape as central to the film and suggests that the forms in the film reflect its underlying ideas:

Here the figure—Saul Bass's credits design it for us—is that of the spiral, or more exactly the helicoid. Line and circle are merged by the imposition of a third dimension: depth. To speak correctly, we will find only two spirals figuring materially in the film, that of the curl on the nape of Madeleine's neck, a copy of that of Carlotta Valdes, and let us not forget that it is the curl which awakens the desire of the detective, then that of the staircase which ascends to the tower. For the rest, the helix will be realized, suggested by the revolving cylinders represented, themselves, either by the field of vision of Stewart who follows Novack in the car, or by the arch of trees above the highway, or by the trunks of the sequoias, or by the corridor that Madeleine mentions and that Scottie finds again in his dream.... Everything forms a circle, but remains uncompleted, the circling always takes us a little deeper into memory. Shadows succeed shadows, images to images, not like walls that disappear or infinitely reflecting mirrors, but by a kind of movement yet more disturbing, because its continuity is unresolved and it combines at once the softness of a circle and the edge of a line. Ideas and forms follow the same way; it is because the form is pure, beautiful, rigorous, astonishingly rich and free that one can say that the films of Hitchcock, and VERTIGO, in particular, have for their objects—other than those which immediately captivate our senses—*ideas,* in the noble, Platonic sense of the word.[19]

Godard and Rohmer provide two of the more radical applications of geometry to film. Even more common, however, is the tendency to see a filmmaker's work, considered as a whole, as something which forms a geometric pattern. To some extent this is clearly a rhetorical device for making the work of a particular *auteur* have a unity which might not otherwise be easily perceived. What it certainly does show, nonetheless, are the geometric terms in which the *Cahiers* critics think. Consider François Weyergrans' review of Pierre Kast's film, VACANCES PORTUGAISES (1962):

> There is a movement in the work of Kast which prefers the steadiness of the straight line to the interruptions of coming and going.
> This straight line, this simplicity, this classicism, whatever one wants to call it, is also an index of a world which is coming undone. The films of Kast talk of passages, and from LE BEL AGE to VACANCES is also a passage, from narration to reflection. A passage also from a lesson to a confiding.... Of *personal* films, here it is: Kast is concerned only with himself, inspired in his circle, but still, a movement which assures the passage from the singular to the universal.... And this passage, at the moment wished, becomes a distancing from himself. This distance allows for the narration. Kast becomes his own ethnologue.[20]

Weyergans uses the geometric metaphor both to describe Kast's work as a whole and to indicate a "circle" which exists between himself and the supposedly autobiographical film, which becomes a "straight line" through a process of distancing the film from himself. The geometric metaphor is not used to indicate the nature of the film itself, but the nature of the director's relationship to his films and the relationships of the films to each other.

Fereydoun Hoveyda similarly uses an extended geometric metaphor to describe Ingmar Bergman's WILD STRAWBERRIES (1958) and its relationship to the rest of the works of Bergman:

> As with our galaxy, the work of Ingmar Bergman develops not circularly but in a spiral. A spiral of which each revolution widens the circle and refines it. In this course toward perfection, the author stops himself occasionally to embrace with a glance the travelled path.

> The greatest ring of the spiral glows then with a particular brightness and seems to hide the rest. The film that comes with it is sufficient unto itself: if it does not render the others useless, it goes beyond them most surely. WILD STRAWBERRIES belongs to this last category. It encompasses thematically all the ideas dear to our *cinéaste*, all his philosophy, or rather his ontology. It recovers in a gripping summary the some nineteen films that we already know. It contains them all, but with something new as well.[21]

Note the spiritually idealist terms used here, such as "this course toward perfection," or Bergman's "ontology." While Hoveyda's astronomical metaphor steps into ground somewhat less conceptualized than pure geometry, it is nonetheless very close to it, for, historically, the development of mathematical and astronomical sciences has been closely related: the movements of the heavens are traditionally considered to be of a pure order.

The *Cahiers* critics are quick to praise films which they can reduce to such geometric terms, and it is not surprising that a film such as Jacques Tati's PLAYTIME (1968) is seen by them as something of a summation of the art of cinema. Numerous articles on it appear in *Cahiers* at the time of the film's release. The film, which has been praised widely for its qualities of abstraction, is also lauded by *Cahiers* for the same reasons, and Tati's work is reduced to its geometrical and mathematical properties. Paul-Louis Martin writes:

> In fact to review the four films of Tati, a fact imposes itself: the itinerary of Tati is rectilinear. In spite of some error, in general corrected, the cinema of Tati is that of a Straight Line as is that of Bresson and opposed to Godard or Renoir who are *cinéastes* of the Dialectic. . . . One can almost say that PLAYTIME is directly deduced from M. HULOT'S HOLIDAY. A deduction or if one prefers a formal succession of signs taken over and modified in each film.[22]

Martin uses a second geometric metaphor to discuss Tati's role as an actor in his films:

> It is very important that Tati has himself played in his films since the beginning and this presence has evolved along two axes. 1) The character tends to become *abstract*. 2) He is more and more disconnected from the world. The character of Tati divests himself of a certain number of characteristics to become a sort of form.[23]

Martin continues to talk about the film as a sort of abstraction of usual cinematic reality and praises its reduction of the usual Tati elements. Admittedly, a work like PLAYTIME lends itself to this kind of discussion, but this may only prove that such formalism is a preoccupation of certain filmmakers as well as critics. It may well be that PLAYTIME represents the accomplishment of an ideal of the *Cahiers* generation—a film of relatively pure geometry.

Where does this obsession with geometry fit in with the direction in which *Cahiers du Cinéma* is to go? The answer must necessarily be somewhat speculative. If one sees *Cahiers* as moving in the direction of the scientific analysis of film, then surely a reduction such as Godard performs on UNE VIE suggests a movement toward a demystified analysis of shots and frames. One might even see the attempt to pinpoint something as imprecise as a film in geometric terms as a move toward a materialist way of thinking about film, despite the idealist philosophy out of which it comes. Indeed, one of the general movements in aesthetics in the twentieth century has been in the direction of materialist analysis growing out of formal analysis (paint treated "as paint" in painting; sounds treated "as sounds" in music, etc.). *Cahiers* is certainly to move in the direction of treating film "as film," that is, not so much as a representation of the real world, but as a communication system in itself. *Cahiers'* desire to treat the forms of film for their own sake may be seen as the first gropings in this direction.

An Art of Physical Relationships

There is a second tendency in *Cahiers'* formalist writing which in one respect grows out of concerns similar to this same leaning toward geometry, but which seeks to apply it to the humanistic concern of man's place in the world. An important group of writings in *Cahiers* sees film's purpose as showing men's physical relationships with the world and each other. On the one hand, this grows out of phenomenology, as discussed above, which tends to see film not as a medium of internalized psychology, but as representing physical relationships seen from the outside, from the surface, despite whatever subjectivity the viewer or filmmaker may lend to them.

This attitude is reflected in Jean Domarchi's review of Jean-Pierre Melville's L'AINE DES FERCHEAUX (1962), a French gangster film modelled on American works of the genre. Domarchi's initial comment is that Melville is put in the ironic position of demonstrating "one of the favorite models of contemporary philosophy," despite the director's disclaimers about in no way being an intellectual. Domarchi's argument reflects the phenomenologist's position:

> To the modern cinema (Bergman, Antonioni, Resnais), which searches to free itself from the American cinema, Melville opposes a return to American classicism (it is not for nothing that America is the chief place of the action), and I think that this option is more fruitful than the other, for in the final analysis, cinema is above all *physical adventure* more than *interior adventure*. Moral conflicts have sense only if they develop by means of physical oppositions (cf., Ford, Hawks, Kazan, Aldrich, etc.) and not by the discourse.
>
> Equal to the great Americans, Melville has a sense of physical relationships. He sees that in the beginning physical relationships are a question of skin, and that as a result, they become idealized: one always finds moral, and thus general pretexts to express one's attraction or disgust toward the other, and it is cinema's job to express the incarnation of these relationships by actors (or actresses) who represent the general types of humanity.[24]

In this quotation one may find repeated one of the rationales for the attraction of the *Cahiers* critics for the American cinema: it is an art of physical relationships rather than moralizing or psychology. (This is the very quality, one will recall, that attracted Brecht to mass-oriented, "vulgar" movies.)

An even more extreme example of this position may be found in Pierre-Richard Bré's review of Valerio Zurlini's FAMILY DIARY (1962). Bré sees the gestures of men (i.e., the physical comportment of the actors) as the guiding forms for film, even more so than a formalism based on strict geometry; he links this attitude to a philosophical phenomenology. He writes:

> For the Past does not mix itself with the Present, it does not burst forth here, as Resnais thinks. It is contained in it; it expresses itself in the situation and the gestures of its trustees. This distinction, already important in philosophy, appears vital for the cinema, art of gesture more than construction (meaning by that construction of abstract elements, and not referring to gestures, that is characters, to others). It goes without saying that the greater the *cinéaste*, the more the gestures of his characters express the totality of their relationships with the world (in the past and also—why not?—in the future), making thus of film an art of the present, indeed an art of a *total present*. To the subtle equations (but so facilely reducible) of a "complex" cinema is the response of the complex simplicity (which cannot be so easily reduced) of works of art for which as art, the gesture is only a sketch, each film only a blueprint. [25]

Bré's brand of formalism, if one can call it that, is here clearly different from that suggested by Godard for UNE VIE (cited above), and indeed may even be opposed to it at some levels. Bré's is a formalism for which the human figure and the gestures it makes are clearly the privileged element of the frame. At the same time, however, the writer seems to share Godard's desire to reduce film to its most important elements (be they geometric or gestural), to those most significant forms of which the film is composed.

Domarchi and Bré share a point of view which is very close to that of a group of critics who briefly invade *Cahiers,* who are known as the Mac-Mahoniens, named after the MacMahon theater in Paris, which they were known to frequent. The MacMahoniens fairly soon broke with *Cahiers* and formed a magazine of their own, *Présence du Cinéma.* Their chief spokesman was a critic named Michel Mourlet, whose writings for *Cahiers, Présence,* and other magazines have been collected into a single volume known as *Sur un art ignoré.*

Mourlet carries auteurism to an extreme and turns his back on the traditional figures of Hawks and Hitchcock to celebrate a pantheon consisting of Lang, Losey, Preminger, and Cottafavi. The basis of this admiration is in these directors' use of actors, their handling of the human figure on the screen, their thinking of film stories in terms of physical encounters. Mourlet celebrates films of violence because they allow for the physical expression of human passions. He observes, for example:

Exaltation of the actor, the *mise en scène* will find in violence a constant occasion of beauty. The hero breaks the evil spells, introduces into a luckless order his personal order, which is the search for a truer, higher harmony. So is defined the type of hero of which the models are Charlton Heston, Fernando Lamas, Robert Wagner or Jack Palance. A brutal and noble hero, elegant and virile, he reconciliates force and beauty (or, for Palance, an admirable beastlike ugliness) and represents the perfection of a master race, made to triumph and to have an inkling of or to know all happiness.[26]

Mourlet's ideas (which have been accused of being linked politically to fascism, a label that Mourlet explicitly refuses to deny himself[27]) are hardly systematized into anything resembling genuine theory. The closest he gets is in one article, called "What is a Scenario?" which, although written for *Presénce du Cinéma,* is still applicable to his *Cahiers* writing. In it, he argues that, contrary to the notion that a good film starts with a good scenario, the scenario is of little importance whatsoever to the quality of a movie. If this were not the case, the argument goes, one could simply publish the plots of films. The *mise en scène* of a motion picture is not just a means but an end in itself. Mourlet continues:

> It would be necessary to specify that the scenarist has no more nor less the right to the title of author of the film than the journalist who reports a detailed news item, than the life which proposes an experiment or an adventure. Elaborated by a specialist, by reality or by the personal memories of the *cinéastes,* the story is a given, doubtless the most important, but something from which everything else still remains to be done: truth, movement, life.[28]

It is the director's gift of animating the scenario in a particular way that produces what Mourlet sees as the art of film.

The ideals of Mourlet are echoed by a colleague, Jacques Serguine, who again reduces the art of cinema to certain formal premises dealing with the gestures of the actors. Serguine is, however, is some ways more systematic:

> What one discovers is that the cinema is not the art of movement—movement is its technique—but rather the art of true movement. He who first has understood the cinema is he who first has rediscovered the gestures of man. Not those arbitrary, overdone, or schematic gestures which are logically made part of those arts usually considered as stylized: the theater, the dance. I say the gestures of men, those which they make when they love or when they suffer, when they eat, when they open a window. Something has moved on the screen, and I have recognized a gesture. A man uses his body to stop up the open hole in the clay of a dam. If I had enough enthusiasm, I would be able to invent this gesture; I recognize it, I have come closer to this man.[29]

The MacMahoniens represent an extreme wing of auteurism; even *Cahiers* found it necessary to print Serguine's article with a disclaimer that his views did not necessarily represent the editorial position of the magazine as a whole. Nonetheless, similar positions can be found in *Cahiers* critics not directly associated with MacMahonism: Jacques Rivette, for example, has argued in favor of the violent American film on grounds very much similar to Mourlet's, claiming that violent subjects allow the director to express himself through the *mise en scène*.[30] And even as late as 1967, Serge Daney writes of Otto Preminger's HURRY SUNDOWN (1967) as a film whose achievements rest on Preminger's fundamental ability at spacing actors.[31] The Mac-Mahoniens represent a certain kind of formalism which is characterized by a lack of interest in specific subject matter; in their time, they are genuinely new and provocative and represent the logical end point of a certain set of attitudes about film.

MacMahonism represents what may be considered an apotheosis of *Cahiers'* apolitical period. The relation to Brecht is certainly tenuous, if existent at all (although we shall see shortly that Joseph Losey is, perhaps, a key connecting figure in this regard). Nonetheless, this extreme concern with the physical gestures of the actors exhibits a certain line of what one might call *Cahiers'* pre-materialist thought. The gestures can well be considered part of the material nature of filmic representation; they are its concrete means of expression. While we are still several steps away from Brecht's notion of the social gest, one can see certain affinities between this phenomenological approach in the early *Cahiers* and the one advocated by the German theorist.

In addition, the notion of theater as both visual and literary spectacle is very strong in Brecht; direction in the Brechtian theater involves very close consideration of all the visual aspects of the production. Roland Barthes and Bernard Dort write of the Brechtian theater that "theory, texts and *mise en scène* form an indissoluable whole with Brecht,"[32] which is a notion very close to *Cahiers'* conception of the art of film. It may be only a superficial affinity, but surely it could not have made Brechtian theory any less attractive to those film critics who were new to the theater of Brecht in the 1950's.

Cahiers' early period is thus one of florid, imprecise, metaphoric language and subjective, impressionist, inductive analysis. Nonetheless, it is an important period in French film criticism in general, for it represents a time of change, controversy, and provocation, a fertile time for critical thought about film. The dozen or so citations given above are meant to offer something of the range of formal approaches (both geometric and gestural) to be found in *Cahiers*. As mentioned earlier, not all *Cahiers* writing is like this, but at the same time, the varied number of different writers and contexts points to some degree of unity of agreement with regard to the importance of form in film. This writing is to become a very significant context for the absorption of certain ideas about Brecht into the general body of *Cahiers'* thought.

Part II

Brechtian Criticism Before 1968

4

Roots of the Brechtian Approach

The assimilation of Brechtian thought into *Cahiers du Cinéma* is a gradual process, one which begins with the introduction of Brecht into the French theater in general in the 1950's but which incorporates a whole set of other preoccupations and interests. One might even argue that there are certain needs in *Cahiers'* film criticism which Brecht proves to be an answer for, as though he were filling a kind of vacuum. The early stages of *Cahiers'* interest in Brecht are tentative ones, but nonetheless interesting, and together this chapter and the one following will aim to explore them. This will include not only consideration of direct references made to Brecht, but also certain other ideas which have strong affinities with his theater and its theories.

This chapter will deal with three essential topics. The first is a brief history of Brecht in French theater up until 1960; the discussion will seek to place *Cahiers'* consideration of Brecht in the context of his place in the general French cultural scene of the time. The second topic will include some of the criticism and preoccupations of Jacques Rivette, who, while he almost never mentions Brecht by name in his writings for *Cahiers,* has nonetheless produced work which demonstrates a progression, conscious or not, toward a Brechtian way of thinking. Rivette's interest in the eighteenth-century French playwright, philosopher, and theatrical theorist Denis Diderot is particularly significant here, for the similarities between Brecht and Diderot are striking. The third section will present several other miscellaneous influences which are nonetheless important to the shift in the direction of Brecht, as several other small streams that feed into the same general channel.

Brecht in France Before 1960

Until 1947, the theater of Brecht was virtually unperformed in France. Postwar productions of Brecht, of *The Exception and the Rule* by Jean-Marie Serreau in 1947 and *Mother Courage* by Jean Vilar for the Théâtre National de Paris in 1951, were resounding critical failures, and it was not until 1954, with the first visit of the Berliner Ensemble to Paris, that the tide began to change. *Mother*

Courage was played by the Ensemble for the first time, and, while the event met with a good measure of critical resistance once again, there was also very vocal defense of the production.[1]

Among the most important defenders of Brecht and the Berliner Ensemble were Roland Barthes and Bernard Dort, who only a few years earlier had founded a theatrical publication called *Théâtre Populaire*. In response to the Berliner Ensemble, *Théâtre Populaire*'s eleventh issue, for January and February 1955, was entirely devoted to Brecht. Barthes' editorial for that issue noted:

> Whatever our final evaluation of Brecht, we must at least indicate the coincidence of his thought with the great progressive themes of our time: that the evils men suffer are in their own hands—in other words, that the world can be changed; that art can and must intervene in history; that it must contribute to the same goal as the sciences, with which it is united; that we must have an art of explanation and no longer merely an art of expression; that the theater must participate in history by revealing its movement; that the techniques of the stage are themselves "committed"; that, finally, there is no such thing as an "essence" of eternal art, but that each society must invent the art which will be responsible for its own deliverance.[2]

Barthes was to become, of course, a major figure in structuralism and semiology in French literary thought, while Dort has also been interested in film, having been, for a period, critic for the left wing journal *L'Observateur*. The 1954 visit of the Berliner Ensemble also resulted in the first French publication of Brecht's complete works and a whole set of critical studies about him.[3]

In 1955, when the Berliner Ensemble returned to Paris with *The Caucasian Chalk Circle,* praise for the production was all but unanimous, although acceptance of Brecht's theories was somewhat more limited. When Brecht died soon after in 1956, he was hailed again by virtually all of the French press as a great dramatist, although the acclaim was once again more accepting of his achievements as a playwright than as a theorist. Bernard Dort reports that even the Jesuit review *Etudes* had high praise for Brecht; while rejecting his Marxism, their critic nonetheless lauded the plays' moral (and, he argued, essentially Christian) values.[4] This acceptance by even Catholic intellectuals no doubt made it all the easier for the still Catholic-influenced, pre-Marxist *Cahiers du Cinéma* to embrace the German playwright.

As a result of this interest, there were an increasing number of French productions of Brecht's plays, and, if their general quality was reportedly inconsistent, Brecht's status in France was still firmly established by the late 1950's. In 1956-58, for example, Jean Dasté produced a fairly controversial version of *The Caucasian Chalk Circle.*[5] Several directors and playwrights had emerged with Brechtian-influenced work by 1960; Brecht was by no means something merely to be imported from Germany. Among the most famous and respected of the home-grown Brechtians was Roger Planchon, whose work for the Théâtre Municipal de Villeurbanne has been considered some of the most successful post-Brechtian work in France. Planchon is even honored in *Cahiers du Cinéma* in March of 1962 with both an interview and an article on his work, despite the fact that he is a man of the theater and not film.[6] In addition, one of Planchon's collaborators, René Allio, was to become a filmmaker in the late 1960's; some of his Brecht-inspired films, such as THE SHAMELESS OLD LADY (1964) or LES CAMISARDS (1971) receive significant attention from *Cahiers* when they are released.

   Cahiers du Cinéma clearly reveals an awareness of the Brecht phenomenon in France. In 1957, in a review of Alberto Cavalcanti's film version of Brecht's *Master Puntila and His Servant Matti,* Louis Marcorelles writes:

   The craze which followed the first visit to France of the Berliner Ensemble in 1954, the systemization of its theories of staging by the review *Théâtre Populaire*, the left wing delirium which heralded the arrival of this company last summer, after the death of Brecht, should not blind us to the scope of the theatrical revolution established by the author-director of *Mother Courage* and *The Caucasian Chalk Circle.*[7]

In his article for the special Brecht issue of *Cahiers* in 1960, Bernard Dort comments on the unprecedented interest in Brecht in French intellectual thought and the threat that it is to pose to film:

   For the Brechtian wave is now reaching the shores of cinema. I don't know if the producers have been touched by it... but the critics, in any case, evoke Brecht, and invoke him sometimes, too, and try to talk of "Brechtianism." *Positif* is now nicely contaminated; *Cahiers du Cinéma* is not missing out either: for several years there already, Louis Marcorelles has done an obstinate, subversive job; last October Eric Rohmer, without self-consciousness, pronounced the name of Brecht. The sign does not fool: A Brechtian epidemic is brewing at *Cahiers*. Perhaps this issue will serve to clinch the matter. I do not despair of seeing the day when those who sing the praises of cinematographic specificity will be studying the "Short Organon for the Theater," or the Hitchcocko-Hawksians rallying at the white dove of the Berliner Ensemble.[8]

   By the time *Cahiers du Cinéma* gets to him seriously, Brecht has been the fashion in France for several years.

Rivette and Diderot

If the influence of Brecht poses something of a revolution for the theatrical arts in France in the 1950's, it is not entirely without precedent. In an essay written in the 1970's entitled "Diderot, Brecht, Eisenstein," Roland Barthes discusses the affinities between Denis Diderot's eighteenth-century theories about aesthetics and theater and those of Brecht (implying, as well, a potential for relating them to film by means of Sergei Eisenstein). A digression into a discussion of these affinities is here well in order. It seems unlikely, Barthes asserts, that Brecht knew Diderot's work particularly well. Nonetheless, he reports how Brecht in 1937 sought to found a Diderot Society in which he invited Erwin Piscator, Jean Renoir, and Eisenstein to join: there was clearly an intellectual relationship between the ideas of the two dramatists.[9]

Jacques Rivette, one of the main forces behind the *Cahiers* of the late 1950's and early 60's, was also apparently profoundly interested in Diderot. In 1964, Rivette directed a stage version of Diderot's *La Religieuse* in Paris with Anna Karina in the leading role. Two years later, he converted this stage production into a highly controversial film which, despite its being taken from a classic of French literature, nonetheless ran into censorship problems for its anti-clericism. In all likelihood, then, Rivette, who appears to have cherished his *La Religieuse* project for some years before achieving it, was more than casually familiar with the eighteenth-century French writer.

Let us briefly, therefore, consider some of the affinities between Diderot and Brecht:

1. Diderot was an atheist and, for his time, a relative materialist. He was, to use Barthes' words, "a man of the theater whose theory aimed at dispensing equally pleasure and instruction."[10] Both men saw a practical, social end to the theater. Diderot writes:

> The pit of the theater is the only place where the tears of the virtuous man and those of the evil man are mingled. There, the evil man becomes angry at the injustices that he would have committed, sympathizes with the misfortunes that he would have occasioned, and becomes indignant at a man of his own character. But the impression is received; it remains in us in spite of ourselves; and the evil man leaves his loge less disposed to do evil than if he had been reproved by a hard and severe orator.[11]

Diderot advocated a change of theatrical form to produce a morally potent theater. He considered tragedy too remote from everyday life and saw comedy as a potent weapon against vice. His new category, which he called the drama, was for him a mid-point between the two that might allow for the instruction of the audience.[12]

2. Diderot, like Brecht, rejected the notion of exact realism as being often artistically uninteresting. Truth in the theater was, to him, a poetic truth entailing a certain amount of "intellectual exaggeration."[13] Diderot admired Jean-Baptiste Racine, for example, because he felt that the language of the street was not necessarily suited to the theater, and vice versa.[14] Truth in the theater was to Diderot not necessarily a matter of painstaking or exact reproduction of life.

3. Like Brecht, Diderot thought of the theatrical presentation as a series of tableaux, in which the composition of the actors and the visual elements was to play an integral part in the development of the meaning of the presentation. (His theories of painting were also related to this notion.) Barthes sees Brecht as

the perfect extension of Diderot's notion of the tableau: "the tableau is intellectual, it has something to say (something moral, social) but is also says that it knows how this must be done; it is simultaneously significant and propaedeutical, impressive and reflexive, moving and conscious of the channels of emotion."[15] In addition, much of Diderot's thought about the tableau is pre-cinematic. In one place, he writes, "Oh! if we could have theaters where the decors would change every time the place of the scene had to change," or in another:

> If the spectator is at the theater as if before a painting, where the various paintings were to pass in succession as if by enchantment, why would not the philosopher seated at the foot of the bed of Socrates, afraid to see him die, be as pathetic on stage as the wife and daughter of Eudamidas in the painting of Poussin? Apply the laws of picturesque composition to pantomime and you will see that they are the same.[16]

One feels certain that Rivette may have also been struck by this marked applicability of Diderot to film.

4. Furthermore, like Brecht, Diderot believed in the use of types, of generalized characters to construct an argument or dialectic. Vexler describes this train of thought in Diderot's writing:

> The French stage, Diderot goes on to say, has known financiers, judges, fathers, etc. But *the* financier as such, *the* judge, *the* father, etc. have been ignored and must now be introduced upon it. Instead of painting portraits of individuals, or even concentrating the most characteristic traits of a given species, say, those of several financiers into the composite portrait or type of *Turcaret,* playwrights ought to construct *pièces à thèse,* sociological plays, in which "the duties of the various professions, social stations, their advantages and dangers would furnish the basis and moral." Moreover, if they should desire to make use of contrast, let them oppose character to *"condition,"* even in the same person, or else one condition to another.[17]

Similarly, Diderot believed that good acting was not based on instinct or emotionalism but on the intellectual comprehension of the actor and his means of expressing the situation, a position very much similar to Brecht's. He writes, for example:

> What confirms me in this view is the unequal acting of players who play from the heart. From them you must expect no unity. Their playing is alternately strong and feeble, fiery and cold, dull and sublime. Tomorrow they will miss the point they have excelled in today; and to make up for it will excel in some passage where last time they failed. On the other hand, the actor who plays from thought, from study of human nature, from constant imitation of some ideal type, from imagination, from memory, will be always at his best mark; he has considered, combined, learnt and arranged the whole thing in his head.[18]

There are other, more minor levels upon which one could draw parallels between Brecht and Diderot, but the essential similarities may be found in the above four points.

The connection between Diderot and *Cahiers* can be made only indirectly and mainly through the figure of Rivette, who in turn has acknowledged a direct interest in Brecht. Rivette has commented, for example, about his first film, PARIS NOUS APPARTIENT (1958): "I'd like to follow the example of Brecht: PARIS NOUS APPARTIENT would be *Drums in the Night;* and the trilogy I am planning set in the eighteenth century, more or less an adaptation of *Edward II.*"[19] Rivette is, therefore, not only interested in Brecht but is doubtless also conscious of precedents for Brecht in traditional French culture. (Here one might also consider Rivette's favorable review of Otto Preminger's ST. JOAN, a film otherwise almost universally considered a failure.[20] Based on a play by George Bernard Shaw, generally regarded as a primary influence on Brecht, the film would unite a theatrical tradition appealing to Rivette, in Shaw, with a cinematic one he would admire as well, in Preminger, one of Rivette's favorite *auteurs.*) Thus, although Brecht's position in the theater is often considered revolutionary, Rivette's approach to him might be classed as evolutionary.

Let us consider, in this context, one text by Rivette, on Charles Chaplin's MONSIEUR VERDOUX (1947), which expresses certain ideas very close to Diderot's. In his critique of Verdoux, Rivette argues that the end of cinema is "that the real world, such as it is offered us on the screen, be also an idea of the world." He asserts that movies which stay simply on the level of physical reality can never understand it. They are, rather, "like the cows who watch the trains that pass, fascinated by the movement or the color, with little chance of understanding what is going on with these objects of fascination." Similarly, the film that starts with an idea risks never being able to give real life or animation to that idea.[21]

Rivette praises those *cinéastes* who start with an idea and then recreate

little by little, under our eyes, a concrete world; different and explained, but more ambiguous, being at once an incarnate idea, then a reality transpierced with sense. It is thus that the idea is already an idea about the world, a conceptual vision (spectacle of metaphor): an image-idea...[22]

Rivette concludes with a reference to Barthes:

The reconstruction of an object "in order to show in this reconstruction the functions of this object": the definition, according to Barthes, of structuralist activity, which rules all of modern art. So VERDOUX, as Landru taken apart and reconstructed by Chaplin-Charlie: an *image,* rigorously non-symbolic and without depth, but *formal:* "neither the real, nor the rational, but the functional."[23]

One finds echoes of Diderot here, both in many of the ideas (the emphasis on the need for guiding ideas in a film, the need for expressing the ideas through concrete imagery) and in the notion of the need for a balance between the intellectual aspects of the work and the more emotional or lifelike ones. VERDOUX would be termed a Brechtian film by some critics, such as Eric Bentley,[24] and surely Barthes' definition of structuralist activity would be how Brecht would describe his goals in the theater, that is, the taking apart of the working of social relations to show the way in which they operate. In context, the passage may also be a response to the MacMahoniens. Their love of *pur regard,* that is, the purely visual and physical properties of a film, makes for a limited kind of appreciation. While the form of a film is important, Rivette would say, the relation of that form to function is the most important.

One thus finds in Rivette one of the strongest links between the old *Cahiers* and the new. On the one hand, his writing still contains vestiges of Platonism (e.g., his looking for the underlying idea in MONSIEUR VER-DOUX), which associate him with the formalism characteristic of Eric Rohmer; on the other hand, he is aware of Brecht, influenced by him, attracted to Brechtian ideas (which, indeed, are at least superficially related to Plato's in their tendency to favor rationality over emotion). Although evidence for the connection is sometimes circumstantial and indirect, the relationship between Brecht and Rivette is undeniable, and the latter is to be considered a major pivotal figure in the changes that occur in *Cahiers.*

Other Influences

In addition, there are three other forces at work in the early *Cahiers du Cinéma* which might be described as pre-Brechtian in that they suggest ideas about film that are similar to Brecht's about theater. These include certain theoretical ideas in Bazin, the rejection of realism as an ideal, and the films of Joseph Losey. Let us consider each in succession.

The Theories of Bazin

At one level, no theoretician in film could be farther away from Brecht than André Bazin. The French critic, who is one of the central, founding influences in *Cahiers du Cinéma,* is a Catholic idealist interested more in aesthetic problems than in political ones. In addition, current attitudes in film theory suggest that in many ways Eisenstein's principles of editing (which Bazin was highly critical of in some of his writings) come closer than any other existing film theory to approximating Brecht's ideals. Brecht's notion of alienation is in some ways comparable to Eisenstein's montage of attraction in that both use techniques of juxtaposing unrelated elements to produce new meanings. By contrast, Brechtian theory would doubtless see the deep focus prized by Bazin as a form of exactly the very realistic illusionism to be avoided.

Some of Bazin's notions, however, particularly taken in the context of their time, point in a direction of interest. Bazin is at times involved in the way in which certain techniques change the relation between the viewer and the movie. Thus, for example, he writes of deep focus in one of his key essays, "The Evolution of the Language of Cinema":

> That it [deep focus] implies, consequently, both a more active mental attitude on the part of the spectator and a more positive contribution on his part to the action in progress. While analytical montage only calls for him to follow his guide, to let his attention follow along smoothly with that of the director who will choose what he should see, here he is called upon to exercise at least a minimum of personal choice. It is from his attention and his will that the meaning of the image in part derives.[25]

Thus, Bazin argues for the type of involved, participating spectator that Brecht sought as well. Bazin continues his argument by advancing the position that deep focus and neo-realist stylistics may be used to create filmic images which are more ambiguous than would be the edited-together images of Eisenstein. While this is not really the same thing that Brecht calls for in asking for the art work to present contradictions, the two thinkers do at least occasionally share the goal of praising works of art for decreasing the passivity of the spectator.

A Reaction Against Realism

Although *Cahiers du Cinéma* champions Italian neo-realism in its early years, at no point does it ever attempt to make realism a single, exclusive, stylistically acceptable mode. On the contrary, there is the frequent denial that truth in film necessarily means objective realism or stylistic naturalism. Rather, there is the common assertion at *Cahiers* that the truths of cinema are invariably based on illusionism. Surely Brecht himself would have no argument with the following statement by Amédée Ayfre:

> It is without doubt with Lumière that one must mark the beginning of cinematographic realism, he who never thought that his invention could be used for anything other than as an instrument of reproduction. But already, the single fact that he placed his camera in a particular spot, that he started or stopped photographing at a particular moment, that he inscribed the world in black and white on a flat surface was enough to admit an infidelity to the real.[26]

Cahiers' rejection of realism takes several forms. When Jacques Rivette, for example, talks of Otto Preminger's ANGEL FACE (1952), he writes that the film's "real problem is less to make us believe in an incredible story than to find a purely cinematic truth beyond dramatic or novelistic probability."[27] This "purely cinematic truth" is to be found in the *mise en scène*. Similarly, a MacMahonien like Jacques Serguine rejects a director like De Sica for his "misérablisme," as not dealing with "Man," but rather with "stagnant, deformed, caricatured life."[28]

One may look at Michel Mourlet's essay on Joseph Losey, "Beauté de la connaissance." In it, Mourlet sees Losey as having a special kind of relationship with the world. Where inferior directors create a "universe," he argues, Losey's films refer to the real universe. But Mourlet continues:

> This is not to say that Losey falls into the rut of realism, and proposes to us banality or ugliness as necessary conditions for truthfulness. The rarest, noblest and most passionate in man is his aim. But this aim is simplicity itself, and it is why it surprises. Our customs of thought form a rupture against exactitude. We are accustomed to their lying to us, so that we believe that they lie to us when they speak the truth: a critic has entitled an article elsewhere on TIME WITHOUT PITY erroneously: "The Splendour of the False," and one talks about expressionism with regard to this film, something which opens the gate to misunderstandings. Expressionism is not in fact content to oppose itself to impressionism by the intervention of an organizing will; it implies the emphasis on what must matter. Now in the *mise en scène* of Losey, what is essential is that *mise en scène* by itself, without external valorization, thanks to the single rightness of the designing gesture.[29]

While the tone of most of these articles reflects the familiar Platonism of *Cahiers* at this time, the writings share with Brechtian thought a rejection of strict empiricism. The aesthetic goal may be truth in each case, but it is not necessarily realism, neither in the naturalistic sense that goes back to Zola nor in the sense of Italian neo-realism. Rather, there is an acknowledgment that film is a medium which often seeks truth through artifice.

In a similar vein, some writings in *Cahiers* discuss this process with regard to the conventions found in the French film. François Weyergans, for example, in his review of Jacques Demy's LOLA (1960), notes that the work "challenges directly and at once the true and the false to wind up with the truer than the true: Demy knows up to what point one must admire Cocteau."[30] Similarly, Jean-Louis Comolli links Jean-Louis Richard's MATA-HARI, AGENT H-12 (1965) to a tradition of French film represented by someone like Jacques Becker, the type of film where "all is false, but one can also find the essential, truer than nature."[31] The theatrical conventions and traditions found in film are not rejected but rather used to make a statement about the real world.

Joseph Losey

Finally, it is impossible to ignore the influence of Joseph Losey on *Cahiers* as a source of the magazine's interest in Brecht. Losey's career began in the theater, and one of his most significant achievements in the 1940's before becoming a film director was his staging of Brecht's *Galileo*. Losey's first film, *THE BOY WITH GREEN HAIR* (1948), is clearly somewhat Brechtian in conception.

Presumably the auteurist critics, seeking to know more about a director they have come to admire, would become interested in one of that director's major influences. One might argue that Losey's applications of Brechtian thought in film have been impure, incomplete, and unacceptable to any sort of Brechtian orthodoxy, but one can hardly be surprised that they should interest the *Cahiers* critics. (By the same token, *Théâtre Populaire* publishes an interview with Losey in 1964; the crossovers of interest between theater and film appear to have been mutual.)[32]

Michel Mourlet's essay on Losey has already been cited above. In the special Brecht number of *Cahiers du Cinéma*, there is an article by Losey on Brecht (which will be discussed shortly), and it may be no coincidence that this special Brecht issue appears only three months after *Cahiers'* special Losey issue in 1960. The growth of interest in Brecht may clearly by attributed to a whole cluster of influences. Losey is surely to be included in that cluster.

Summary

In this chapter we have surveyed some of the events whereby French theater people, critics, and audiences became interested in Brecht's plays and theories in the 1950's. We have noted the influence of Denis Diderot on Jacques Rivette and the similarities between many of Diderot's ideas and Brecht's. We have suggested that in certain of Bazin's ideas, in the magazine's frequent rejection of realism, and in its interest in Joseph Losey, *Cahiers du Cinéma* may have been inadvertently preparing itself for an acceptance of Brechtian thought.

5

Key Brechtian Texts

This chapter will treat two types of Brechtian film criticism in *Cahiers du Cinéma* before 1968. Some of the writings deal with Brecht directly, seeking to apply some of the theories and standards of the German theorist to the cinema. There is a second group of articles, however, which do not always mention him directly but which rather advance ideas that show close affinities with Brechtian thought, either consciously or not. The following survey will treat the two separately, but they appear in the magazine simultaneously, suggesting that directly Brechtian thought was supplemented by theorization that was moving toward some of the same goals independently of a Brecht-influenced doctrine.

Writings About Brecht

The following section will have three general objects of study: *Cahiers'* special Brecht number in December 1960, the writings of Louis Marcorelles, and Fereydoun Hoveyda's review of Joseph Losey's EVA (1962).

Cahiers No. 114

Cahiers No. 114 is perhaps the most important single issue of the magazine in terms of this discussion. It begins with an editorial on Brecht by the *Cahiers* staff, which asks the questions, "Why this issue on Brecht? Is Brecht a *cinéaste?* Is Brecht a *Cahiers auteur?*" It answers the questions with a list of responses, among which are:

> No, if it is true that the cinema, such as we are trying to define it here, does not need to follow up, we believe, on this modern art of which Brecht, in the theater, embodies the most intransigent idea. It is this belief in a *free* cinema which serves as the common denominator to the diverse tendencies expressed in our review.
> No, if it is true that a "Brechtian critique of cinema," such as Bernard Dort describes it, aims to destroy all the objects of our former and current adoration: actors, works, and the approach to these works and these actors.[1]

Thus, *Cahiers* embraces Brecht as an alternative, not to the exclusion of other modes of cinema, but in addition to them. While this can be seen as missing the point of Brecht's work, *Cahiers* does at this time see the need to expand its interests, to start to treat the problems raised by him. The editorial continues:

> But, if we mistrust a cinema which looks to its neighbor for sole inspiration, we do not yet condemn our art to its formerly fruitful, today sterile isolation. We think that, henceforth, the points of convergence between the two arts are not only necessary, but desirable.[2]

Part of the interest in Brecht stems in this issue from *Cahiers'* interest in film history. The magazine publishes, for example, a translation of Brecht's original scenario for THE THREEPENNY OPERA (1931) and portions of his text on "The Threepenny Lawsuit." Also linking Brecht to the history of film is an article by Joseph Losey, in which Losey describes his having worked with Brecht and Brecht's influence on him. While Losey's article is mainly a kind of reminiscence, it also outlines some theoretical concepts important to the consideration of Brecht in the cinema. Losey sees two kinds of thinking with regard to Brecht: the first understands Brecht through observation, on an intellectual level; the second responds to Brecht on a far more internalized level. Losey reaches several conclusions in the course of the article, which he summarizes at the end. These are:

1. Brecht was not really a theorist. While he may have written much theory, he was far more interested in the practical effects of the techniques he advocated. Brecht was interested in the end result of his works; he never saw his plays as fulfilling prearranged aims.

2. Although Brecht had political interests, he was not really a politician. Losey sees Brecht's political interests as almost somewhat peripheral and certainly lacking in dogmatism. Again, he views Brecht as a practical man rather than a theorist.

3. Although Brecht's work can be stylistically austere, it is not at all cold or uninteresting.

4. Brecht had a Germanic temperament but was blessed with a sense of humor as well.

5. Brecht was, personally, an alive, vibrant man.[3]

In sections, Losey, rightly or wrongly, all but reduces Brecht to technique. Losey writes of him, for example, "I had interpreted it as significant for Brecht not that truth is absolute but that it is precise, that there is a good manner of having access to it: justice of observation, economy of means of expression."[4] From this, Losey sees a Brechtian cinema as made up of:

> The stripping down of reality and its precise reconstruction by means of a choice of symbols-reality;
> The importance of precision of gesture, of texture and line in objects;

Economy of movement, actors and camera; to have nothing moving without a reason; a sense of difference between calm and motionlessness;
The focus of the eye by the exact use of lenses and camera movement;
The fluidity of the composition; the juxtaposition of contrasts and contradictions, helped by montage and by the text, is the simplest fashion for obtaining the very highly regarded distancing effect;
The importance of the exact words, sounds and music;
The exaltation of reality to ennoble it;
The extension of the vision of the individual eye.[5]

In Losey's view of Brecht, form follows function, the expression of the film is an integral part of the content. While *Cahiers'* later critics would doubtless reject Losey's interpretation of Brecht, it is easy to see the great compatibility of this view with the *Cahiers* of 1960. If part of *Cahiers'* interest in Brecht comes out of the magazine's interest in Losey, Losey clearly emphasizes the side of Brecht attractive to *Cahiers*.

The December 1960 special Brecht number also contains two theoretical essays, one by Bernard Dort, the other by Louis Marcorelles. Dort begins with a somewhat pessimistic observation about the lack of applicability of Brecht to the cinema.

I know well; this proposition has all the air of a paradox. *A priori*, the work of Brecht has nothing to do with the cinema. I would say further—it pushes away, refuses the cinema violently. It wishes itself to be, with ostentation, theatrical, purely theatrical.[6]

From this initial observation, that the medium of film rejects a Brechtian approach by nature, Dort works forward to a reconciliation of Brecht and film through a kind of reanalysis of Brechtian theory:

Let us in fact characterize the epic Brechtian theater no longer by the necessity of a distanciation or alienation effect (it is only the means to an end, and to consider it alone, one risks freezing the theater into rhetoric), but as the essential will of Brecht to offer to the spectator, through the medium of art, images of social life that are recreated, that is, rendered comprehensible, from which the spectator can, by an incessant movement between identification with the character and the comprehension of an historical situation which makes these characters what they are, draw forth a valuable lesson for its period....
One sees it; understood at this level, the Brechtian system does not exclude the cinema. What art is better than cinema to elicit such a new look, to allow for a grasp of everyday life in that which is most concrete, and by means of this grasp lead to an historical understanding?[7]

Dort's analysis bears fruit when he seeks to apply it to specific examples. A first example is André Bazin's critique of Chaplin's MONSIEUR VERDOUX. According to Dort's argument, Bazin surely unconsciously applied a Brechtian analysis to the work. According to Bazin, we identify with the character of Verdoux partially because we see him as Charlie; at the same time, the acts he does in VERDOUX run counter to our sense of morality, so we are forced to examine them objectively, in terms of the conditions which have made Chaplin the way he is in the film. The movie is, as it were, a dialectic between our identification and our comprehension. As we see society judge Verdoux in the film, so we come to judge society. This is a particularly pointed observation for Dort to make in *Cahiers,* for it links Brecht to *Cahiers'* spiritual father, Bazin.

Dort repeats the same argument, applying it to two films by Antonioni, IL GRIDO (1957) and L'AVVENTURA (1960), comparing them in the process to Brecht's *Mother Courage.* According to Dort, on the external level, both the Brecht play and the Michelangelo Antonioni films contain characters whose fortunes seem ruled by fate. Yet in the play, Brecht emphasizes two aspects: one, the effect of social forces as being that which makes Mother Courage what she is; two, the potential for her to change: she alone is responsible for her fate. Dort sees the Antonioni films as working from identical premises. Antonioni underlines the social status of his characters, presenting them as products of their society. At the same time, however, one of his chief themes is the potential for the individual to change, to refuse to accept the society which constrains him.

Dort discusses two recent French films as well, Claude Chabrol's LES BONNES FEMMES (1959) and Louis Malle's ZAZIE (1960). In each case, he sees a surface realism in the films linked to a metaphoric structure in their stories. The movies are not just naturalistic recreations of Paris life but presentations from which more generalized conclusions can be drawn. This leads to Dort's central thesis: that film can by nature be a Brechtian medium because the techniques of the fictional film are a kind of mediation between the rough naturalism that the director often shows and the generalized observations about society that a Brechtian aesthetic requires him to make. Film is, to Dort, an art of *mediated* reality, of a reality which is carefully reshaped by the artist. It is this mediation which makes film Brechtian and resolves the supposed problem. Dort's dialectic is here linked further at the end to Bazin and to Bazin's rejection of what he called the "cult of personality" in extreme auteurism; Dort's critique can be seen as a reaction against such extremists and their recent popularity at *Cahiers.* At the same time, however, it puts Dort's preoccupations in a straight line with the *Cahiers* tradition coming forth from Bazin. Like Losey, Dort never addresses himself to directly political questions.[8]

Louis Marcorelles applies himself to the question of Brecht and the cinema somewhat differently. He addresses quite specifically the question of acting, first discussing the lack of interest in the actor in the modern cinema. To Antonioni, the New Wave directors, even Hitchcock, the actors are mere servants to the director, tools whereby he can create his own personal vision. He sees the emphasis on realism in the film as the reason for this decline in acting traditions.

Marcorelles then draws a parallel to literature. Modern literature, he says, has emphasized a destruction of the real, of realism (he cites James Joyce and Alain Robbe-Grillet). Modern film, by contrast, has destroyed the unreal conventions of acting, to be found, for example, in Max Ophuls or Jacques Becker, to talk only of the French cinema.

Brecht can serve, Marcorelles' careful argument continues, as a basis for the reintroduction of artifice into the cinema and as a reintroduction of the importance of the actor. According to Brecht, a good performance is a dialectic between the faithful recreation of a person's external behavior and the actor's ability to comment on that behavior. In addition, Brecht, because he used a communist model, saw the actor as a co-creator with the playwright. (Thus, in this context, Marcorelles sees such filmmakers as Jean Rouch or Karel Reisz as more Brechtian than anyone, to the extent that their films are co-creations between the filmmaker and the actor.) Thus, to Marcorelles, the problem of applying Brecht to the cinema is one to be solved through the actor, through the development of styles of playing which imply a dialectic between actor and director, between external reality and comment on it. To demonstrate his points, Marcorelles takes examples from the acting of the Berliner Ensemble.[9]

Marcorelles' essay is also somewhat anti-auteurist, seeing film as a collective endeavor. It reacts against "pure cinema," emphasizing rather the relationship between film and reality. This article, perhaps more than any other, suggests a new direction to come at *Cahiers:*

> That would signify, finally, that our critics, above all our young critics, will make up their minds one day to descend from the planet of so-called "pure cinema" and look at the world around them, to help a bit with its transformation. Not to be content with idealist speculation on the genius of directors, above all American, without control over their art and who must submit to the necessities of commerce. It has been accorded to us by nature to live right in the middle of the scientific century to which Brecht wished to give an art worthy of its ambitions. The cinema will or will not be this prodigious revelator of the contradictions of modern man; of that which is frozen and dies. It will teach us to live fully the instant, without losing the view that this instant is inscribed in an historic or even a cosmic continuity.[10]

There are several conclusions to be drawn about *Cahiers'* special Brecht number:

1. The articles (excluding those by Brecht himself) seek a kind of evolution, rather than a revolution, in cinematic forms and criticism. While Dort and Marcorelles call for change and criticize extreme auteurism and "pure cinema," they also link themselves to both current art works and to previous precedents in *Cahiers du Cinéma.*

2. The articles are technically biased. Losey talks about techniques and purity of forms as inseparable from intentions in a film; Marcorelles discusses the role of the actor. Only Dort talks about film from the point of view of the critic rather than the filmmaker.

3. While the articles acknowledge Brecht's Marxism, they do not emphasize it. Brecht's artistic importance takes precedence over his political importance. (In this respect they may really be a distortion of Brechtian thought.)

4. The articles tend to treat the problem of making Brecht applicable to the cinema, taking for granted that Brecht *should* be made applicable to the cinema. In other words, they take the importance of Brecht as accepted.

5. The articles are future oriented. Brecht is seen as a wave of the future (perhaps even the next wave after the New Wave). They suggest, not a culmination or summary of interest in Brecht, but rather a commencement. This attitude did indeed turn out to be a self-fulfilling prophecy. Brecht was to become a major guiding force at *Cahiers* by the late 1960's. This special number on Brecht is an early indication of things to come.

Louis Marcorelles

Of the critics who contribute to the special Brecht number of *Cahiers*, the one who does the most to bring Brecht to the magazine in general in the later 1950's and early 60's is Louis Marcorelles. Although he tends not to be so strongly associated with *Cahiers* as many of the other critics (especially those who became filmmakers), he is a major name in the magazine at this time and produces articles or reviews for almost every number. Marcorelles could not be described as a Hitchcocko-Hawksian or a MacMahonist but rather has far more eclectic tastes. He is certainly interested in the American cinema and writes articles on films by the likes of John Ford and Leo McCarey, the new school of directors to come out of television, and a new American semi-documentarist like John Cassavetes, to mention only a few of his subjects. This same critic is also concerned with other international cinemas, particularly behind the iron curtain and in Germany and Britain. Indeed, his writings only very infrequently deal with French film at all.

Among Marcorelles' many interests is Brecht, and he even writes drama criticism for the British theater review *Encore,* some of it dealing with Brechtian considerations.[11] Marcorelles is probably the first *Cahiers* critic to mention Brecht at any length; in 1956, in a discussion of the Actors' Studio, he compares Elia Kazan to Brecht, much to the former's disparagement:

> Elia Kazan, like Bert Brecht in Germany, puts realism of *mise en scène* and acting to the back, but to ends essentially contradictory. Brecht insists on the necessity for the spectator to keep all his lucidity, to be able the better to criticize, whereas Kazan always has cards up his sleeve and aims in the end at a hypnotic effect rather close to that dispensed by the cinema. The critical lucidity of Brecht is pitilessly opposed to the exaggerated sentimentalism, heavy with all possible neuroses, of Kazan.[12]

In December of 1957, Marcorelles gives *Cahiers* its first lengthy article dealing with Brechtian thought, the opportunity being a review of Alberto Cavalcanti's film version of Brecht's play, *Master Puntila and His Servant Matti.* By way of introduction to his review, Marcorelles gives historical information about Brecht and places him in the history of theater as well, as an anti-Aristotelian, closer to Elizabethan theater, which sought to relate history to its present society's concerns. The critic then continues to outline Brecht's idea of the place of the spectator in a drama and his notion of the *Verfremdung* effect, relating the latter both to acting styles (opposing it both to the Stanislavsky/Actors' Studio Method and the French boulevard theater) and to music and decor. Marcorelles concludes his introduction with the somewhat eccentric suggestion that Bresson, in his handling of actors, would be perhaps the most Brechtian director working at that time.[13]

Applying these ideas to the Cavalcanti film, Marcorelles proceeds to demonstrate the ways in which Cavalcanti's efforts, despite their desire for fidelity to Brecht, are essentially a betrayal of him. Marcorelles' conclusions suggest that there is an essential incompatibility between Brecht and the cinema, an idea he will repeat later and one which will ultimately put him in opposition to the post-1968 *Cahiers.* He finishes by noting:

> Brecht attempted in all his work to obtain a maximum of *critical* realism. For him art is inseparable from the transformation of Society: a new Society requires a renovated art. From which comes epic theater, all but disregarded in Moscow where bourgeois-socialist realism always reigns. The cinema by nature possesses first off this hypnotic power so feared. Eisenstein, the other great genius of the socialist world, adopted an opposing position, in every function of the instrument he was making use of. What is, in the final analysis, his "montage of attractions," an offspring of Meyerhold's "bio-mechanist" theater (the mechanics of life), of which he was a disciple, if not a grandly elaborate instrument to stimulate the spectator? And in the last article that he wrote, on stereoscopic cinema, the director of POTEMKIN and IVAN THE TERRIBLE envisions the cinema, endowed with the fourth dimension, as a sort of dynamic theater, thrust into space, realizing a synthesis of all the other arts. All theater, up to the new order, is inevitably based on the constraint of three walls, supposing the absence of a fourth, thus anti-realist. Brecht mitigated these limitations by the most rigorous aesthetic system that one could imagine (it would be necessary to talk of the quasi-cinematographic quality, by this definition, of Brecht's *mise en scène);* he joined realism by a maximum of sophistication. The cinema is born realist: Cavalcanti has completely forgotten that.[14]

Although the post-1968 *Cahiers* critics are to argue that Eisenstein extends Brecht's theories, that montage is a way of producing an active spectator, the above paragraph is nonetheless of fundamental historical importance, for it is *Cahiers'* first lengthy consideration of the issues it raises.

Part of Marcorelles' interest in Brecht clearly comes out of an interest in socialist art; he repeatedly discusses the Eastern European cinema. His interest in Brecht becomes a way of reaffirming a concern with the issues of revolutionary art, while rejecting the so-called bourgeois, academic socialist realism associated with Stalinism. He praises, for example, the first two films of Andrezj Wajda as providing alternatives to the duller forms of communist art (though interestingly, in a later review of ASHES AND DIAMONDS (1958), Wajda's third film, he criticizes the director for seeking to revive an outmoded expressionism related to Pabst—the corrupter, Marcorelles states, of Brecht's *Threepenny Opera*).[15] By 1960, Marcorelles sees socialist art as clearly providing an important alternative to the art of the West. In a review of Konrad Wolf's STARS (1958), an East German film written by the Brecht-influenced Angel Watenstein, Marcorelles sees in several Eastern European films a tendency toward the construction of careful argumentation which uses the poetry of cinema in the service of a social conception of society. STARS becomes a prime example, a film which uses, not the "vulgar realism" rejected by Brecht, but rather "precise indications in the acting, the decor, indications as rigorous as the composition in someone like Stravinsky or Eisenstein, aiming at another realism, of subject."[16]

One of Marcorelles' most important applications of Brecht is in his review of Ingmar Bergman's THE VIRGIN SPRING (1960). One may remember that *Cahiers* had been one of Bergman's chief defenders when his films were being introduced into France in the 1950's, and thus Marcorelles' examination of the connections between Brecht and Bergman is a linking of *Cahiers* to its own traditions. Marcorelles is, in his own words, obsessed by these connections and seeks to explain them. He writes:

> The Marxism of Brecht acquires all its sense only in reference to Christianity; the Christianity of Bergman has little to do with Catholicism. With both of them the imprint of Protestantism is ineffaceable, but corrected and modified in the need to dramatize the problems of man, be they social or metaphysical.[17]

Marcorelles describes the way in which Bergman treats his subject in a Brechtian way, substituting his own brand of Christianity for Brecht's Marxism:

> Bergman, an agnostic by temperament, preoccupies himself more with dramatizing his subject through the problem of good and evil; with his mournful, unhealthy tension inseparable from his manner, he relates what is above everything a fable, exactly like Brecht in *The Good Woman of Szechuan* or *The Caucasian Chalk Circle*. Like Brecht, he leaves the question open; with a Marxist interpretation in Brecht's case, the choice arises whether to opt for socialism against capitalism, the source of all ills; with Bergman, it is the background of Christianity, where nothing is ever given in advance.[18]

In other words, Marcorelles' argument is that Bergman's choice between believing or not believing in God is presented open-endedly, just as Brecht presents the choice between socialism and capitalism. The difference between the two is merely one of subject matter. This is in one way typical of *Cahiers* at the time, of a tendency to see Brecht as an important formal innovator, assuming implicitly that the form can be applied to a different type of content. For indeed, Marcorelles devotes much of his space to Bergman's "flat" style and the way in which his *mise en scène* allows each character to develop separately. Following Brecht's ideal, Marcorelles argues, Bergman deals with the growth of his characters.[19]

A far more scholarly text deals with a film with which Brecht was actually connected, Fritz Lang's HANGMEN ALSO DIE (1943). Marcorelles gives a considerable amount of historical information on the film and comes up with the conclusion that Brecht's theories are not really applicable to the cinema. He writes:

> All this to repeat what is plain evidence, that the admirable theatrical theories of Brecht are not transportable to the cinema, that if the reflection and the very concrete experience which produced them maintain, indeed, their value as an example, and are able by analogy to allow the *cinéaste* to become conscious of the formal and economic traps which he risks falling into, they nonetheless oblige him to find a new solution inasmuch as he is preoccupied with the problem of critical realism, at the heart of Brechtian thought.[20]

Marcorelles is saying that Brecht's ideas are valuable as a stimulus to solving comparable problems in the cinema but that they do not provide genuinely cinematic solutions. Rather, he carries this generalization about film to a specific level in talking about Lang's film and why it is not really Brechtian. He notes:

> For Brecht the truth of the moment does not exclude a more profound and more general truth. Contrary to this, the truth with Lang takes its place only in the moment, on the level of appearances. Both men claim to have an "idea." But with Brecht, the idea is first in the content, a point of view about the real world; with Lang, there exists only the space of its apparition on the screen, an open window on the imaginary world. If Brecht never really took the cinema seriously, it is perhaps because he feared the terrible power of cinematographic illusion, which magnifies indiscriminately anything and everything.[21]

Marcorelles' articulation of the problem, namely the fear of the capacities for cinematic representation, suggests exactly what *Cahiers'* subsequent treatments of Brecht will develop further. For it will become the argument in *Cahiers* that the Lang point of view is exactly what is to be rejected in the film, that the imaginary world of the cinema is by nature repressive.

As the 1960's progress, Marcorelles writes increasingly less frequently for *Cahiers du Cinéma;* he becomes something of a champion of the *cinéma vérité* movement, and his relation to this, Brecht, and the post-1968 *Cahiers* will be discussed later in Chapter 7.

Hoyveda on EVA

One of the most extreme but interesting texts in *Cahiers* on Brecht and film is Fereydoun Hoyveda's discussion of Joseph Losey's film EVA. Hoyveda considers EVA one of the great works of the whole history of cinema, on a par with CITIZEN KANE (1941) and other classics. His chief argument is that Losey's cinema is formal, that its emphasis on formal values is what makes it great:

> If I might summarize in a lapidary formula the new film of Losey, I would say: *for the first time in cinema, meaning is found entirely in form.* Cinematographic language achieves here a complete independence. To understand the purpose of the author, it does not suffice to question only the dialogue, the decor, the expression and the gestures of the actor. But also it is necessary to examine closely the movements of the camera, the lighting and the construction together in their dialectical relationship to the rest. More than ever one must say with Godard that a travelling shot is a moral consideration. Nothing gratuitous in the *mise en scène.*[22]

Hoyveda attempts to link Brecht to this attitude about the film, citing at great length the article by Losey which had appeared two years earlier in the special Brecht number of *Cahiers,* specifically the part, cited above, in which Losey describes the elements of Brechtian technique that are applicable to the cinema. Hoyveda writes:

> I would like first to insist on the general construction of the film. One might, without the risk of being mistaken, qualify it as Brechtian. . . . [Hoyveda here quotes Losey on Brecht at some length.] All this is in the *mise en scène* of Losey and results in an impeccable distancing which refuses all possibility of identification to the spectator, and leaves him, to participate in the work, only the free exercise of his intelligence beyond ease or constraint. . . . In truth, EVA appears cold only to those who do not see and who remain insensitive to the beauty of the form and the idea. The second degree emotion which goes back to the intellect, is it not superior to that immediate one that makes use of the primary process of identification and projection?[23]

This way of reasoning draws us back to several of the indirect roots of *Cahiers'* interest in Brecht, such as formalism, Platonism, the admiration for Losey. Hoyveda's review may thus be seen as a kind of extreme point in *Cahiers'* formalist line, one defined (by Losey) as Brechtian. It is a particular interpretation of Brecht and a questionable one, but, even if it is a corruption, it also marks an acceptance of certain key Brechtian notions—lack of identification and distancing. Hoyveda accepts Brecht as a stylistic influence and concludes his review with a discussion of the movie's stylistic approach:

> Losey's style goes counter to the current of a cinema which reasons, explains and calculates. By opposition to what I would call the filmmakers of the "soul" (for example, Antonioni or

Bergman), one might say that Losey is a *cinéaste* of the "body": to the attempt at penetration into the "subjectivity" of beings, he prefers an objective relationship which is limited alone to cinematic means. In this sense, he makes "pure cinema."[24]

Such an approach to Brecht presents his theories as an alternative to conventional Aristotelian drama. While it does distort Brecht, Hoyveda's review nonetheless highlights the points of continuity one can find through Brecht between the early, formalist *Cahiers du Cinéma* and its later, politicized period.

Other Criticism Related to Brecht

There is another kind of criticism appearing in *Cahiers* which is related to Brecht's theories but which does not always mention him by name. It is not always possible to tell if the critics in question have been thinking about Brecht and are familiar with him or if they have arrived at similar ideas independently. What is important, however, is that the kind of criticism employed comes straight out of some of the lines of thought already discussed; it appears periodically in *Cahiers* and is not centered in one or two writers. Rather, it would seem that many of the critics who write for *Cahiers* on occasion praise a film for some quality that might be described as Brechtian, or at least anti-Aristotelian.

There are, interestingly enough, three main kinds of films for which this type of criticism appears. The first kind consists of films of the New Wave, specifically the films of Chabrol, Godard, and, in a somewhat different context, Jean Rouch. The second is the new Italian cinema of directors like Francesco Rosi and Vittorio de Seta. The third group of films for which analysis reflects these concerns consists of two films from the American cinema, by classic established directors. A fourth consideration of this section will be two essays, one by Michel Mardore, the other by Jean-Louis Comolli. Both discuss the question of politics in the cinema and reach conclusions which are a kind of foreshadowing of the direction *Cahiers* is to take.

Cahiers and the French New Wave

The early films of Chabrol, Godard, and Rouch produce an interesting critical phenomenon at *Cahiers du Cinéma*. Both Chabrol and Godard had enjoyed critical and commercial success early in their careers with THE COUSINS (1959) and BREATHLESS (1960), respectively. Both directors had been former critics for *Cahiers,* and their success as filmmakers might in some ways be seen as a vindication of the magazine, although each man's career fell into something of a slump following these initial successes. In both cases, Brecht-related theory is employed in *Cahiers'* pages to justify such critical and commercial failures as Chabrol's LES BONNES FEMMES and OPHELIA (1962) and Godard's LES CARABINIERS (1962).

The case of Chabrol is particularly interesting, for there is little in Chabrol's writings or statements about his films to indicate an interest in Brecht. Rather, the *Cahiers* critics seem to want to justify a certain coldness of attitude they find in his work, a certain refusal to work on the level of strict naturalism, for which he substitutes a tendency to combine elements of stylistic realism with other elements of theatrical convention. Since *Cahiers* at this time develops a reputation for reviewing favorably films made by its former critics, it is difficult to say if this theory is used as convenient justification for films that would otherwise be considered artistic failures or if the effects described were intended by their makers. In any event, the arguments are of substantial interest in establishing the beginnings of a Brechtian bias.

LES BONNES FEMMES is a film by Chabrol which at the time of its release received a particularly universal negative response, although critical attitudes toward it have become far more favorable in recent years. We have already discussed Bernard Dort's application of his notion of mediation to the Chabrol film. André S. Labarthe sees the film as ushering in "a new era, the era of realism, of syntheticism, of objectivity."[25]

Labarthe's argument is that the Chabrol film is objective, not just in the sense of being free from bias, but also in the sense that it renders its various subjects like objects, like things which can be scientifically studied. Thus, he writes:

> The study of human mores does not differ by nature from that of animals: it differs only by its object. This takes place in the long scene at the swimming pool and above all at the zoo, where the impossibility of the objective [the French word here is *"objectif,"* which can also mean "lens"] juxtaposes, like a collector his stamps, the cries of the animals with the laughs of the *bonnes femmes*. For it is not only the gestures, the attitudes of the *bonnes femmes* which appear absurd, it is also their language, from which we can seize the formal characters before the meaning. The language itself is objectified, one might say even reified.[26]

Chabrol, Labarthe argues, wants the audience to observe his *bonnes femmes* objectively, dispassionately, rather than with the cinema's usual emotional charge. In the critic's words, LES BONNES FEMMES "deprives us of our comfortable habit of going from the sense of a film to its form."[27] Rather, we see the film at first through its forms and only from there work out to more generalized meanings. It is this emphasis first on intellectual observation which makes this argument so modern and, in the end, so allied to a Brechtian line of thought. Labarthe's comparison of the film to scientific study and his praise for the work's objective observation of gestures and behaviors can also be related to both Brechtian scientific ideals and the social gest.

Much the same approach to Chabrol is employed some three years later by Jean-André Fieschi, writing about Chabrol's OPHELIA and LANDRU

(1962). Fieschi, however, takes his discussion of Chabrol one step further than Labarthe and sees Chabrol's use of stylization as praiseworthy for being analytical and dialectical:

> In any case Chabrol's characters, whether they be the manipulators or the manipulated, are spectacles in themselves. From being just the following of rules, this extreme theatricalization which is so often reproached becomes (and it is here that it also unites with expressionism) a means of *analysis:* all the givens of the *mise en scène* unite together in an aesthetic and a morality of the scalpel—supremely cold, the commercial failure of LES BONNES FEMMES is not to be found elsewhere. The treatment of gesture establishes a distance between the author and the characters, just as it does between the characters and the audience. The sense is no longer in what one sees, but *next to it*. The same holds true for the dialogue. The text (and whether it is by Gégauff or Sagan matters little) becomes a kind of vocal material in which the delivery unveils a different meaning from that of the words used.[28]

The example Fieschi gives—of the delivery of dialogue being in opposition to the meaning of the words—is a characteristic technique of Brechtian alienation.

Fieschi continues his discussion, treating LANDRU[29] as a film which historicizes the reality it presents (again, another Brechtian ideal). Fieschi sees two methods for approaching an historic reality on film, the first being to use the neo-realist style of Rossellini, the second being the one employed by Chabrol, whereby history and myth are related. Fieschi emphasizes the benefits of a spectacle which presents an event at the same time that it comments on it and notes that LANDRU is a film for which the audience maintains its objective, critical faculties:

> The side of Chabrol which is an entomologist here finds almost a moral justification: he has succeeded in presenting us with the document (no matter if it is reconstructed, since it comes off more honest and convincing, by this bias, than the most humble appearing montage compilation film) and the judgment on this document. The honesty here consists of never for an instant seeking to make us believe that we are living in Landru's time. The spectator always remains aware that this is a film in 1962 and the processes of distancing employed by Chabrol in his preceding films here take all their weight.[30]

Only at the end of his critique (and in its title) does Fieschi indicate a definite link to Brecht, but he clearly sides with this Brechtian stance and sees it as the quality that makes Chabrol modern. (This is in contrast to Labarthe, who appears to be working independently of any Brechtian influence.) Fieschi concludes:

> The tour de force of Chabrol has above all been, utilizing such means, to avoid dehumanizing his film to the point of making it a fable. I mean that he has known how to obtain a truth, an emotion, in spite of challenges to the conventions used, and if our Brechtians were more lucid in that which concerns the seventh art.... [ellipsis is Fieschi's][31]

This line of argument about Chabrol continues in other reviews of his films in *Cahiers*. For example, when Luc Moullet reviews the director's purely commercial project, THE LINE OF DEMARCATION (1966), he suggests that Chabrol works from a realistic framework to come up with something other than pure naturalism. Moullet observes that "Chabrol's realism is a more profound realism, it goes beyond the framework of film and concerns its consequences: it brings the audience back to its own realities, reestablishing a public scale which the comedy film, the demagogic or message film, tend today to split into several layers."[32] In other words, Moullet is again concerned with the relationship of the audience to the spectacle (and indeed, with a film that can reach a large audience rather than a bourgeois one). The critic's praise for Chabrol's use of deliberately stylized, stock, typed characters is right in keeping with the same theoretical concerns:

> And the superiority of THE LINE OF DEMARCATION over La Patellière, Verneuil and consorts [purely commercial French directors] is in the fact that Chabrol proposes to us only characters that are visibly fabricated...rather than the character played by Gabin or Ventura which is falsely presented to us as spontaneous, natural and without problems. As if this personality were not the most complex, the most fabricated of all...as if, after fifty centuries of civilization, the spontaneous, the natural, the absence of problems were not the very index of deceit.[33]

The case of Godard is somewhat different. Godard has acknowledged the influence of Brecht throughout much of his career. As early as 1962, for example, he is reported to have written, "One must not forget that the cinema should today more than ever keep for a rule of conduct this thought of Bertolt Brecht: not how are true things but how things are truly."[34] In an early film like MY LIFE TO LIVE (1962), Godard breaks up his story into ten episodes or tableaux through the use of titles, an effect which clearly relates to Brechtian technique. In like manner, one might be able to see Brechtian implications in almost every *Cahiers* article on a Godard film: the films lend themselves to such an analysis.

Let us therefore consider only two particularly interesting responses to films by Godard before 1968, Paul Vechialli's critique of LES CARABINIERS and Jean-Louis Comolli's review of ALPHAVILLE (1965). Vechialli begins with a discussion of the lack of success of the earlier film and attributes this to its lack of a satisfyingly emotional treatment of the subject of war. He notes:

> If the spirit is always overwhelmed, it is never excited. All reflections being included, the film becomes a necessary passage to its end, and refuses any evasiveness.[35]

The critic sees LES CARABINIERS' chief virtue as providing no solution for the problem of war that it presents: it presents its war as neither revolting nor justified but simply as useless. The lack of a solution is what bothers the audience; the movie offers no reassurances.

Vechialli suggests that the way the movie does this is to render all of the characters equally unsympathetic. He writes:

> The objective sympathy that an author can grant to his characters is very quickly transformed into a subjective sympathy by the viewer who, recognizing the chosen side, accuses the author of demagoguery toward the others.... The only honest approach is to make them all equally antipathetic.[36]

This is not a completely Brechtian notion, in that Brecht would say that it is important to take sides in a war but that it is necessary to do so objectively. Yet the notion of subverting the traditional narrative structure of the war film, whereby the audience empathizes with one side over another, certainly does suggest the direction forthcoming at *Cahiers.* And while Vechialli's approach to the work is certainly apolitical ("What is important in this film is thus for us to move up to a more precise, more lucid morality, that of total kindness: a morality of Indulgence"),[37] he praises aspects of the film which have affinities to Brecht.

The transition from the old to the new *Cahiers* is demonstrated remarkably in Jean-Louis Comolli's review of ALPHAVILLE. Early in his essay, Comolli introduces an analogy to painting, which, while certainly formalist, indicates the movement (which has taken place in art criticism as well) away from an idealized, Platonist formalism to a more materialist one, in which what is important is the physical, material nature of the paint itself. Comolli complains that no one, in looking at a still life by Braque, seeks further information about the objects that make up the composition ("what the fish may be telling each other, why they are there and not in the sea, to whom the lemon belongs, and whether the plate is exploiting them"). In cinema the opposite is true: "an actor cannot put one foot in front of the other without the spectator wanting to know where he is going, why, whether the woman he loves has broken with him, and whether that is his last pair of shoes."[38]

Comolli praises Godard for having made in ALPHAVILLE a film for which the images have no special meanings, for making a cinema of "non-interpretation, non-commentary, non-signification." He explains later in the review:

> This equivalence of elements is a characteristic quality of the cinema of Godard. There is a refusal to privilege one sign at the cost of others. All things are given, are shown, as equal. Everything is on the same plane: the "negative" sequence seen from the same distance and even on the same level as the scenes of the scuffle, the drive, or the closeups of the headlight; not a unity of tone, a uniformity, but a unity of measure and an equality of weight. The smile has the same worth as tears, the gesture in air and the gesture that kills are charged with the same intensity. The cinema of Godard is not a preferential cinema; in it nothing is stressed—

or rather, everything is stressed in the same manner, which does not go without shocking people: that "hollow" moments, the words or the gestures that most directly concern "the action," confers on them an increase of presence, a vexing insistence, a place that seems all the more invasive because it does not exist at all in conventional cinema.[39]

Clearly, this view of the film is not directly Brechtian, for Brecht advocated anything but a rejection of explanation and emphasis. Where this point of view does link to Brecht, however, is in its calling for a comparable objectivity, for a comparable lack of concern with the problems of empathy and identification. The "presentation of contradictions" that Brecht calls for requires a similar lack of privilege toward either side of the contradiction. Comolli's explanation of ALPHAVILLE may more properly be seen as a kind of terminus of *Cahiers* formalism: the "non-interpretation, non-commentary, non-signification" suggests a theoretical point of no return. But it is an end point which, with a few shifts of assumption, can be converted without too much difficulty to a Brechtian point of view.

One of the key events of the 1960's in French film is the development of the *cinéma vérité* movement, which seeks to revolutionize the conceptions usually held about the documentary film. The key figure in the movement is Jean Rouch, whose anthropological films call into question the nature of filmic reality by freely mixing documentary materials with staged or semi-staged sequences, all of which feature non-professional casts. Rouch's intent has been to underline the illusory nature of all film but also the corresponding truthfulness of the medium. In addition, his work implies a different set of priorities in dealing with the narrative. Plot is no longer of central importance; things become important not because they fit into a preconceived notion of the subject but because they occurred during shooting and were captured by the camera. His films are also marked by a technical freedom and a lack of polish (e.g., occasionally mismatched editing, bad photography).

Rouch has been consistently championed by *Cahiers du Cinéma,* and much of this admiration may be seen as stemming from the fact that he treats the very nature of film, i.e., both the filmmaker's relationship with the reality he photographs and the viewer's relationship with the film he sees, offering an alternative to the conventional narrative film and conventional notions of representation on film. He is defended at *Cahiers* by Michel Delahaye, whose writings about Rouch raise some points which clearly relate to *Cahiers'* subsequent positions. Delahaye raises, for example, the question of film as an ideological discourse. His argument, that any film not only presents but also interprets reality, has already been suggested by both Amédée Ayfre and Jacques Rivette, but it is to become a cornerstone of later *Cahiers* theory. Delahaye writes:

What is not "authentic" are the facts, the ideas, and the ideas about the facts: their interpretation. For the fact is always contaminated by an at least latent interpretation. Once the interpretation reveals itself as such, then the truth, on this static group, becomes possible. But one will only be able to approach it by giving in to its dynamic of impossible truth, looking to make possible its impossibility, in a dialectic which involves the fact interpreting itself and the interpretation realizing itself, of the interpretation as a moment of reality, of the false as a moment of the true. Inversely, the search, offered from the beginning, of objectivity makes of the truth the ultimate moment of falsehood: nothing is given to that which pretends to straightforwardness, everything to that which captures it in the night of opposites.[40]

In other words, the only true approach is to acknowledge the subjectivity of the filmmaker (and the nature of film) in approaching the objective world.

Similarly, Fereydoun Hoyveda has discussed a film like Rouch's CHRON- ICLE OF A SUMMER (1962) in terms of the work's use of a structure that goes very much contrary to the traditional Aristotelian one found in the conventional narrative film:

> . . . let us affirm that rather if, as Rouch himself would say, LA PYRAMIDE HUMAINE is a film of a film, CHRONICLE OF A SUMMER is simultaneously a film and the film of this film. Habitual logic would ordinarily demand that we talk about each of these two aspects, each one in turn. But it is advisable to distrust the traps of our Aristotelian heritage. A film *and* the film of this film, yes; but mixing without end their images to wind up with something absolutely new, arising of its own force.[41]

This notion of a cinema which reflects on itself, of a film which comments on its own processes is one very much related to Brecht. Indeed, the Brechtian truth in *cinéma vérité* would be in the acknowledgment of all the interventions of the filmmaker. The problems raised by *cinéma vérité* with regard to reality run very much parallel to those raised by Brecht for theatrical realism. They will become particularly important after 1968, in Jean-Louis Comolli's "Le détour par le direct," a theoretical essay on *cinéma vérité* which we will discuss shortly.

Cahiers and the New Italian Cinema

If the *Cahiers* critics apply Brecht to the French New Wave films of the early 1960's, they do much the same thing with some of the new Italian cinema of the same period. Unlike their French counterparts, however, directors like Francesco Rosi and Vittorio de Seta are politically committed, and, while they make films that come out of Italian neo-realism and are semi-documentary in tone, Jacques Joly, in a 1962 number of *Cahiers,* seeks to relate their work to Brecht:

> This role of the spectator, this will to create works which do not alienate is another characteristic of the new Italian cinema. It is not a question of making us feel the anguish, the misery, the injustice of a world, but of teaching the observer to open his eyes, and since

Brecht is the bedside reading of the young Italian directors, let us borrow from him the end of *Arturo Ui:* "Aspire to see instead of looking stupidly." In pushing to its limit the will to provoke the spectator's lucidity, one ends up at two "documentaries" of feature length: Vittorio de Seta's BANDITS OF ORGOSOLO and Francesco Rosi's SALVATORE GIULIANO.... There was only one way: for the analysis of an objective reality, to employ the most real and objective tone possible. Not to call on the spectator's sensibility, or his heart or identification, but to trick the intelligence by talking to it in the language of evidence and historic truth.[42]

While Joly praises this branch of the Italian cinema, he by no means does so to the exclusion of other cinematic forms: his discussion of Rosi and de Seta comes in an article in which other approaches in the Italian cinema are lauded as well. *Cahiers,* typically pluralist in its interests at this time, again accepts the Brechtian cinema alongside other forms of film as well.

The significance of Rosi for *Cahiers,* and particularly of SALVATORE GIULIANO (1961), his film about the Sicilian bandit, is not to be underestimated. Jacques Doniol-Valcroze, one of the main editors of the magazine for a long period of time, is later to discuss the work in a review of a later Rosi movie. While his article makes no mention of Brechtian theory, much of what he talks about (historicization, presentation of contradictions) is remarkably similar to it:

SALVATORE GIULIANO marks, in my opinion, an important date. All that makes up the essence and originality of neo-realism can be found in it.... Rosi adds here a lesson that comes from elsewhere (and perhaps even from CITIZEN KANE): a dedramatization of historic givens by breaking the usual narrative structures. He does not recount the life and death of Giuliano, he reflects before his cadaver and invites the viewer to this reflection by turning the pages of an enigmatic dossier. To account for the complexity is to be obscure with precision, imprecise with lucidity.... He [Rosi] reconstructs *everything* with the greatest fidelity to existing documents, but only that which had been seen and heard and from the manner in which that evidence had been available. The assembly of material is thus a method, and this method is that of intellectual liberation.[43]

Again we can see a link between the old *Cahiers* and the new. Just as in the Italian cinema the neo-realist tradition could be seen as growing in a Brechtian direction, it would be appropriate for *Cahiers* to adopt critical methods appropriate to the new cinema being produced. There is doubtless a two-way process: *Cahiers* is influenced by the films its writers see and admire but, just as much, it exerts an influence on the cultural climate in which films are made. Much of *Cahiers'* writing is practically oriented toward dealing with new films as they appear, way before it enters the realm of the theoretical.

Two American Films

If some of *Cahiers'* pre-1968 writing responds to films intended to be Brechtian in style, some of it, in turn, works with films whose intentions have nothing to do with theory but whose results are particularly compatible with a similar theoretical framework. This is the case with two writings on the American cinema, Michel Mardore's review of Billy Wilder's IRMA LA DOUCE (1963), and Jean -Louis Comolli's analysis of Raoul Walsh's OBJECTIVE BURMA (1945).

Mardore, for example, praises Wilder's "realism," even though he sees that realism as something stylized, something that goes beyond mere surface faithfulness to appearances. He argues that Wilder's satire on the French *flics* is far more pointed than anything which could appear in France about the police yet acceptable because it is in an only semi-naturalistic context in the film. Mardore values the Wilder work for its dialectical approach:

> Ambiguous, for in this coming and going between stylization and naturalism, between the burlesqued and the serious, the true level on which the film should be read appears difficult to grasp. According to our position, one side destroys the other, and vice-versa. Like all truly modern creators, Billy Wilder has not escaped the problem of a certain "distanciation," even involuntary. This is not the facile categorization that it might seem to be, but, on the contrary, a reason for the tearing apart of each artist. The originality of Wilder (and this process is imposed on IRMA) consists of rendering the decision impossible for the spectator. One no longer knows what is distanced, and what distances. The stupidity of any sort of definition indicates the discomfort of the spectator as a fundamental motivation in the work.[44]

For another genre, the war film, Jean-Louis Comolli talks of the several layers of the film's realism. On one level, he notes, the film is characterized by a high level of technical accuracy (unlike many Hollywood war films): it was even used as an instructional film for guerilla fighters. In the mixture of superficial accuracy with the movie's plot, he sees the result as "an explosive mixture of the abstract with the concrete." Comolli raises an argument that seems to come out of phenomenology, one which discusses the nature of cinematic reality:

> The greater number of works place themselves in double reference to the world and to the viewer, between which they play, very simply, the role of mediator. But here is a film considered by its privileged spectators as a piece of the world itself: its reality is no longer of expression; it can no longer be a mirror of the world, since one makes of it a mirror *in* the world. Also, between OBJECTIVE BURMA and its spectator is established a relationship more direct than is customary: in fact, the spectator finds himself face to face with the film in the same manner that he is face to face with the world. The film and the world are put on the same level. From here comes the concrete dimension of the film. But from there also comes the fact that the work loses its mediational function between the spectator and the world: no longer in contact with the spectator as a work. For, if it is put on the same level as the world, it is not necessarily merged with it: it is like the world, but alongside it. And it is this alternation

(necessary in order that the work not be absorbed by the real and still be a work) which provokes the receding series of passages, of oscillation between opposed and complementary terms: the more the spectator takes the work as reality, the more it must become unreal to subsist on its own and be all the same with the concrete, the abstract, the material and the spiritual.[45]

What is Brechtian here is not the general argument but the recognition that a film's nature as a discourse comes from its unrealistic element as a film. The differences between a film and the world are what allow us to understand the way in which the film is *about* the world. (The reverse is implied: the less manifest those differences, the less the film says.) Comolli's is not a materialist analysis of the film, but, as with his review of ALPHAVILLE, it suggests certain points of continuity between his critical work of 1964 and that of five years later.

Two Significant Essays

In 1966, both Mardore and Comolli produce essays which discuss theoretical issues and which indicate the direction that *Cahiers du Cinéma* is shortly to take, bringing the magazine one step closer to the adoption of a Brechtian line. The first to appear, in February of 1966, is Mardore's "Age of Gold (Buñuel), Age of Iron (Rossellini): Notes on Politics and Cinema." In it, Mardore begins with an examination of French politics—the victorious fashionability of the left—and the usual notions of political cinema—contrasting the complete propaganda film, in which the entire work centers around a political theme, e.g., POTEMKIN (1925), SALT OF THE EARTH (1954), with the entertainment film which contains occasional political references, e.g., VIVA MARIA (1965), IRMA LA DOUCE, THE TIGER SPRAYS HIMSELF WITH DYNAMITE (1965).

To Mardore, this dialectic accompanies a second one, the classic discussion of form and content, which in turn suggests yet another controversy, one of intellect vs. passion. He writes:

> Passion is choice sustenance for the artist, and at some moments fury rightly prevails over reason. But these works possess the same sort of beauty as music or painting, whose inspired disorder the constraints of socialist realism, no more than those of other doctrines, have not succeeded in curbing. By its nature, the film of passion loathes political analysis.[46]

Mardore links this problem to the tradition from which *Cahiers* has grown, noting that the classic Hollywood cinema, made by so-called reactionary *cinéastes* like John Ford, King Vidor, Howard Hawks, and Samuel Fuller, has often been far more interesting than the deliberately leftist cinema. He finds inadequate the two usual solutions to the problem, either that the films should be dismissed as right wing films or that they are right wing only in content, progressive in form.

Mardore continues the line of argument with a discussion of Sartre's notion of engagement, whereby, for example, with the Algerians during the war, "it was better to be carrying bombs than to direct films of carriers of bombs." The critic sees this as a narrow view: "If we want an adult cinema, it is necessary to discover politics where it actually is, in the totality of man and of society, not in anecdote and sectarian interests."[47] The subject of political film is the whole of man. Mardore continues his attack on the Hollywood cinema with this idea as his chief arguing point and in so doing makes the statement which, in varying forms, is to become the battle cry for a new generation of political film critics: "In our eyes, everything is political." He points out that all the seemingly insignificant details of a film, in decor, costume, or behavior, all "verify some political option. ... The total vision that one takes from a film is singularly more important than the 'political' details gargled by the chronicler of opinion."[48]

Thus, a change toward a politicized cinema must be a total and fundamental change. Mardore's formulation prefigures the declaration that will be repeated constantly in the later *Cahiers* that films will ordinarily support the ideology under which they are produced. Mardore's solution is to seek a cinema that would acknowledge and treat the political contradictions of its time. To Mardore, the true political cinema is not a cinema of propaganda, but rather "an objective cinema, serene, complex, pitiless, in the measure of the mysteries and of the cruelty of our time." He cites SALVATORE GIULIANO as such a film, praising its "really dialectical research."[49]

Mardore thus concludes with an opposition between two types of political cinema. The first would be a cinema of "pure contestation, of integral anarchy and whose sublime prototype, unequaled, would be L'AGE D'OR." It is an alternative Mardore rejects in favor of an approach he sees derived from Rossellini. He writes:

> The aim of politics in the cinema is not to repeat the action of the combatants, with derisory weapons, but to supply the intelligence with facts, to teach the spectator the art of reinventing the world by himself. One should no longer evoke strikes, unions, the contradictions of capitalism, without having patiently assimilated the rudiments of political economy. One should no longer cite the Vietnam war without taking into account the complexities of international politics. Nothing is played in advance, nothing is "white" or "black."[50]

In other words, Mardore calls for a didactic cinema, a mode of film not tied to bourgeois theatrical forms of identification and passion but to the objective assessment of facts. He calls for genuine political discourse.

Comolli's essay is shorter and less involved. "Notes on the New Spectator" begins as an assessment of the purely physical conditions under which most people see films, i.e., the use of the *salle obscure* (darkened theater) as reflective of the nature of film as a medium of transference, fascination, myth. The piece is Freudian in approach, but, like Mardore's, it is also a qualified attack on the Hollywood cinema. Comolli writes, "what the absolute supporters of American cinema love in that cinema is not, never has been, the beauties, the audacities, or the new forms, that the Hollywood freelances of genius dealt out; on the contrary, it was, and sadly, it always is, an automatic satisfaction, without problems, of their desires (if we can call these impulses desires)."[51]

The *Cahiers* critic continues by attacking the passivity of the usual cinema audience, citing the very same qualities of those audiences that repulsed Brecht.

> Entering the cinema, the spectator is at first prisoner of the dark theater; conditioned by it to receive certain impressions, to expect certain thoroughly standardized series of emotions, he must carry through a real effort at resistance, he must undertake to detach himself, in order to appreciate the slightest *film d'auteur*, film that, by definition, does not conform to the norms fixed by the tradition of the *salles obscures*. Once in the darkness, the spectator must remain awake in order to understand something of the film that refuses to consider him as a spectator asleep.[52]

To this, Comolli opposes the notion of the *salle claire*, in which the spectator would watch the film in an alert, non-sleep-like state, a cinema which would play to the audience's intellect. And the purpose of the *salle claire* would be to help create a cinema which relates to the real world: "Of course this *salle claire* is also a dream: but no longer the dream of a cinema of escape, the dream of a cinema that would derive from life, and, in the end, would be truly our reflection of life (it is in this sense that today one can "live the film")."[53]

These two essays are particularly important and prophetic for the following reasons:

1. They no longer reflect the old *Cahiers'* pluralism but seek for an improvement of cinematic forms. They do this in a nearly polemical fashion.

2. They qualify very severely *Cahiers'* admiration for the American cinema and reject rather strongly certain extreme factions of auterism.

3. They seek an active audience that is alert and unmanipulated, that exercises its intellectual capacities in an active way. They reject audience passivity.

4. They seek to relate film to the real world, to treat film not just as an art form that exists in a closed universe but one that involves the whole of mankind's reality.

We have thus sought to trace, in the preceding pages, the introduction of Brecht into *Cahiers,* beginning with the influences and precedents which prefigure this introduction, moving through the actual texts in *Cahiers* which deal with Brecht, and concluding with a selection of articles which reveal affinities to Brechtian thought (some in response to films which begin with a Brechtian attitude; others on films less intentionally modelled in this way; and yet others more theoretically based in considering the nature of film in general).

Part III

Brechtian Criticism After 1968

6

A New Politicization

The year 1968 is generally regarded as one of the most significant dates in recent French political and cultural history. The date also marks a break between what is often referred to as the "old" and the "new" *Cahiers du Cinéma,* the former being apolitical and formalist, the latter not only politicized but Marxist-Leninist in its avowed line. As a result of the events of May 1968, most French film criticism takes a decided shift to the left, to a point where by the mid-1970's virtually all major intellectual French film reviews may be said to characterize themselves as leftist.[1] Thus, *Cahiers du Cinéma* on the one hand reflects certain trends which are felt more generally in French writing about film; on the other, it proves to be a major force in reformulation of film theory taking place at this time.

The preoccupations of Parts I and II of this study, formalism and Brecht, are both particularly relevant to more recent critical writings in *Cahiers du Cinéma.* The post-1960's work in the journal represents in part an extension of the formalist concerns of the earlier years, in part a rejection of them: in many ways, form is still seen as the major point of critical discussion, but it is always viewed as inseparable from content, which in this new light means *political* content. The efforts of *Cahiers* since 1968 represent a vindication of Brecht's postulate that the form of the work is as much a political question as the overtly political implications of the content.

For practical purposes it will be necessary to separate *Cahiers'* theoretical and practical writings. This chapter and the one following deal with theoretical issues; the next two treat practical writings. This is done somewhat more easily in principle than in actual practice, for much of *Cahiers'* theoretical writing is written in the discussion of practical examples, and much of its specific criticism draws from or exemplifies some of these new theoretical approaches. Nonetheless, the separation is justified. For one thing, after 1968, there is an increasing amount of theoretical work done in *Cahiers;* the editorial choices made in the magazine become linked less to recent releases of films than to the more general problematic concerns of the authors who write for the magazine. While some of this writing does arise in direct response to problems raised by certain contemporary films, much of it is far more theoretically involved with the nature of the film medium. Thus, it is only for select films that advances in theoretical thought arise out of specific stimuli: these films will be treated in the Chapters 8 and 9 of this study, but they will necessarily be preceded by two chapters devoted to an analysis of *Cahiers'* more generalized, theoretical discussions.

Roots of the New *Cahiers* Approach

The changes that arise in *Cahiers* are hardly without precedent even in writings from before the influential events of May 1968. By the mid-'60's, there is evidence in some of *Cahiers'* articles that many of its writers have started to look for new, alternative critical methods and conceptual frameworks. In November of 1965, for example, *Cahiers* publishes a round table discussion of the *politique des auteurs* which is essentially critical of many of the excesses and abuses that the theory had produced. One of the conclusions of the article, for example, is that *auteurs* are the exception rather than the rule in the American cinema, that the great American directors are those who have managed to escape the system and produce personal work in spite of it. In some ways, the article may be seen as a result of the shift in *Cahiers'* interests away from the American cinema and towards the new *jeune cinéma* movements in Europe, Asia, and South America: implicit in it is the assertion that the film medium's major revelations are no longer to be found in the American cinema but elsewhere.[2]

Jean-Louis Comolli, a relatively new critic at *Cahiers* at this time but one who is to play an increasing role in the shaping of the magazine, articulates this need for new critical approaches in his review of René Allio's THE SHAMELESS OLD LADY. It may be no accident that the film in question is based on a short story by Bertolt Brecht and that the director in question, René Allio, was to go on to do several Brechtian films which were to be followed very closely by *Cahiers* in the development of the magazine. Comolli writes:

> Ten years of *Cahiers* criticism contemplates in vain certain key films of today (from GERTRUD to ALPHAVILLE, from MAN'S FAVORITE SPORT to THE FIANCEES). All the critical apparatus which up to the present has taken in charge Bergman or Hitchcock stalls before the youngest iconoclasts, but also before the recent works of these consecrated authors. . . .
> The question thus is to know how this new criticism will forge itself; the response must be that the work henceforth is not just the anvil that it was before but must become the blacksmith himself. In fact, if one looks for an effective base for this critique of modern works, this can only be what one finds already in these works to participate in a critical movement. The films we are concerned with now have in common a quality of being at once the work and its conscience; they proceed by a creative movement (always obscure, mysterious, inexplicable, as creation) and by a reflection on this movement, extracting from the mysterious order a disorderly logic.[3]

Comolli is talking about two kinds of things here: first, about films that comment on their own being, the processes whereby they are made, their own achievements; in other words, the type of film that is involved, not just in illusion-making but in an analysis of its own structure. Secondly, he is implicitly saying that the relationship between the viewer and the film is changing, partially due to these kinds of films but also, perhaps, to a new kind of viewer sensibility, one which rejects passivity. This new sensibility is often provoked by the films themselves.

This new type of relationship between the viewer and the film is suggested later by Comolli in his response to Jean-Luc Godard's LA CHINOISE (1967). Comolli discusses the notion of "reading" a film. This idea of "reading" or *lecture* in film is no doubt in part borrowed from semiotic analysis[4] and at the same time implies that formal analysis is of utmost importance to the full comprehension of the work of modern cinema. Comolli observes about LA CHINOISE:

> LA CHINOISE demands expressly what every film timidly suggests to its spectator, to read the images: the image is there to be read, and there is nothing there not to be read, and anything that can be read is there. To read the image—or rather to decipher it as for a handwritten text which one glances over for the first time—is not to make an interpretation of its signs, nor to decode its ciphers, nor to analyze its pre- and post-suppositions. Rather the patient spelling out, shot by shot, task by task, of its "constituents"—but with this nuance that the image in itself constructs the constituent parts, makes them visible and manifest. Beginning with such a marking—an operation of a scientific rather than critical nature—of the *facts of the image,* a second, more global, critical reading can be constructed.[5]

The active analysis of a filmic text is a notion that forms a cornerstone for the writings of Noël Burch which appear in *Cahiers du Cinéma* in 1967 and which have been translated into English in the book *Theory of Film Practice.* In some respects, Burch may be considered the apotheosis of formalism in *Cahiers du Cinéma.* Burch's main thesis is that the most creative use of the film medium is in those works that are most keenly aware of the medium's structural possibilities, its purely physical limitations and qualities. Burch has summarized his point of view on this:

> The contemporary film narrative is gradually liberating itself from the constraints of the literary or pseudo-literary forms that played a large part in bringing about the "zero point of cinematic style" that reigned supreme in the 1930's and 1940's and still remains in a position of strength today. It is only through systematic and thorough exploration of the *structural* possibilities inherent in the cinematic parameters I have been describing that film will be liberated from the old narrative forms and develop new "open" forms that will have more in common with the formal strategies of post-Debussyian music than with those of the pre-Joycean novel. Film will attain its formal autonomy only when these new "open" forms begin to be used organically. What this principle involves is the creation of a truly consistent

relationship between a film's spatial and temporal articulations and its narrative content, formal structure determining narrative structure as well as vice-versa. It also implies giving as important a place to the viewer's disorientation as to his orientation.[6]

Some of Burch's notions, such as his assertion that the space outside the frame of a film is as artistically important as the space inside the frame, have been subsequently attacked in *Cahiers du Cinéma* as idealist and as just as regressive in their own way as Bazin or any non-materialist criticism.[7] In this respect, Burch's writings may be seen as merely a sophisticated extension of *Cahiers'* previous line, a taking of principles of formalist criticism to a logical end point. On another level, however, they form a bridge to the newer, politicized *Cahiers,* for in his preoccupations with the material qualities of the film medium, Burch does write materialist film criticism. The writing is a rejection of Platonism in that it refers not to any sort of essential forms but to the forms materially present in the given film. In his introduction to the English language edition of the book, Burch writes, "Although no special emphasis is placed upon the fact in this book, my entire approach was, even then, implicitly predicated on the conviction that the illusionist approach to film-making—comparable to what Brecht condemned in the theater as 'identification' and what the nineteenth century called 'the pathetic fallacy' and which is in fact the *raison d'être* of what I call the 'zero point of cinematic style'—contains a fundamental principle of alienation that degrades both film-maker and spectator."[8]

In addition, Burch introduces in his book the notion of what he calls "dialectic," and while he acknowledges that his use of the word is not as rigorous as some Marxist theoreticians would like, he nonetheless makes use of some ideas which will be refined and developed further in the politicized *Cahiers.* Particularly important is his championing of certain films, like Marcel Hanoun's UNE SIMPLE HISTOIRE (1958), for the dialectic they contain between the visual and sound tracks. This same separation is insisted upon, as we shall see, by the theorists of the *Groupe Dziga-Vertov,* among others, as a means both of combatting the illusions they seek to avoid and also of making precise the nature of the image being presented on film.

The other key influence on *Cahiers* at this time is that of structuralism and semiology, i.e., the study of film as a branch of the linguistic study of signs and symbols. The first major indication of this is in the December 1966 issue of *Cahiers,* an issue called "Film and Novel: Problems of Narrative."[9] From this point on, articles with a semiological bias appear in *Cahiers* with increasing frequency.

The primary attraction of the semiological approach is its presumed scientific nature. The comments by Comolli on LA CHINOISE quoted above indicate a desire to understand the filmic text fully before being able to comment on it critically. The desire to rid film criticism from its ideological biases and to approach it scientifically is in keeping as well with the Marxist vision of history as a science. It is a notion also found in the writings of Louis Althusser, a key influence in French cultural history of the time.[10] Semiology thus becomes the science whereby one discovers the determinations which make films what they are, an idea expanded and modified in later *Cahiers* criticism.

The history of semiology has long had this leftist bias. As early as the 1950's, Roland Barthes (whom we have already discussed somewhat as an influence) was writing about semiology and Brecht together, as related problems in aesthetics. Barthes notes in one of his essays:

> For what Brechtian dramaturgy postulates is that today at least, the responsibility of a dramatic art is not so much to express reality as to signify it. Hence there must be a certain distance between signified and signifier: revolutionary art must admit a certain arbitrary nature of signs, it must acknowledge a certain "formalism," in the sense that it must treat form according to an appropriate method which is the semiological method.[11]

Thus, any movement in *Cahiers* toward the direction of a scientific analysis of a given filmic text may be linked also to an analysis of the way in which the signifiers which comprise that text are used. A materialist reduction of the art work, such as Brecht would advocate, ends in its political and economic determinates. If an Althusserian view of Marxism equates politics and history to a science, then the new film criticism may be seen as equating political criticism of the art work to scientific analysis.

Cahiers du Cinéma following 1968 is formed out of a collection of disparate influences and approaches which manage to converge and interrelate to form a relatively unified system. In the pages to come, an analysis of the sytem—which uses both a new kind of formal analysis and Brechtian theory as its cornerstones—will be attempted.

A New Politicization

May 1968, as a point of revolutionary change for contemporary French cultural history, is a key event in *Cahiers du Cinéma's* changeover to a political line. The effects of the political events on French film criticism of the time have been analyzed by both Sylvia Harvey and Maureen Turim and in Thomas Elsaesser's study of the periodical *Cinéthique.*[12] Turim notes the emergence in the 1960's of a movement composed of students and young workers which provided a leftist alternative to the *Parti Communiste Française,* one which allowed for organized anti-Gaullism that would also eschew the pro-Soviet line of the establishment Communists. Turim talks about May 1968 in particular. She writes:

The student-worker uprising of May 1968 can be seen as the turning point for the *Cahiers* staff, just as it was for many French people. The Gaullist regime proved more vulnerable than anyone had dreamed and the lines of demarcation between the right wing and the gauchists were so clearly drawn that there remained no comfortable middle ground. The French Communist Party aligned itself with the Gaullists against the far left and in the crisis one was either a revolutionary or a fascist.[13]

If the "events of May" clearly serve to traumatize the *Cahiers* critics as they did other French critics, Elsaesser suggests an even more complex web of theoretical, intellectual influences. Elsaesser describes two of *Cahiers'* main writers and editors at this time, Jean-Louis Comolli and Jean Narboni, as followers of Philippe Sollers, head of the literary magazine *Tel Quel.*[14] *Tel Quel* is published by the French publisher Editions du Seuil, a publishing house with a distinctive type of product, and source of the editions of Barthes' and Christian Metz' writing, as well as the French semiological review *Communications* (with which these authors have also been associated). Thus, we may see the development of a sort of network of influences and affiliations. Barthes becomes a senior figure from whom both semiology and ideological analysis develop (to the point, one will grant, where they are to disagree with each other), in both literature and film. He is also, as has already been mentioned, one of the key men responsible for the introduction of Brecht into post-war French culture. Thus, this network which develops from Barthes by way of Editions du Seuil and Philippe Sollers has certain fundamentally unifying points of assumption, despite much in-fighting within the group, and is a primary influence on the branch of it indirectly established in *Cahiers du Cinéma.*

A particularly significant event, and one which appears to influence *Cahiers du Cinéma* profoundly, is the founding in 1968 of *Cinéthique,* a film magazine also attached to Editions du Seuil, Phillippe Sollers and the materialist philosophy connected with them. *Cinéthique* proves to be a determining factor in *Cahiers'* shift of position. *Cahiers'* attempt to define its new stance may be seen most directly in a two-part article written by Jean-Louis Comolli and Jean Narboni entitled "Cinéma/idéologie/critique." The first of these articles is a statement of the new *Cahiers* position; the second is a response to *Cinéthique,* a critique of the newer magazine which attacks it even while accepting implicitly several of its fundamental assumptions. Let us consider these two articles in somewhat more detail.

The first begins with an examination of the relationship of both *Cahiers* and the film medium to the economic system. Both are seen as commodities, implying they need a certain amount of complicity with a capitalist economic system. Because films are made to be sold—and this applies even to so-called revolutionary films—they tend to reflect the dominant capitalist ideology. In effect, this text argues that all film is ideological and that the ideology of most films is capitalist. (This is hardly far removed from Brecht, although the authors' formulations may well have been drawn up independently of him; Brecht's text on the lawsuit of THE THREEPENNY OPERA, for example, seeks to demonstrate how the capitalist system under which the film was made distorted its message.)

The culprit, as it were, for Comolli and Narboni, is cinematic representation (just as realism was for Brecht). Their argument is that representation and realism are not real, nor are they true:

> One knows that the cinema, "quite naturally" because the camera and film are made for this end (and that the ideology imposes this end), "reproduces" reality. But this "reality," so susceptible to being reproduced, reflected by instruments and techniques which are otherwise a part of it, one indeed sees as completely ideological. In this sense, the theory of "transparency" (cinematographic classicism) is eminently reactionary: it is not the world in its "concrete reality" which is "seized" by (or, rather, imbues) a non-intervening instrument, but the vague, unformulated, non-theoretical, thoughtless world of the dominant ideology.[15]

Comolli and Narboni acknowledge their sources in Althusser in the article: they call for film to be looked at as ideology because it deals with man's relations with the world, rather than as a science, that is, a direct relation with the world. Thus, representation becomes a dishonest form of expression, in that it seeks to create the impression of a direct treatment of reality when what really takes place is interpretational, indirect, and ideological. According to the *Cahiers* authors, "The most important task of cinema, knowing the nature of the system which renders it an instrument of ideology, is thus to put in question this very system of representation: to question itself as cinema, to provoke an alternation or a rupture with this ideological function"[16]

The critics then proceed to divide all films up into seven categories, each of which demands a different type of treatment. They are:

1. The greater majority of films which unthinkingly reflect the dominant capitalist ideology. The critical approach required for these films is to point out their ideological assumptions and determinations.
2. Those films with both political subject matter and political form. These films are the only films seen as capable of reacting against the dominant ideology. [Examples given: Jean-Marie Straub's UNRE-CONCILED (1964), Robert Kramer's THE EDGE (1968), Glauber Rocha's THE EARTH ENTRANCED (1967).]
3. Those films whose content is not explicitly political, but whose treatments of filmic forms are perceptive about the nature of film in a way that becomes progressive and politically advanced. [Examples: Jean-Daniel Pollet's MEDITERRANEE (1963), Jerry Lewis' THE BELLBOY (1960), Ingmar Bergman's PERSONA (1966).] For these

films, as well as those of category 2, Comolli and Narboni require a dual analysis, of both the signifiers and the signifieds and how they unite in a political message.

4. Those films produced within the dominant ideology whose politics are leftist but whose forms are not. [Example: Costa-Gavras' Z (1969).] Here what is seen as necessary is an examination of how the political signification is weakened by the use of reactionary forms.

5. Those films whose intentions are in keeping with the dominant ideology but whose result is out of keeping with the manifest intentions, i.e., those films which in spite of themselves point to political and economic realities in the world. (Examples: some films of Ford, Dreyer, and Rossellini.) These films require an examination of the ways in which they escape the dominant ideology.

6. Those films of the *cinéma direct* movement (i.e., that branch of filmmaking, which includes *cinéma vérité,* that favors the use of direct sound, lightweight cameras, and an improvised approach) which do not escape the dominant ideology. These works are therefore to be treated like those films of type 4, as films which do not see how their underlying forms are self-defeating. In other words, these *direct* films still fall into the trap of representation. [Example: Richard Leacock's CHIEFS (1968).]

7. Those films of the *cinéma direct* movement which question the system of representation, to be treated like type 2 and type 3. [Examples: Pierre Perrault's LE REGNE DU JOUR (1966) or LA RENTREE DES USINES WONDER (1968).][17]

The major link between this article and *Cinéthique* is that both take as their most important premise the economic nature of cinematographic production: film is a commodity, and this existence as a commodity affects every aspect of its nature. From its very inception, this has been *Cinéthique's* major critical premise; it is one that Comolli and Narboni also seek to adapt for *Cahiers.* Where the two differ is in the application of this premise, and indeed, *Cahiers'* second article on "Cinéma/technique/idéologie" is an attack on *Cinéthique* for working from these principles ineffectively. In it, Comolli and Narboni discuss what they see as *Cinéthique's* readings of Althusserian principles, and seek to show that Marcel Hanoun's OCTOBRE A MADRID (1965), for example, a self-reflective film about the process of making a film, championed by *Cinéthique,* hardly escapes the capitalist marketplace either. For them, *Cinéthique's* methods of favoring science over ideology, as Althusser advocates, only fall into further ideological traps.[18]

One suspects, too, that a category like type 3 (as described by the *Cahiers* authors) may be included as something of a response to *Cinéthique,* for the films which the newer magazine has found principally praiseworthy have been not films with directly political content but those which research formal properties of the film medium, such as Pollet's MEDITERRANEE. The two magazines differ significantly, however, at least in Elsaesser's view, in that *Cinéthique* sees this type of film as the *only* politically advanced cinema whereas *Cahiers* would advance that it is only one of several. Indeed, *Cahiers* rejects interest in pure formalism as bourgeois and lacking in political effectiveness. There is the suggestion of an ironic contradiction here, for on the one hand this concern with the formal properties of political works provides the new *Cahiers* with a link to its old, formalist past; on the other hand, the extremes of formalism practiced by *Cinéthique* have now become more radical than *Cahiers* and are rejected by it.

The extent to which *Cahiers* begins to define itself in terms of *Cinéthique's* line of thought may be seen in Jean-Louis Comolli's review of Ingmar Bergman's SHAME (1969). Almost all of Comolli's review is a response to a negative critique of the film by Jean-Paul Fargier, a writer associated with *Cinéthique,* who attacked the film violently in the *Tribune Socialiste*. Comolli quotes at great length from Fargier's article and implies that Fargier's comments are very important for a Marxist critique of the film.

Fargier's main argument is that, to the extent that Bergman's SHAME is a film about war, it is a reactionary work. Bergman's refusal to specify the nature of the two sides fighting and his concentration on the reactions of the individuals caught in the middle becomes, to Fargier, an attempt to escape the economic and political realities of war: to imply that all sides are essentially equal in a conflict is an essentially bourgeois notion. The refusal to specify particular political, economic, and social realities becomes a form of obscurantism and mystification.

Comolli's response goes back to Fargier's main assumption, that SHAME is a film on the subject of war, and attacks it. (Comolli even goes so far as to dismiss Bergman's own claims about his film.) Thus, his defense of the work is, essentially, that it is unfair to attack it as an unclearly defined film about war, because it is really a film about a human relationship for which war is an accompanying metaphor. The primary focus is in the disintegration of the relationship between the two main characters, not on the specific war, nor on any notion of war in general. Comolli argues that war is used by SHAME to support a discussion of psychology, rather than psychology a discussion about war.[19]

While it is possible to see Comolli's defense of the film as a rationalization for his liking the film and Bergman, the fact that Comolli sees it necessary to argue on Fargier's terms in itself indicates an acceptance of his basic assumptions. The Comolli review is a direct example of *Cahiers'* being forced on the defensive by a more radical segment of French film criticism.

Statements of *Cahiers'* general political policies continue to appear at regular intervals for the next few years, through the writings of one or another critic for the journal. Certain texts signal the expansion and development of *Cahiers'* ideology during this period; these warrant study in some detail to see how their main arguments are organized, outlined, and summarized, to provide a direct statement of the magazine's positions.

The *Groupe Dziga-Vertov*

The next major, generalized statement of political policy comes with a text on the *Groupe Dziga-Vertov*, that filmmaking collective formed by Jean-Luc Godard after May 1968. In 1972, the group released TOUT VA BIEN, which may now be considered its main achievement, and *Cahiers'* primary statement on it occurs at about this time. (*Cahiers'* analysis of the film itself will be treated in the last chapter dealing with "practical" rather than "theoretical" criticism; this text is, beyond doubt, a major critical effort of this period.)

Cahiers' main theoretical text on the *Groupe Dziga-Vertov* begins with the statement by Godard (and his partner of the time, Jean-Pierre Gorin) that one must make political films politically. The authors contrast this with the usual notion of the "political film," i.e., one which uses a political subject to produce an effect of sensationalism and, as a result, something which can be marketed. In their words, "to make political films politically" should produce films where: "1. the subject is political and dictates the *mise en scène* (the subject has a decisive role); 2. the *mise en scène* is subordinate to a working in the film for political practice which fights specifically on the level of filmmaking itself against a profit-motivated ideology."[20]

This same text links this process directly to Brecht, and most specifically to Brecht's struggle against the passivity of the spectator. It draws from the distinction which Brecht makes in his introduction to *The Rise and Fall of the City of Mahagony* between "dramatic" forms and "epic" forms, the former being, in *Cahiers'* terms, "metaphysical, idealist, and petty bourgeois," the latter "materialist, dialectical, revolutionary."[21]

On one level, it is this use of Brecht which distinguishes the *Cahiers* approach from that of *Cinéthique*, for *Cahiers* never goes so far as *Cinéthique* in the rejection of all drama. Indeed, this article notes: "It is not a matter of simply eliminating drama; the epic form is the critique of the dramatic form, by the principles of narration and *mise en scène* which are antagonistic to dramatic effects and the metaphysics they imply (for example, the *Verfremdungseffekt*—the effect of distanciation which renders unnatural—distorts—the events of the plot.)"[22]

Thus, the techniques of Brecht fight against the audience's passivity, and this fight is waged in favor of the construction of a dramatic narrative which would allow for a different set of moral decisions than those of the traditional dramatic form. "To demolish the mastery of the dramatic scene is to demolish that of morality, of subjectivism; to present political problems, that is, *problems of decisions* to be made—politics is the science of making decisions (to choose at every moment between two positions, two ways, two lines)."[23]

The article provides a kind of summation of the position taken against representation, against realism: "The image is no longer innocent, it no longer reflects the world as it is mechanically and truly, it is no longer the immediate duplication of a world made ambiguous by essence ... the cinematographic image is a human discourse, an ideological discourse." Because of this, in the films of the *Groupe Dziga-Vertov,* "each shot, each fragment of each film is the object of questioning, of study, of discussion, of knowledge, in its relation and linkage to the others."[24] The text repeats the fundamental message of Brechtian thought: that realistic theatrical representation is basically false.

Having established this, however, the essay "Le 'groupe Dziga-Vetov,'" moves onto a far more sophisticated level of argument about the nature of the filmic image and its relation to the use of sound in film. It argues that the conventional film is "epistemophilic," that the place of the audience in the conventional film is to recognize and name what it sees, to identify for itself what is presented. The audience is always left with the role of interpreting the images it sees. The conventional film always refers to a reality which is "beyond," in the world, never to itself. Sound is used to cement this structure: "Put another way, there is a concurrence between the sound of the film and the silence of the spectator."[25] It is rarely used as a dialectic with the images, to explain what is being shown, largely because attempts to use sound this way usually result in a sense of *unreality* about the image. Yet this is exactly the use of sound (to produce a sense of unreality, or, in Brechtian terms, "alienation") that the article's writers call for, for this use of sound would create an awareness of what the audience really is seeing—not reality but a discourse about reality.

The *Groupe Dziga-Vertov* argues for a filmmaking practice in which the filmmakers consider the political implications of every image, sound or technique they use.

A New Set of Issues

Further efforts to establish a precise theoretical base for *Cahiers* were the result of a conference held by the editors in Avignon in 1972, to reassess *Cahiers'* position and its place in the class struggle. One result of this conference was a breaking of the writers for *Cahiers* into task forces to examine specific problems related to *Cahiers,* namely, "cultural animation" (a reevaluation of the recent *Cahiers* efforts toward a Marxist-Leninist line), the teaching of film, the notion of a "positive hero," and the production of revolutionary cinema.[26]

Early in 1973, the first reports from these groups appear, and among the most interesting is the one on the reevaluation of *Cahiers'* editorial policy, written by Jacques Aumont. In his report Aumont outlines the four major themes which have been studied in *Cahiers:*

1. The place of the spectator in the cinema, particularly in the light of recent psychoanalytic theory.
2. The relationship of film to the real, e.g., representation, realism, the functions of montage.
3. Narrative structures, studied in the context of semiology.
4. The use of characters and the fundamental questions of identification and distanciation.[27]

One may see where the positions taken by *Cahiers* on all of these issues cause them all to be interrelated. As was demonstrated in the argument about the *Groupe Dziga-Vertov*, the passive role of the spectator is a function of representation and surely has to do with character identification. Thus, Aumont's four major concerns are not to be considered separately but as a matrix of preoccupations which work with one another to develop a fairly unified framework of theorization (this, despite an eclecticism and diversity of which Aumont talks, i.e., a seeming lack of organization). In the discussions of *Cahiers'* writings to follow, these four areas of concern will reappear again and again.

The examination of what the functions of criticism should be continues with another series of articles by Serge Daney. Daney's first essay is in some ways a self-criticism of both the old and new *Cahiers*. He attacks the old *Cahiers* for equating aesthetics with politics, for saying that "any lacking of a film on a formal level must necessarily go back to a lacking on a political level," without seeing that the politics of a film often produces its forms (which means that its politics, not its form, really is primary). Similarly, however, he auto-critiques the new *Cahiers* for using its Marxist-Leninist orthodoxies too facilely and mechanically and too exclusively on the level of form.[28]

As an alternative, Daney suggests that one must examine "the relationship between two terms: *l'énoncé* (what is said) and *l'énonciation* (when it is said and by whom)." It is not enough to say that every film is motivated by the bourgeois ideology; one must specify how each film does this. He then goes on to suggest samples where the *énoncé* predominates (television documentaries that seem purely functional), those where the *énonciation* dominates (the *film d'auteur*), and the borderline cases ("progressive" films, critical of capitalism but still made under it).[29]

What Daney is saying here is that the political aspects of film are the most primary, that they should be the point of departure for the critic, and that the political signification of the work is as much a function of the context in which the work is produced as it is the form and content of the work.

Daney continues this line of argument in another article of the same "Critical Function" series. Daney begins this article with an example from THE NIGHT PORTER (1974), which he uses to discuss the nature of narrative in general. All films, he argues, force the spectator to choose between one of two sides; narrative conflict always implies taking sides. Repressive films tend to offer a choice only between two evils (as in choosing a Nazi who is less evil over one who is manifestly more evil) or a notion of arbitration (whereby a political conflict is settled on a middle, humanistic ground). "In film, as in the reality which produces film, FICTION IS A POWER STRUCTURE" [upper case is Daney's].[30]

That narrative forms must be understood and mastered by the proletariat for a genuinely progressive cinema is implied in one of Daney's footnotes, which suggests a new refinement in the statement of the problems of politically advanced filmic forms:

> The famous thesis of the "neutrality of forms" needs another thesis to live: that there is only one ideology, the dominant ideology. These two theses, put together, permit us to propose two others: one which says that forms are not neutral, that they return to their sources (that is, they are linked directly to the ideologies that invest in them), the other which states that there is something which resists the dominant ideology and which it is necessry to call, for lack of a more precise word, proletarian ideology. This ideology has, will have need for forms, need to know that fiction, for example, is not an open mould, but a power structure, before posing to it the question of its own power of its ideological hegemony.[31]

We can thus see in the years since 1968 a process of continual reaffirmation and refinement of the ideas expressed in the first article by Comolli and Narboni. The problem hinges on a film's form as well as its content being political, or, put in Daney's terms, the realization that politics dictates not only the content of a work but also the form that content takes. There is thus a constant suspicion at *Cahiers* of the "progressive" film, the film that seeks to make advances on the level of content but not of form. The task of the critic is therefore to examine how this process operates for each film; not, as Daney states, to accept that pattern (of progressive statements in reactionary structures) as stereotyped doctrine. The achievement of this goal is attempted to some extent by the practical criticism of *Cahiers* and that theoretical criticism which deals with specific techniques and issues of film form. If many of the texts err in the direction of generality, it is doubtless because this period is one of theoretical fertility at *Cahiers,* one in which attempts are made to reevaluate the basic concepts about film that have been too long taken for granted.

7

Reassessment of Classic Film Theory

Following 1968, virtually all of the theoretical assumptions of traditional film theory come under fire in *Cahiers du Cinéma,* and the magazine becomes devoted to a reformulation of principles and standards about cinema. The shape which such reformulations take is at times dictated by the personalities and preoccupations of the individual writers for *Cahiers* who seek to systematize their observations into a film theory that will proceed from a Marxist, materialist base. At other times, the writings seem more addressed to specific issues, and one will find pieces by several different authors which address themselves to comparable points of discussion.

This chapter will examine both types of writing. First, we will consider the work of two major theorists in the post-1968 *Cahiers du Cinéma,* Pascal Bonitzer and Jean-Louis Comolli, both of whom produce a series of articles aimed at the restructuring of the general conceptual framework for the discussion of film. Second, we will treat writings on four major theoretical issues: montage and post-Eisensteinian thought, the political implications of *cinéma direct,* naturalism and its corresponding codifications, and the applications of Lacanian psychoanalysis to film.

Two Major Theorists, Bonitzer and Comolli

The articles by Pascal Bonitzer and Jean-Louis Comolli represent an attempt at a complete revamping of traditional film theories and the vocabulary used to talk about film. Bonitzer and Comolli rebel against what they see as the dominant idealism of most writing about film and seek to direct their attention to making materialist formulations about the medium, to correct and adjust the generally accepted notions of how film should be considered.[1]

Pascal Bonitzer

While Comolli's series of articles, "For a Materialist History of the Cinema," are the more deliberately structured of the two authors' writings, Bonitzer's are in some ways more thorough and systematic. Seen as a whole, Bonitzer's writings move through all the standard areas of assumption about film (film as a reflection of reality, the notion of the close-up and of editing as "fragmenting" reality, or even the notion of the cinematic shot as being film's necessary primary structuring device). Bonitzer sees all of these assumptions as based in ideology; he criticizes them for being a set of repressively capitalist dictates produced by the economic sources at the root of the medium's development; all exemplify the repressive use of filmic fascination which results in viewer passivity. Let us examine some of Bonitzer's writings in greater detail, following a chronological order.

In the first part of " 'Réalité' de la dénotation," Bonitzer builds largely on an article by Jean-Louis Baudry, "Effets idéologiques produits par l'appareil de base," originally run in *Cinéthique,* which attempts to get at the fundamental ideological effects of the cinematic reproduction.[2] Bonitzer points to the notion of the close-up as demonstrating the way in which a seemingly apolitical notion is really ideologically based: we define close-up in terms of the human form and its proportions, a notion which historically can be traced to the Renaissance concept of the primacy of man and his proportions as a metaphysical model for the correct proportions of art. The notion of the "fragment" in the cinema always implies the presence of a whole (when in reality that whole need not exist for the creation of the effect of a whole). Bonitzer sees the way in which filmmakers customarily frame shots as an implicitly ideological attempt to reinforce the illusion that something exists beyond the frame. This in turn further aids the deceptive presentation of film as a reproduction of reality, rather than an ideological discourse on reality. (In this respect, Bonitzer's text is even a critique of Christian Metz, who continues to talk about film in terms of its analogic nature.) Bonitzer writes:

> What is hidden here [in the notion of the analogic nature of cinema] is the ideological/ symbolic reality of the "spontaneous" effect of recognition instigated by the mechanical production of a certain type of figuration, the apparatus of production "disappearing in what it has produced," the *eye* of the subject/spectator coming then to substitute itself for it, thus closing the imaginary scene. This effect of recognition, and this imaginary scene, which are purely ideological, are literally consecrated by the "scientific nature" of a semiology which sets up at the origin of the filmic text a purely denoted level.[3]

What Bonitzer here ultimately is arguing for is that there is no "pure" denotation in film, that everything recorded by the medium has a strong level of connotation which renders the filmic text ideological. Thus, while Bonitzer's text is a critique of Metzian semiology, it also reaffirms the necessity for genuinely scientific filmic analysis (which in this case would mean Marxist analysis).

Bonitzer's attacks become even more specific in an article dealing with the notion of the "shot" as the fundamental unit of film, "Fétichisme de la technique: la notion de plan." In this article, Bonitzer sees the use of the word "shot" (in French, *"plan"*) as something which aids in the avoidance of discussion of films' ideologies. "Shots" are generally defined either in terms of their function as linking agents (e.g., the *"plan-séquence,"* that is, a sequence or scene done all in one shot) or else in terms of their size (close shot, long shot, etc.). With the former, the use of the shot as a linking agent, the shot is therefore a fundamental agent in the building of narrative structures, which by definition cannot be separated from subject matter and ideology. The initial uses of differing shots by Griffith were essentially for the purpose of making film closer to the bourgeois theater that he idealized.[4]

For Bonitzer, the cinematic "scene" is defined in terms of the shot, and there is no scene without ideology. This article is in part a response to a series of articles on film and ideology by J.-P. Lebel, which appeared at about the same time in *La Nouvelle Critique,* a magazine closely linked to the establishment French Communist Party. Bonitzer's argument, like Comolli's to be discussed shortly, is that there are no filmic practices without ideologies, whereas Lebel takes the point of view that events like the development of montage are due merely to the technological limitations of the medium. Thus, to Lebel, it is not the montage *itself* which is reactionary but Griffith's bourgeois theatrical influences. To Bonitzer, Lebel condemns himself in his own words: why should one want the illusion of continuity in film when the nature of the medium goes against it? Bonitzer accuses Lebel of operating outside of history in his refusal to link the devopment of montage to the society that produced it.

With definitions of shots by size, Bonitzer makes the point again that they are measured by the human body, that our conception of shots is ideologically charged. Indeed, he points out, shots are perceived in terms of a figure in a ground; there is no way that one can talk about shots without talking about subject matter. Thus, the primacy given to the shot by theoreticians like Bazin is seen by Bonitzer to be merely a redoubling of the ideological inadequacies of the films themselves.

In addition, Bonitzer takes a psychoanalytic approach toward the primacy of the shot in literature on film. He describes the idea of the shot as fetishist (there being a conflicting desire to continue the scene without cutting and a desire to cut), which he in turn links to an obsession with castration. Bazin, he argues, wants to deny the castration of editing; this fetishistic approach to castration is fundamental to the use of editing in the film medium.[5] Thus, like Brecht, Bonitzer sees the techniques of representation in theater or film as being dictated by economic factors; unlike Brecht, Bonitzer applies a psychoanalytic layer of interpretation to this.

A link to Brecht may be made even more closely in discussing an article by Bonitzer which appears the following month in *Cahiers,* in which he treats the question of "off-screen" space in film. The creation of the effect of off-screen space is fundamental to the creation of the illusion of reality, which Bonitzer sees in turn as fundamental to film.

Bonitzer argues that the fundamental "ideological gesture" in moviegoing is the perception of a fictional depth in a two-dimensional image. "This depth," he writes, "denotes the reality in the fiction, the reality of the fiction."[6] He condemns this as the movies' greatest ideological hold over the viewer. This rejection of the "impression of reality," comparable to that of Brecht, relates to a notion of cinematic fetishism similar to the one advanced in the previous article:

> The "real" constitutes the ideological boundary around which all criticism revolves, the divided and blocked reading, between neurotic hesitation and the fetishist turnstile (denial), where the paradigms of "true" and "false" alternate. This alternation of "judgment," inhibition of reading and its results, that is to say its productivity, defines summarily the mechanism of *deception spec(tac)ulaire* [a pun meaning both specular, and spectacular, in the sense of theatrical]; the "taking distance" is a moment necessary to representation, which permits the foreseeing, the toleration and the mastery of gaps in "credibility."[7]

This structure of combined truth and falseness, combined belief and rejection is the main structure of the bourgeois cinema. Bonitzer argues that, when one objects that these devices are needed to make a film acceptable to the masses, what one is really saying is that they must be acceptable to the "masses of petty bourgeois viewers intoxicated with dramatic cinema, Aristotelian realism, the credible."[8]

The impression of reality, the argument continues, is never absolute; rather the fascination of cinema derives from its lack of completeness. The cinema is, according to Bonitzer, "interested in 'what it cannot be,'" on two levels: a *diachronic* level (the linkage between the shots) and the *synchronic* level (off-screen space). The effect of the latter helps produce the former.[9]

Bonitzer then proceeds to analyze some of the previous studies of this area of filmic phenomena. It is interesting that the first figure he attacks is Noël Burch, whose essay on the use of off-screen space in Renoir's NANA is one of the writer's most important pieces of work. He criticizes Burch for non-materialist thinking about the use of "off-screen" space, the talking about this space as though it were real. Significantly, Burch's writing is taken as a point of definition for Bonitzer's treatment of the subject: the Bonitzer article seems almost like a direct answer to Burch. Bonitzer then proceeds to criticize Bazin for making the same errors, for seeing the picture frame as a *cache* (referring to a blinder or curtain), making film like a window, rather than a *cadre* (frame) into which things are put. He similarly turns to a manual from the French film school IDHEC to attack the ideal of film's goal being "continuity, intelligibility, and homogeneity"—all seen in terms of unified space:

> The values of continuity, intelligibility and homogeneity are coextensive, since in this system, *reality signifies the exemption of contradiction.* . . . To introduce dialectic, contradiction, into the representation, is necessarily to alter the system, to alter the "reality" which is the key word, the fetish key word.[10]

Bonitzer then moves into an attack on the *Cinéthique* treatment of this same problem (and specifically, in part, the Jean-Louis Baudry article mentioned earlier). His assertion is that Baudry merely adds one more level of fetishism to the system. *Cinéthique*'s solution to the problem lies, in Bonitzer's interpretation of it, at least, in the inscription of the technical apparatus into the film (as mentioned earlier, a Brechtian notion). What the *Cahiers* critic objects to, however, is that such an inscription can turn into one more level of illusionism. What is a positive technique in Vertov and Godard for the building of an awareness of cinematographic illusion is a negative one in Rouch and Perrault (two members of the *cinéma-vérité* movement). The films of the latter do not escape the identification which is at the root of the problem but rather only make it all the more intense, because the technique is all the more deceptive.[11]

Rather, Bonitzer offers a different solution, a different formulation: "The classic scene, divided, is supposed total in each of its fragments. The 'materialist' scene, divided, constructs-destructs itself in an articulation and interaction of its fragments." In this respect Bonitzer critiques even advanced films like Jean-Marie Straub's OTHON (1969) and Marguerite Duras' JAUNE LE SOLEIL (1971) for not analyzing thoroughly enough the effects of ideology on their own technique. (He sees the films of the *Groupe Dziga-Vertov* as much more responsible here.)[12]

"Hors-champ: Un espace en defaut," is one of the most lucidly structured and instructive of the Bonitzer essays. It is an essay with a theoretical territory which establishes that almost all film, at least as film language has developed, presents certain problems of realism that must be dealt with. It is an essay which demonstrates a cognizance of the formalist traditions which have preceded it in *Cahiers* (both in Bazin and Burch) but which at the same time reacts against a contradictory return to formalism with *Cinéthique*. It is an attack on cinematic illusionism and representation which deals with the problem on the most fundamental level, while also being an attack on those branches of film criticism which it sees as having only confounded the problem by treating as existent in reality the illusions which most films strive to create.

Bonitzer's essay on "off-screen" space does not conclude his preoccupation with the fetishistic nature of the film medium. One of his next essays, written with Serge Daney, is a discussion of the writings of André Bazin, the key influence at *Cahiers* in the earlier years, in terms of fetishism, i.e., the desire to believe in cinematic illusionism even when one knows it is false. Bonitzer and Daney see Bazin's theories as something of a reduction of the notions of a "classic" cinema of continuity and transparency. Bazin's bias against montage, seen as the key element in his work, is the fundamental point of discussion for Bonitzer and Daney.

These later *Cahiers* critics perform a kind of psychoanalysis on Bazin and assert that the content of many of the examples he gives in his writings is also significant: they are not exclusively about technique. Invariably, they say, Bazin's most pointed examples of why montage should not be used involve men in the same frame with wild beasts. The force of the example lies in that they are thus life-death situations: montage would allow one to film death without its really occurring. The uncertainty that the actor or cameraman might be killed by the wild beast provides the viewer with an archetypally fetishistic stimulus (in, it is argued, classically Freudian terms). Thus, the passivity of the viewer is further encouraged by the passivity of the filmmaker; the image will only stop if that stop comes from the other side (the beast killing the cameraman).[13]

Bonitzer's and Daney's dismissal of Bazin is one of the strongest anti-Bazin pieces of writing that the magazine has run. What makes it particularly significant is its use of psychoanalysis to examine the same passivity of the audience about which Brecht had written so intensely. Bonitzer's writings (along with Jean-Pierre Oudart's, to be discussed shortly) are significant because they go beyond being a statement of the passivity of the viewer as a given, to the theoretical dissection of how that passivity arises.

Bonitzer's ideas develop to an even more extreme point in later writings. He continues to attack traditional notions of specularity, as applied to the cinema, but seeks to push his arguments to their furthermost points. In his review of the Canadian film by Denys Arcand, REJEANNE PADOVANI (1973), he discusses the use of space in film in general and questions Roland Barthes' essay, "Diderot, Brecht, Eisenstein," discussed earlier in this study. The Barthes essay comes out in favor of the use of the tableau as a revolutionary effect.

Bonitzer counters that while the tableau and the social gest are important in Eisenstein, the "division and difraction" of Eisenstein's tableaux by montage is equally important. By itself, the tableau is comparable to the Italian scene in theater or perspective in the classic painting in that it inscribes the viewer into a position of passivity before the image.[14] This is a notion we will discuss further in the section treating the writings of Jean-Pierre Oudart. What is important here is that Bonitzer rejects Barthes' notion of the tableau as being not at all advanced:

> What fails here is not an avant-garde conception: it's on the contrary the old conception of cinema as photography-in-movement, the classic conception tied to representation, the adventures of the *camera obscura:* photography substituting for painting, and the cinema adding movement to it.
>
> It is time to see something else in the cinema than the obsessional perfecting of the copying of the real, something else than this theory of the "impressions of reality" for which the concept belongs to the most classic psychology, that is to say the most metaphysical. A film is not a perfected tableau, it is not a moving tableau, nor a succession of tableaux. It is that only for a reductionist and extremely limited conception of it. [15]

Bonitzer hereby provides an implicit addition to *Cahiers'* attitude toward Brecht—that a cinema founded on Brechtian principles will not necessarily result in film that looks like Brechtian theater. Rather, he represents an attempt to perfect and refine a theory of non-illusionist, materialist cinema.

In 1976, a number of Bonitzer's essays were collected into a book, *Le Regard et le Voix.* [16] Two subsequent essays from 1977, both published under the heading "La notion de plan et le sujet du cinéma," continue his theoretical interests. In the first, entitled "Voici," Bonitzer continues to argue that the very concept of a shot (*"plan"* in French) remains theoretically ambiguous and confused in most writing about film. For example, one cannot describe a shot as either a "long shot" or a "close-up" if the camera moves and changes distance within the shot. Similarly, one cannot categorize a shot as either a long shot or a close-up if there is both a foreground subject and a background subject in it. Bonitzer chides such theoreticians as Jean Mitry and Christian Metz for their fuzzy thinking on the subject. [17]

Instead, Bonitzer links the theoretical concept of a shot to the rise of the narrative cinema and Griffith. Thinking in terms of shots would allow for the dramatization of points of view—not for the characters within the movie but for the audience. Bonitzer contrasts the way shots are conceived in D.W. Griffith or Hitchcock to the work of the Soviet montage filmmakers. Where Hitchcock tries to manipulate and modulate the point of view of the audience, Eisenstein offers fragments that may seem discontinuous to the perceiving audience. There is the difference between a passively directed audience and an audience presented with dialectical oppositions, for which no one viewpoint is necessary. In Eisenstein, Bonitzer argues, everything is in close-up, for the film is not conceived in terms of a subject the audience can either approach in close-up or retreat from in long shot. [18]

In the second article, Bonitzer discusses the common rule of cinema prohibiting the actor from looking at the camera. Bonitzer argues that such a look can either block a sense of realistic illusion, or it can redouble the sense of fiction in the film, providing for a fantasy involving the audience's taking a voyeuristic place behind the camera, becoming, in a sense, the fictional eye of the filmmaker himself. [19]

Bonitzer synthesizes many of these preoccupations into a particularly Brechtian piece of criticism entitled "Les dieux et les quarks." In it, he argues that the modern cinema, such as that of Jean-Luc Godard, Jean-Marie Straub or Hans-Jürgen Syberberg, is deliberately non-realist, deliberately fantastic. It challenges the effect of reality by creating a sense of the film performer addressing the viewer directly, rendering the movie, in Bonitzer's terms, slow, heavy, and theatrical rather than suspenseful. The motion picture becomes a "text" rather than a "story," in a manner that relates directly to Brecht. Emotions are no longer the simple ones of the classic cinema, because the spectator cannot respond to them automatically.[20]

Bonitzer links this whole form of filmmaking to the way in which *cinéastes* like Godard or Straub conceive of the shot. Close-ups no longer have dramatic emphasis but rather serve to make the reality they present strange. The shot is no longer a part of a whole narrative continuity but rather is a fragment without a whole, an image that no longer suggests any further world outside the frame. In this sense, the modern Brechtian cinema challenges conventional film theory.[21]

Pascal Bonitzer has remained a major figure on the *Cahiers du Cinéma* staff throughout the 1970's and into the 1980's. We will see in later chapters how changes in the magazine's direction seem specifically to mirror changes in Bonitzer's attitudes as he writes for the magazine.[22]

Jean-Louis Comolli

The writings of Jean-Louis Comolli on film theory begin from many of the same starting points as Bonitzer's. One of Comolli's first tightly theoretical pieces, "Technique et idéologie: Caméra, perspectif, profondeur de champ," begins from the same starting points as Bonitzer, that the basic techniques of cinema as customarily practiced are ideologically determined. (Comolli sees his writings also as being an answer to J.-P. Lebel.) Similarly, Comolli begins with references to the *Cinéthique* position of Jean-Louis Baudry, that the invention of the base apparatus was ideologically determined in the nineteenth century by social and economic forces. Indeed, Comolli's main point throughout the writings is that the historical development of the cinema is due to social and economic factors, that film as a medium is within the realm of ideology rather than being, as Lebel would argue, a scientific development which has been used to ideological purposes.

Thus, Comolli devotes many paragraphs to a discussion of the development of cinema and to the way historians have customarily written about it. Comolli analyzes the observations of Bazin about the invention of cinema[23] and sees that the very invention is the result of an idealist ideology which sought to reproduce life "as it is," mixed with certain economic determinations of the profit motive. Thus, Comolli agrees with Bazin that the creation of the cinema grew out of a "dream" that man has had about making a perfect image of the world as it is, but he sees this "dream," this desire, as being rooted in a bourgeois ideology.[24]

Comolli then proceeds to attack Bazin in a second section of the article dealing with depth of field. Implicit in Comolli's argument is that at the root of the develoment of deep focus are certain ideological motivations, which are in turn the same ideological factors that Bazin ultimately defends: that deep focus is supportive of the dominant ideology which produced it. Bazin defends deep focus as being closer to reality because (like reality) it is more ambiguous and allows the viewer more interpretation. Or, to state in Comolli's own words his summary of Bazin's theories:

> Thus: 1) the real is ambiguous; 2) in giving a fragmentary representation (by the montage: stylistically developed), one reduces this ambiguity and substitutes for it a "subjectivity"(one can read that as a signification, that is to say a "vision of the world," an ideology); 3) because depth of field brings the cinematographic image closer to the "normal" retinal image, closer to "realistic" vision, and because it shows literally *more* of the things, *more of the real,* it permits anew the game of "ambiguity" which "frees" the spectator, that is to say it aims to abolish the differences between film and reality, representation and the real, to confirm the spectator in his "natural" relationship with the world, to thereby redouble the conditions of his vision and of his "spontaneous" ideology: it is not for nothing that Bazin wrote (not without humor): "Depth of field in William Wyler wishes itself to be liberal and democratic as the conscience of the American spectator and hero of the film."[25]

Comolli's objections to Bazinian realism are, ultimately, the same as Brecht's toward realistic theater. Where Bazin sees the film which approaches reality as being preferable, Comolli obviously looks upon that process as a mystification, as a prevention of true discourse about reality.

Comolli treats two responses to Bazin, by Jean Mitry and Gérard Leblanc of *Cinéthique,* as falling into basically similar traps. While Comolli agrees with Mitry's critique of Bazin that the filmic image is inherently different from reality because of the presence of the frame, he criticizes Mitry for offering only empirical descriptions of the differences. Mitry, he argues, implicitly accepts and approves of a maintenance of the deceptions whereby we still see film as reflections of reality. "On condition that one does not make depth of field an omnivalent principle which substututes for all other formulation about *mise en scène,* Mitry here declares himself 'in perfect agreement with Bazin.' "[26]

Comolli criticizes Leblanc of *Cinéthique* for accepting in his own arguments some of the same assumptions of Bazin about linear perspective. In the end, the *Cahiers* theorist sees certain basic misunderstandings as being common among all three theorists. What is most important about this article is that it reaffirms *Cahiers'* stand against cinematographic representation and that it defines this stand in terms of classic conceptions of cinema, i.e., Bazin,

Mitry. It establishes *Cahiers* as attempting to offer a genuine alternative to traditional notions of film theory.

Comolli essentially repeats, expands, and elaborates on these same ideas in his continuations of this article, which he entitles "Pour une historie matérialiste du cinéma" ("For a Materialist History of Cinema"). In some of them, he continues to attack Mitry and Bazin, arguing for a treatment of the cinematic object as an historical object (historical again in the Marxist sense of viewing history as a science). To discuss the techniques of cinema without relating them to specific films in which they are used is, according to Comolli, ridiculous, for it is only in the practical use that the techniques are at all meaningful. Thus, he calls for a history of film which would talk about *le practique signifiant* (literally translated, *signifying practice*), i.e., both the technique and the way in which it is used are important.[27] He thus criticizes Mitry's history of film as being obsessed with the phrase "for the first time," as though the major achievements of film were wholly technological and as though one could separate the form used in film from the content. Comolli writes, for example, "It is not the close-up that has meaning, it is the system that gives the close-up meaning."[28] The history of cinema must be an economic, ideological, and technological history. Only in the interrelation of the three does one find the reality of film's past.

In 1976, Comolli directed the film LA CECILIA, about a nineteenth-century Italian anarchist commune in Brazil, and on its release Comolli wrote in *Cahiers du Cinéma* about his attempts to put theory into practice.[29] He followed this film with TOTO, UNE ANTHOLOGIE (1978), a compilation film about the Italian actor Toto, and L'OMBRE ROUGE (1981), another period film set in Marseilles in the 1930's. Presumably as a result of all this activity in production, Comolli's work as a film critic becomes less significant by the late 1970's, but, given the man's interest in historical reconstruction in his feature films, it is not surprising that much of his subsequent theoretical writing should center on questions of cinema and history.

In the late 1970's Comolli wrote a series of articles under the heading "La fiction historique." The series includes a detailed analysis, co-written with François Géré and continued through three issues of the magazine, comparing Fritz Lang's HANGMEN ALSO DIE, which was based on a script by Bertolt Brecht, with Ernst Lubitsch's TO BE OR NOT TO BE.[30] Both were anti-Nazi films made in Hollywood in the same year—1942.

Comolli and Géré's central thesis is that Nazi ideology involved the creating of an image of Hitler, a kind of *mise en scène* of Hitler in the media. To fight Nazi ideology, the filmmakers had to attack not only the philosophy of fascism but the images and techniques used to present it to the world. In other words, Comolli's central thesis is a post-Brechtian one: to understand the movies' effectiveness as propaganda, one has to understand how they fight against both the content and the form of Nazi ideology and culture.[31] The final article in the series deals with Hans-Jürgen Syberberg's HITLER (1978), an unabashaedly post-Brechtian epic dealing also with Hitler as a public image or myth, an almost abstracted, imagistic embodiment of what Naziism meant to its supporters.[32]

We will return to the writings of Pascal Bonitzer and Jean-Louis Comolli in subsequent chapters. Of the two, one might see Bonitzer as the theoretician of cinema, Comolli as the theoretician of the history of cinema (and later, of history and cinema). A reading of their writings establishes that the two approaches are, in effect, inseparable, for both would doubtless argue that cinema exists in its history (rather than as any essential form). Together with Jean-Pierre Oudart, whose main interest is psychology, they form a triumvirate of major theoreticians in the post-1968 *Cahiers du Cinéma*. They are, understandably, intensely involved in questions of film form, and in the central issues found in Brechtian theater theory: representation, the place of the spectator, the relation of the presentation to reality.

Four Theoretical Issues

Let us now discuss four theoretical subjects which become particularly important in the politicized *Cahiers du Cinéma:* montage, *cinéma direct*, naturalism, and psychoanalysis. In each case these subjects will refer back to the more generalized conceptualizations about film found in essays by critics like Bonitzer and Comolli as well as the more generalized political writings found in the preceding chapter; these particular subjects represent workings out of somewhat more specific theoretical problems. They nonetheless are an integral part of the critical system formed at *Cahiers* after May '68, a system quickly and sometimes extravagantly elaborated in the magazine's more politicized pages.

Montage

It should come as no surprise that any reevaluation of film theory by *Cahiers* should also include a reevaluation of questions of editing and montage, since the issues raised by them have been central to film theory since almost the beginning of cinema. While *Cahiers* had periodically discussed the Russian theorists even in the pre-1968 years (as part of its general interest in film), there is an increased involvement in the Russian silent cinema which accompanies the magazine's switch to a more political line. Of the fifteen issues of the magazine published in 1969 and 1970, for example, nine contain writings by or about Sergei Eisenstein, in addition to a special number of the magazine (No. 220-221) devoted to the Soviet cinema of the 1920's, published in May-June of 1970.

Cahiers' major statement on questions of montage comes early, in 1969, when the magazine runs a round-table discussion on montage which includes Jean Narboni, Sylvie Pierre, and Jacques Rivette. The discussion is the direct result of a conference on montage that was held at Avignon at that time and therefore includes many references to specific films that were shown as part of that conference. Several major lines of thought are nonetheless evident from the text, and, put together, they make for a logical discourse on the subject.

The first is the assertion, made by Sylvie Pierre, that all film uses montage. Pierre sees montage as the fundamental structuring element of cinema. She allows for two sub-categories, "rarified montage" (in films which, for example, use cutting very sparingly) or "effaced montage" (in films which try to use "invisible" editing). She criticizes both, arguing that, where effaced montage favors illusionism, rarified montage encourages a kind of fascination on the part of the spectator. She argues, in opposing to them Eisensteinian techniques she finds politically correct:

> In the two cases, it is the impossibility of escaping from what *is* on the screen. Presumably, as opposed to the real world. That which one can, by opposition, characterize as "progressive" about Eisensteinian montage, is paradoxically that which is the most dictatorial: the passages from one shot to another take away from the spectator all possibility of escaping from rationality, to the necessity of putting oneself in relation to the shot in a state of reflexive distance. Thus no means of abandoning oneself to representation.[33]

Thus, montage becomes a way of both defeating cinematic illusionism and representation and achieving the distanced effect desired by Brecht, to overcome the passivity of the audience.

Related to these assertions are the ones by Jacques Rivette that montage is always a form of criticism, a means whereby the work criticizes itself. Rivette presents this as a hypothesis: "if all coherent thought on montage is *de facto* critical thought, all form of refusal or disdain of montage implies a theological mentality, that is to say the accepting of the world such as it is, if not the resignation, or at very least the passive contemplation of the 'being-there' as pure presence, without history or mediation, and all the concepts of permanence and destiny related to this ideology."[34]

Rivette goes on to assert that the critical thinking required by montage can extend to all the levels of the film's production. He calls at the same time for a montage that is not one of fixed "effects" but an active montage which prevents the spectator from abandoning himself to the plot, making him a part of the critical work that occurs in the film itself.[35]

The article also works toward an historical appreciation of montage. Thus, what is the product of bourgeois ideology for Rivette under Griffith is rendered with a new political meaning under the Russian silent masters. Similarly, Jean Narboni points to certain elements of accuracy in the writings of Bazin about montage. Narboni argues that Bazin really was right about the cinema of Pudovkin, that the manipulativeness that Pudovkin gave to montage was genuinely contrary to aesthetic and political rightness, whereas he feels that the analysis of Bazin toward the work of William Wyler and Orson Welles (i.e., that it provokes participation in the audience) may in some ways be more accurately applied to Eisenstein. In a later section, Narboni even compares the Pudovkin version of THE MOTHER (1926) to Brecht's stage version, seeing in the former a film which "takes abusively the mask of a dialectical Marxist film," while the latter has a true analysis of a revolutionary situation and the relationships existing in a society as a whole.[36]

This rejection of Pudovkin is echoed again by Rivette, who sees in Pudovkin a bourgeois perversion of Eisenstein's practices for the sake of a conventional narrative. Rivette argues that through Pudovkin Soviet montage was transferred to the commercial cinema and turned from "montage" to *"découpage"*—the framing and direction of actors.[37] Rivette thus breaks film history up into four movements: the invention of montage (Griffith, Eisenstein); the deviation by Pudovkin and Hollywood; the rejection of the propaganda film (by the cinema which would extend from neo-realism to the New Wave); and finally the revival of montage in contemporary cinema.[38]

The article "Montage" suggests two main arguments about montage that fit in directly with the general direction in which *Cahiers* is headed at the time:

1. The panelists value montage for its analytic qualities, for its ability to allow for an intellectual, rational discourse in film. They see montage as a tool to help the spectator be active and alert.

2. Economic factors cause the decline of montage following the Soviet silent period, thus causing a direct link between montage and ideology. The commentators see the suppression of montage as a kind of suppression of free, revolutionary thought.

"Montage" represents the last major appearance of Jacques Rivette in *Cahiers du Cinéma*, apart from interviews, but it further establishes his position as a major transitional figure in the magazine. Though his name is often associated with the older line of *Cahiers* critics like Truffaut and Chabrol, the attitudes Rivette expresses are as Marxist as anyone else's on the round-table. While Rivette's subsequent work in film has not revealed a great concern with Marxist-Leninist thought, one cannot ignore the directness of Rivette's statements in the article. They suggest that the transition at *Cahiers* from a formalist, apolitical journal to a leftist, revolutionary one is not as discontinuous or abrupt a change as might be thought.

Cinéma Direct

One of the phenomena of the 1960's in film is the development of what the French call *cinéma direct,* a term for which there is no precise equivalent commonly used in English. *Cinéma direct* subsumes much of what is customarily included in *cinéma vérité* but includes films which are not exclusively documentaries but are nonetheless shot on real locations, with direct sound, often improvised acting, and lightweight mobile cameras. *Cinéma direct* represents one of the prime innovations in film during the 1960's, and it is inevitable that *Cahiers* should respond to it. The primary response to the movement is found in a two-part article by Jean-Louis Comolli entitled "Le détour par le direct," which runs in February and April of 1969.

One of Comolli's earliest statements about *le direct* is cautionary, for he sees in it the same dangers of representation and manipulation that exist in regularly staged cinema. He writes:

> The fundamental lie of *cinéma direct* is in fact that there is a tendency to pretend to transcribe truly the truth of life, to give oneself as a witness and the cinema as a mode of mechanical recording of facts and things. When, most certainly, the very fact of filming already constitutes a productive intervention which alters and transforms the material recorded. From the intervention of the camera starts a *manipulation;* and each operation— even one so limited in its motive as turning the camera on, stopping it, changing the angle or the lens, then choosing the rushes, then editing them—constitutes, to a greater or lesser extent, a manipulation of the document. One may have every good will of respecting this document, but one cannot avoid fabricating it. It does not pre-exist as reportage, but is a product of it.[39]

Comolli decries a certain hypocritical tendency linked to some thought about *le direct,* namely, the treating of the manipulations and interventions described above as though they did not exist or were not important. Thus, one of Comolli's fundamental principles is comparable to that of Brechtian theater, the need to acknowledge the means whereby the illusion is produced, even in something like a *cinéma vérité* documentary.

Comolli proceeds from this assertion, however, to discuss a phenomenon found in *cinéma direct,* namely, a sense of *irréalité* which surrounds many of the films of this sort. Comolli asserts that this sense of unreality tends to be greatest when there is a minimum of manipulation, that those films which seek to intervene the least become the most dream-like (he offers as a radical example Andy Warhol's film of the Empire State Building, where the lack of intervention is virtually total). By contrast, he argues that films seem most meaningful, coherent, and forceful exactly when their materials are most manipulated and falsified.[40]

The author then proceeds to examine the historical precedents for *le direct,* which he finds in the Russian cinema of the silent era, namely, the *kino pravda* films of Dziga Vertov and Abram Room's BED AND SOFA (1927). As with montage, as discussed in the previous section, Comolli sees the suppression of direct cinema as linked to economic causes, that the results of direct cinema ran contrary to what was needed by a bourgeois capitalist cinema. Comolli links the renaissance of *cinéma direct* to the renaissance of montage, seeing the two as related, and notes how, even with the revival of *le direct*, its growth has been outside the commercial industry's usual parameters. Comolli attributes the resurgence of direct methods to technological improvements; particularly important to him is the emergence of direct sound as a common technique. For while he sees the emergence of sound as a bourgeois tool to keep films artificial and manipulative, the use of direct sound allows for an alternative to the traditional bourgeois Hollywood talking film.[41]

The technical tools of *le direct* affect the content that is used in the films, Comolli argues. He writes:

> The techniques of *le direct* do not suit themselves to the industry nor the aesthetic of the cinema of re-presentation. *Le direct* does not permit the filming of *the same* things as *le non-direct* in a better and newer fashion: it permits the filming of *other things*, it opens up new horizons for the cinema in the fact that it changes the object of cinema, and by that its function and nature.[42]

Thus, Comolli sees *le direct* as a way of escaping the economic restrictions of the capitalist system: he sees the films of the *direct* movement as being political whether they intend to be or not, because they provide an alternative to traditional, capitalist forms. *Le direct* thus allows for a chance to escape representation; by creating a cinema which intervenes in reality, the direct film no longer merely reflects the dominant ideology. Rather, it has a chance to shape that reality, to be a "producer of political sense."[43]

In the second part of the article, Comolli proceeds to give an example of the positive principle that he sees governing *le direct*, namely, the films of Miklos Jancso. Comolli points to the ways in which Jancso's films avoid realism. Rather, they are constructed *for* the camera; movements of figures in the films are made to correspond to movements of the camera. The spectacle is performed for the camera and is never intended to have any real existence apart from it. The camera is not recording an event; the event is in the recording. Thus, despite the fact that Jancso's films use no direct sound whatsoever, Comolli classes them as part of the direct movement; indeed, he sees them as radical examples.[44]

From this, Comolli begins to explore an idea which relates directly to Brechtian theater, the idea of inscribing the process of producing a play (or film) into the play or film itself. Comolli observes:

In many musical comedies (THE BANDWAGON is the prototype of it), as in THE GOLDEN COACH, THE RULES OF THE GAME, numerous Bergman films, THE PATSY, etc., the phenomenon of re-presentation becomes part of the fiction of the film, one of its dramatic motors. This supplementary bid—to the principle of the film there is already re-presentation of the re-presentation—produces an effect, if one may say it, of "frankness." The film designates itself (not to say "denounces itself") here as illusion, there as reconstruction or spectacle: for that which it is.... But also, when self-avowed re-presentation takes itself for its explicit theme, and films itself, the re-presentation of this re-presentation (the film) becomes in a way primary, direct. To film a play is effectively to make an act of reportage, to reintroduce the documentary into fiction.[45]

Such a process allows the film, Comolli implicitly states, a greater degree of honesty. The film Comolli sees as "the extreme end point of this dialectic of re-presentation/re-presentation of a re-presentation, fictional play and fiction of a play," is Jacques Rivette's L'AMOUR FOU, a film which presents the rehearsal of a play and includes the shooting of a documentary film on that rehearsal in the film itself. Rivette's prominence and importance is again apparent as a transitional figure between the old and the new *Cahiers*.[46]

Thus, one may summarize Comolli's argument by repeating (as he does himself) that the advantage of *cinéma direct* is that it does not seek to reproduce reality but works rather from a framework that the reality of the film is inseparable from its being photographed (this is true for both documentaries and fiction films made under the system). Because of this lack of a completely predetermined reality (in the fiction film, by means of improvised cinema), Comolli argues, the film is no longer bound by the conventions which allow false representation. A genuinely truthful cinema can thus emerge.

One should remember that this pair of articles was written early in 1969, before the full effects of May 1968 were felt by *Cahiers*. As an early piece of writing, it is not as extreme as some of *Cahiers'* later writings. The attitude of French leftist criticism toward works of the *cinéma direct* movement becomes much more critical as they move into the 1970's. Consider, for example, Bonitzer's comments on Rouch and Perrault in " 'Réalité' de la denotation" (cited earlier). Some of the statements of Godard and the *Groupe Dziga-Vertov* have heavily attacked the *cinéma direct* movement for being just a more sophisticated form of representation. While later articles in *Cahiers du Cinéma* will soften this position somewhat, there is a clear hostility to aspects of the *cinéma direct* movement as the magazine becomes more politicized.[47]

At about the same time as the Comolli article, Louis Marcorelles stops writing criticism for *Cahiers du Cinéma* and becomes one of the primary champions of the *cinéma direct* movement. The realignment of Marcorelles is a significant event for it suggests a split in sensibilities that reflects a division in French thought about film that is broader-reaching than individual disagreements. In his book, *Eléments pour un nouveau cinéma* (translated in English as *Living Cinema*), Marcorelles devotes several paragraphs to a discussion of

Bertolt Brecht. His comments echo his assertion (made in the special Brecht number of *Cahiers* from 1960, cited above) that the primary contribution to be made by Brecht to the cinema is in the changing role of the actor in the presentation. Important in this notion is the idea that the acting of a play should not just present the text realistically, and by means of realistic performance, but be a stylized reduplication of the codifications of social behavior.

In his book, Marcorelles suggests that what Brecht criticizes in theater, representation, is all but automatically avoided in *cinéma direct.* He writes:

> But in direct cinema, and first of all in Leacock's films, reality is given to us raw with all its instant, provocative qualities. Unlike Brecht's theater, which rejects the fake realism of the bourgeois theater and seeks to give us social reality by distancing the audience from the stage and the action, Leacock's cinema, denouncing the fake realism of what is said to be the only possible cinema—that of performance—moving us to take a more intense part in real action, gives us the tool needed to discover on the screen how things *really* happen. Here "reality" can be seen at first glance, if it has been filmed with the right skill. Then the social fiction that underpins all our actions can be revealed, the drama we act out each day for society. By this new relationship with the lightweight synchronized camera, the person filmed, whether an actor or not, appears to our eyes and ears in a new dimension. . . . In other words, it is possible to forget the written word in favor of a living, lived word, flung out by man *en situation.*[48]

Thus, Marcorelles begins with Brechtian ideals but ultimately concludes that they can be achieved in the cinema not by imitation of theatrical forms but by a use of cinema that is faithful to what he sees to be the capacities of film to intervene in real life. Although this viewpoint is similar to Comolli's, it may be seen, in another sense, as the other side of a two-pronged progression from the old, somewhat Brecht-influenced *Cahiers* to the film criticism of the 1970's. While Marcorelles implicitly confirms what he has suggested earlier—that film as a medium is at odds with Brechtian theatrical ideals—the principles behind Brecht are, granting that Marcorelles' reading of them is open to discussion, assumed and incorporated into his system.

Naturalism

The 1970's witness a resurgence of naturalism in the French cinema. Michel Ciment, reporting in the 1975 *International Film Guide,* lists a good half dozen new films from 1974 as partaking of this trend, which he sees as one of the most significant new directions in the French film.[49] A handful of new directors (Pascal Thomas, Joël Seria, Jacques Doillon, Daniel Duval, and others) join with several more established figures (Jacques Rozier, Jean-Daniel Simon, Jean-Louis Bertucelli, Yannick Bellon) to make for what may indeed be seen as a movement or trend. Many of the films they produce enjoy significant critical and box-office success. In some ways these films are off-shoots of the *cinéma direct* movement: their makers often use lightweight cameras (shooting, on occasion, in 16mm which is subsequently blown up to 35mm for commercial distribution), improvised acting, direct sound.

Cahiers du Cinéma takes a dim view of most of the films of this movement and rather uses their appearance to rearticulate and reevaluate the arguments against naturalism which have been used all along. The first generalized reaction to this wave of realism occurs with Pascal Kané early in 1974. Kané's immediate conclusion is:

> this naturalism here, not only is it not "natural," it is a code—we already know that—but, above all, it determines its contents very precisely. Nothing left to chance: a representation where everything "goes without saying" implies necessarily a content of the reactionary class.[50]

Kané then proceeds to examine how in several films of this type there is a use of young, teenage girls who have neither professional nor ideological identities in the context of the film. Thus, these characters, by exemplifying no *types*, condense nothing of French society. (Kané refers here directly to Brecht and his calling for the use of types.)

Kané builds his piece around a discussion of the films' avoidance of typage and refers again near the end to Brecht, in praising only one French film, Gérard Guerin's LO PAIS (1971). He cites from the film a scene in which a worker from Brittany puts up an advertising poster over a political poster that seeks to encourage him in the class struggle. By representing "typical conduct over a typical situation," Kané argues, Guerin achieves something comparable to Brecht's social gest.[51] By contrast, Kané agrees that a director like Pascal Thomas has nothing to condense except what might be called idealist essences of human nature, because his characters are detached from genuine social roles.

A more extensive and definitive discussion of naturalism occurs in the May-June 1975 issue of *Cahiers*, which features a collective discussion on the subject of naturalism, entitled "Une certaine tendance du cinéma française" (a clear reference to the famous *Cahiers* article by Truffaut of the same title, which attacked the overly academic, paralyzed French cinema of the 1950's). The general thrust of the discussion is that the "realism" of the new French cinema really avoids reality and is instead conventionalized. Serge Daney talks of a "new stock of filmable visuals" which includes certain visions of the working classes, has a nominal social conscience, but which uses stereotyping (in the bad sense of the word rather than a Brechtian sense) as a way of avoiding genuine issues. In other words, naturalism is seen as meaning certain new subject matters for the French cinema, subject matters which include social themes but social themes (Jean-Pierre Oudart asserts) as seen by the bourgeoisie.[52]

The article introduces the notion of what the critics call "segregation," that is, the idea that naturalism is always what is "real" to the social majority. This majority, in turn, never considers itself as a group which can be typed: it is, in effect, a group without a self-image. The majority types the minority, but it is incapable of typing itself. Thus, the naturalism of these new films may include certain segments of society formerly excluded (such as the workers in Daniel Duval's 1974 LE VOYAGE D'AMELIE), but this in itself implies new exclusions.[53]

By contrast, the use of stereotyping in some of these new films (such as the racist Frenchman in DUPONT LAJOIE) is such that the bourgeois audience cannot see itself in these stereotypes. Naturalism is used on the side of the majority to exclude from itself what it does not want to think it is. Thus, the new films tend, Oudart asserts, to reduce political issues to personalities (to characterization, in the sense that Brecht would attack). In contrast to the films of the New Wave or those of Robert Bresson, which dealt with marginal characters in isolation, the new French cinema deals with defensive, socialized groups, groups with which the viewer can identify.[54]

Kané thus can conclude with a critique of Costa-Gavras' SPECIAL SECTION (1975) on the grounds that the film reduces a real social issue (Pétainism) to a metaphor for the individual against society, with little discussion of how power is wielded by social forces. The film thus has no difficulty uniting disparate social segments in its audience: by presenting power as an abstraction, the film avoids any genuine discussion of history. The Fascist is always the other person.[55]

Significantly, this article contains little discussion of techniques: the assumption is implicitly that they fall into the mold of representation even when they borrow certain methods from *le cinéma direct*. One imagines that they would claim that such *direct* techniques, when used at all, had been co-opted by the dominant ideology. One might also read the article as a protest against what might be called certain cultural products representing the organized leftist establishment (the *Parti Comuniste Française*), in that some of the films discussed (Jean-Daniel Simon's IL PLEUT TOUJOURS OU C'EST MOUILLE, dealing with difficulties between left and right in an election in a rural French community, Jacques Doillon's LES DOIGTS DANS LA TETE, or Philippe Condroyer's LA COUPE A DIX FRANCS, all from 1974) reflect rather closely a kind of establishment leftism. Thus, the situation of their being attacked by *Cahiers* in some ways parallels the attacks by Brecht on the socialist realism that was required under Stalin. The 1975 "Une certaine tendance du cinéma française" is in this sense as much a critique of France's non-revolutionary communist movement as it is of any films or their techniques. As indeed the critics would argue: the political backwardness of the former is inseparable from the aesthetic backwardness of the latter.

Psychoanalysis

One of the significant aspects of French intellectual life in the period following 1968 is the renewal of interest in Freud and psychoanalysis, particularly under the influence of Jacques Lacan. Many of the writings in *Cahiers* during this period are influenced by Lacan and his post-Freudian school of thought. The section which follows is intended to be neither a complete presentation of these ideas and their effect on film theory nor a complete analysis of those writings in *Cahiers* influenced by Lacan. Rather, the author will discuss certain key ideas in some of the writings which both augment and relate back to *Cahiers'* interest in both formalism and Brecht, to show how changes in French psychoanalytic thought are incorporated into *Cahiers'* whole theoretical system. (Lacan's influence on *Cahiers'* film theory had been summarized rather effectively by Daniel Dayan in his article "The Tutor-Code of Classical Cinema," a work which on occasion will be referred to below.)[56]

There are three main notions in this school of thought which complement and extend (even though it would be difficult to discover any direct influence) the theories of Brecht. These ideas may be labeled as *passivity, identification* and *representation.* Let us consider them in succession.

There is an often unstated assumption throughout *Cahiers* (which reflects the assumptions of Brecht) that the passivity of the spectator must be considered ideologically suspect. This fairly constant discussion of passivity takes on further meaning when considered in the light of Lacanian thought. Jean-Louis Baudry, in his *Cinéthique* article "Ideological Effects of the Basic Cinematographic Apparatus" (already cited above as having markedly influenced thought at *Cahiers*), discusses the film medium in relation to what Lacan refers to as the "mirror stage" of the child's development, the moment which occurs between the ages of six and eighteen months when the child is able to recognize his image in a mirror. At this point, Lacan argues, the child forms a conception if the "I," of himself. It is an "imaginary constitution," that is, a condition whose existence is based on images. Baudry writes of the relationship of this to cinema:

> But for this imaginary constitution of the self to be possible, there must be—Lacan strongly emphasizes this point—two complementary conditions: immature powers of mobility and a precocious maturation of visual organization (apparent in the first few days of life). If one considers that these two conditions are repeated during cinematographic projection—suspension of mobility and predominance of the visual function—perhaps one could suppose that this is more than a simple analogy. And possibly this very point explains the "impression of reality" so often invoked in connection with the cinema for which the various explanations proposed seem only to skirt the real problem.[57]

Yet this passivity is not linked exclusively to the physical immobility of the spectator at a movie. Rather, it is seen additionally as partaking of the whole tradition of Western linear perspective. (Baudry points out that the idea of a "normal" length lens, for example, is derived from Western linear perspective, which is not a scientific notion but an ideological one.) Thus, film (like traditional perspective painting), constructs itself around a "subject," the viewer (the acknowledgment of whose presence is usually suppressed, even though the exploitation of that same presence is built into the work), who sees the work as a "reflection" of himself and of reality, when actually the work is very highly codified. By exploiting at the same time the way in which the viewer constitutes his sense of self, film, like classical painting, operates on certain essential deceptions which are built into the apparatus used.[58] This idea is used by several writers in *Cahiers*, namely, Jean-Louis Schéfer[59] and Jean-Pierre Oudart,[60] to demolish the notion of the "impression of reality." The whole system of linear perspective inscribes a physical (and, by implication, a moral) passivity for the viewer into the painting. Dayan describes this process:

> When I occupy the place of the subject, the codes which led me to occupy this place become invisible to me. The signifiers of the presence of the subject disappear from my consciousness because they are the signifiers of my presence. What I perceive is their signified: myself. If I want to understand the painting and not just be instrumental in it as a catalyst to its ideological operation, I must avoid the empirical relationship which it imposes on me. To understand the ideology which the painting conveys, I must avoid providing my own imaginary as a support for that ideology. I must refuse that identification which the painting so imperiously proposes to me.[61]

There are two things to note here. The first is the apparent irrelevance of content. The primary ideological signification of the work is made a question of form: perspective itself is seen as repressive. The second is that this repression is, for practical purposes, built into the nature of representative film. To counteract it, therefore, requires all the more effort and consideration on the part of the filmmaker. The task of making a Brechtian film, in this context, becomes all the more difficult, for the filmmaker must compensate for the negative ideological biases in standard film practice. Thus, Marcorelles' observation, cited earlier, that the theatrical theories of Brecht must be considered antithetical to cinema would still hold, but out of this antithesis, one would then argue, would come a deconstruction (to use Dayan's term) of the cinematographic system.

These ideas about the passive spectator lead directly to consideration of the role of identification in the cinema. Again, Baudry's article, while not from *Cahiers*, proves to be the seminal work from which others follow in *Cahiers*. Baudry distinguishes two types of identification in film. The first is the traditional type of narrative identification with the characters, the type dealt with by Brecht with regard to the theater. The second identification is an identification with the camera, as it were, with the camera's form of vision as analogous to the viewers'. "Thus the spectator identifies less with what is represented, the spectacle itself, than with what stages the spectacle, makes it seen, obliging him to see what it sees; this is exactly the function taken over by the camera as a sort of reality."[62] Thus, if one wishes to extend Brecht to the screen, it would seem implicitly that one would have to argue against both kinds of identification (as indeed the *Cahiers* critics do).

One of Jean-Pierre Oudart's key essays, "La suture," deals with these two issues of passivity and identification and extends them more precisely to film. Oudart deals with the use of cutting in a film to create the illusion of a unified space, through the system of shot/reverse shot. In the first shot one sees a person or an object; in the shot which follows one either becomes, subjectively, that person and sees from his point of view or occupies the space that one has previously seen and sees the character who had been perceiving the previous shot, or spatial field. The sense of a whole is built up by the succession. The structure of the film is built around an interplay of these two kinds of identification: one sees what many of the characters see, but one also has a position of mastery, an ability to see all. Thus is created a *false* illusion of reality, for the film seeks to create the impression that there is no camera recording each shot but rather that there is "real," unified, and whole space.[63]

Related to both of these concepts is the third one of representation. One can see where what Oudart calls the system of the suture is one of the primary techniques of filmic representation, of the creation of an artificial illusion of reality. Implicit in these arguments, however, is the idea of filmic representation as repeating and reconstructing the system whereby one develops a notion of reality, of "self." Just as, to Lacan, the notion of self comes from an unreal mirror image, the notion of filmic reality comes from a comparable unreal mirror image. Cinematic representation thus differs integrally from stage representation: where the latter need only reproduce the physical properties of events by putting the needed objects and people on stage, the former is involved with a far more complex method of producing the effect of reality, for it becomes necessary to deny and hide the apparatus whereby the film is produced.

Needless to say, the above paragraphs are a reduction and a simplification of Lacanian psychology and its manifestations in *Cahiers du Cinéma*. There are, however, certain fundamental qualities to this approach which unify it with both *Cahiers'* formalist and Brechtian preoccupations. On the one hand, there is, once again, the assertion that forms are not neutral, that the formal aspects of a work have as much political signification as the aspects of content: the two cannot be separated. The explanation for this is that all such formal properties are historically determined, and this materialist way of thinking seeks to find the historical determinations for the forms of film. Secondly, rather than just assert that the conventional film puts the viewer in an undesirable position of passivity, these writings attempt to seek out the ways in which this passivity is produced. These analyses go beyond the assertion suggested throughout Brecht, that the production of blind emotion prohibits clear, rational thought. Rather, this passivity is linked to the physical position of the audience and to certain structures which put the audience into such a position, either physically (through structuring into the work the place from which the viewer will passively watch) or symbolically.

This line of pursuit produces a whole set of writings about specific films, particularly those of Jean-Pierre Oudart, which are essentially outside the realm of this study but nonetheless tangential to it. For example, Oudart writes very deliberately about Robert Bresson and the way in which his films circumvent the usual mode of the suture.[64] His piece on the new model for the European film, "Un discours en défaut," examines the structures of the European art film of the late '60's in terms of identification and the resolution (or non-resolution) of political conflicts.[65] With Serge Daney, Oudart writes about Visconti's DEATH IN VENICE (1971) in terms of the work's multiple levels of identification, reading in these levels the attitude of Visconti himself as director (reflected in the audience's appreciation for the film as a Visconti film) as paralleling the relationship between the film's main character and the boy of a lower class, which in turn provides the bourgeois audience with a comparable level of relating to the proletariat; all of this sees DEATH IN VENICE as a fantasy about bourgeoisie and proletariat that is worked out in terms of the various levels of passivity, specularization, identification, and representation present in the film.[66] Such articles are very important in the definition of the new *Cahiers,* but they reflect certain rather specialized preoccupations. These preoccupations form an important branch of the *Cahiers* of this period, but it is in another group of writings that the preoccupation of formalism and Brecht reach a definite, direct end point.

Theoretical Writings—Summary

Let us review the various areas discussed above. Seen in terms of a battle or struggle, the fight which *Cahiers* wages against what it sees as conventionalized bourgeois cinema occurs on several theoretical fronts:

1. *The rewriting of film history and theory.* The writings of Pascal Bonitzer and Jean-Louis Comolli strive for a rethinking of previous assumptions about film. They attempt to expose the deceptions and idealism of many older writings and suggest materialist alternatives. They argue that one must not treat film history and theory in terms of specific techniques alone, but rather, link technique directly to the content it expresses.

2. *Montage*. The *Cahiers* commentators see montage as an inescapable fact of cinema. By montage, the director can comment on his material. The right kind of montage provides for an active, alert audience. From this point of view, the history of the capitalist film is a history of the suppression of revolutionary montage.

3. *Le direct*. Writing in 1969, Jean-Louis Comolli sees direct cinema as an alternative to conventional cinematic representation, since it is concerned not with reproducing events for the camera but with producing events that could not exist without the camera. While *Cahiers du Cinéma* does not permanently adopt Comolli's position, his formulations about *le direct* are of major importance.

4. *Naturalism*. The *Cahiers* critics describe naturalism as a set of codes that reflect the dominant ideology. It becomes a way of introducing new stereotypes into film, of preventing the audience from seeing itself in the work.

5. *Psychoanalysis*. Lacanian psychology provides the *Cahiers* critics with further levels of theorization about the nature of the passive viewer in film, the ways in which cinematic identification takes place, and the way in which filmic representation reflects the constitution of the sense of self and reality found in direct childhood perception experiences.

These writings provide a theoretical background for the practical writings to be found in *Cahiers*. The basis for discussion of most of the films in the forthcoming sections may be found in these more generalized writings. The *Cahiers* of the post-1968 period is a far more theoretical journal than it has ever been in the past. These issues above provide the basis of such theory.

8

Practical Writings

While there is a great increase in theoretical writing in *Cahiers du Cinéma* after 1968, there is still significant attention paid to practical criticism, to following developments in recent films, to analyzing and criticizing specific works at the time of their release. In many cases, critics for the magazine raise theoretical issues in their reviews and make theoretical points through the use of examples from recent releases.

Nonetheless, one can discern in the early 1970's an attempt to move *Cahiers* away from journalistic treatment of current films. Since the editors would then obviously consider the practice of film reviewing, in the conventional sense, to be an adjunct of the standard, commercial, capitalist method of film distribution, an arm of the commercial publicity machine, the kind of writing in *Cahiers* on current films undergoes considerable change. There is a decreasing emphasis on the coverage of every major release; there is a greater willingness to allow for a time lag between the release of a film and an article on it. Often questions of whether the film is "good" or not are ignored; what becomes relevant is the film's ideological expression. While we will discuss in Chapter 10 *Cahiers'* shift back to a more cinephilic, more traditional approach, this ambivalence about practical, applied movie reviewing continues through much of the 1970's.

As *Cahiers* moves further to the left in the early 1970's, it treats, not surpisingly, more and more films with leftist leanings, films that would be characterized as "progressive." (The not quite translatable French word is *"progressiste"* and often the quotation marks are retained around *"progressiste"* to indicate a certain skepticism about the true progressiveness of the works.) For convenience sake, the practical writings discussed below will be divided into three sections: the first will treat certain general writings about the *film progressiste;* the second will discuss some of *Cahiers'* reassessments of film history; the third will treat *Cahiers'* reaction to the historical film and the attempt to develop a theoretical framework for the treatment of historical subjects in the cinema. In almost every case, there is an affirmation of the theoretical requisites discussed in the preceding section; in many cases Brecht is referred to directly; invariably the discussion treats the form of the film as being as important as the content.

The *"Film Progressiste"*

Cahiers du Cinéma in the 1970's periodically runs critical attacks on political, leftist films which were nonetheless made through the conventional means of financing and production. One of the first of these is Pascal Bonitzer's article, which appears in July of 1970, entitled, appropriately, "Film/politique." Bonitzer notes that most films hide a latent political discourse behind certain devices which attempt to mask it and that often in presumably "leftist" film there is an underlying discourse which supports the dominant ideology. Thus, Bonitzer sees what he calls an inflation of films on politically controversial themes as evidence that there are definite inequalities in the system, and he sees a process whereby the discourse of these films is "clouded." He cites, for example, Marin Karmitz's CAMARADES (1970), a French film about workers' problems, as a particularly symptomatic film. It had been the aim of Karmitz to reach a mass audience, which implies, to Bonitzer, two things, both related to one another. First, the film would have to be shown in a normal distribution pattern. Second, the film would have to have a familiar, commercial, and therefore inoffensive and non-revolutionary story line.[1] The message is a familiar one: the method whereby a film is produced and marketed reflects the actual content it presents.

Bonitzer goes on to describe specifically how CAMARADES' form affects its content. He talks of the way in which the film seeks to separate content and form (quoting from an interview with Karmitz to prove his point) and then goes on with this description:

> Besides, every film, whether the *cinéaste* wishes it or not, talks of itself: so the long lenses photographing the beautiful construction yards of CAMARADES do not express simply that the bosses do not easily let cameras film what goes on in their yards, but the will to be content with long lenses, that is to say a vision, not "distanced" (though some people have, in fact, talked of this film as Brechtian), but far away. Like the conception of a character who is a weak dreamer, which is the level at which the fiction remains; why *one* character, if not to avoid showing wholes, structures, real forces?[2]

Similarly, Bonitzer criticizes a film like Robert Kramer's ICE (1970) for its treatment of what might be called "neurotic projections" of fascism as a castrating agent: to Bonitzer, only to the extent that ICE acknowledges it presents a projection process and offers it to the audience *to read* (again the notion of *lecture,* discussed in the beginning of the preceding section of this study) is the film praiseworthy. Similarly, he criticizes the South American THE HOUR OF THE BLAST FURNACES (1969) for containing a somewhat unclear discourse which confuses and condenses Third World ideology, Latin-American cultural nationalism, and the Argentine class struggle into a single "subject." To Bonitzer, THE HOUR OF THE BLAST FURNACES develops its own system of fascination, "for which the most significant political operation is the systematic reabsorption of *real contradictions* into the artificiality of *conflicts,* of events, the *effect of presence* of direct cinema here working fully."[3] (This is another indication of the disillusion with the *cinéma direct* movement which takes over the *Cahiers* line.)

Thus, Bonitzer demonstrates the insistence on form to be found in the new *Cahiers.* In all three cases these are films which have been generally regarded as leftist but which Bonitzer seeks to criticize for not being *clearly* political enough, for not making every aspect of the discourse show an awareness of underlying political significations. The fact that all three films could be considered significantly leftist as compared to the general product being exhibited in French theaters clearly matters little to Bonitzer. What is important to him is to refine the question of political signification down to its most precise points. In every case the movie's form prohibits a lucid political discourse.

A little over a year later, Jacques Aumont responds to a different production phenomenon, the sudden number of French films dealing with police themes, e.g., Philippe Labro's WITHOUT APPARENT MOTIVE (1971) or Yves Boisset's THE COP (1970). Once again, the films contain certain elements which label them as political or leftist. Aumont sees this phenomenon as a fetishization of political issues in order, in the long run, to repress political comment all the more violently. He sees the films as having a vaccination effect: the criticism is far from accurate or of the sort needed to treat the real issues of the place of the police in the France of 1971.[4]

Aumont's article is as much a critique of the French critics who praise many of these films as it is a critique of the films themselves. Aumont notes that the films are often seen as good largely in comparison to other films, particularly American films of comparable genres, rather than in terms of the discourse that is contained in them. He notes, for example, the way in which criticism becomes a part of the marketplace, seeing a complicity between the statements of the critics and the avowed intentions of the filmmakers, regardless of the real product. For example, he points to the way in which the films are praised for their realism (citing as an example Robert Chazal of *France Soir* writing about Yves Boisset's THE COP), when in reality they are very truly stereotyped. What becomes more important in these films (and even more important in dealing with their characters) is the Aristotelian notion of probability or verisimilitude, for in reality the characters are idealized: the main policeman is often given a position of omniscience, of fabulous, almost superhuman qualities. Indeed the heroes of these films have the qualities of a movie director themselves.[5]

Aumont comes to three conclusions about these films, the first of which cites Brecht directly for contrast:

1. Credited with an absolute mastery over their own acts, the exceptional characters that they present all benefit by the overvaluing that is due to their position as "heroes"; everything in their behavior that is given as condemnable monstrosity is easily reabsorbed in their crises of conscience, everything can be redeemed by an adequate sacrifice, and at the minimum, they will be much pardoned for having much suffered. Knowledgeable at every instant of all the determinations of their situation, they are the opposites of the characters, blind to their own behavior, in the didactic plays of Brecht: they can serve no other purpose than to elicit the admiration, identification, and blindness of the viewer.[6]

2. The immorality of the policemen in these films is constantly shown in terms of individual morality or lack of it.

3. The films criticize police corruption without ever taking account of the class system which produces it.

Thus, Aumont ultimately critiques the new French police films for their lack of typing and their attempted naturalism, which he sees not as being realism but as a way of avoiding a genuine criticism of the French police system. The films reflect bourgeois ideology, and the bourgeois press, as a part of the same system, only reinforces this in its praise for the films.

In 1972, two Italian political films, Francesco Rosi's THE MATTEI AFFAIR and Elio Petri's THE WORKING CLASS GOES TO HEAVEN, shared the grand prize at the Cannes film festival. Both were films made within conventional commercial systems, and, rather predictably, *Cahiers* finds elements in them to criticize. Pascal Kané faults the films for the fact that they have, for him, no true political discourse but rather mimic political discourse. In his collective review of the films, he criticizes them for not giving, as Brecht explicitly advocated, the *totality* of a political situation. He attacks THE MATTEI AFFAIR for presenting only a part of its situation, for dealing with the oil magnate Enrico Mattei in a way that very well treats his political significance to the developed world but ignores the way in which the problems extend as well to the underdeveloped countries. One needs, Kané concludes, to present a problem in all its contradictions.[7]

Kané also approaches the problem of what is called the "positive" hero, a type of hero which appears neither in the Elio Petri film nor in Francesco Rosi's. The difficulty with the heroes of these films is that, according to Kané, they fall into the category of traditional heroes from classical bourgeois narrative forms; that is, they are what he calls the *héros agissant (agissant* meaning active in both the sense of busy and effective). The presentation of contradictions cannot genuinely include this classical form of hero, for he cannot be contradictory and active at the same time. In both the plays of Brecht and some classical cinema (Mizoguchi, Renoir), there is an abandonment of

the *héros agissant,* so that, Kané explains, in THE RULES OF THE GAME
(1939) the class contradictions are spread across the various members of the
cast. The implied objection to this sort of hero is that he is never seen as a *type*
(in the sense that Brecht advocated) but always as an exceptional case. And the
exceptional case is invariably inapplicable to the audience's particular
problems and behavior.

Kané articulates the problem directly:

> The most urgent problem that this question raises is, today, this one: can one still be
> content with negative heroes, divided, simple revealers of class contradictions? How can one
> conceive of the positive hero from a political point of view, that is to say for whom the
> opposition to the bourgeoisie is active? But then, how does one avoid that this character
> might be perceived in a reflex manner as a "hero occupied with politics" (a *héros agissant)*
> and not fall into classic, edifying exemplarity. Thus the hero of the Petri films is indeed a
> proletarian, which does change the traditional lack of definition of the classic hero. But this
> exception alone produces neither (negatively) a critical division of the scene [into
> contradiction], nor (positively) an image of real struggle.
> ...Volonté is received by the spectator as a character *agissant,* in the continuity of classic
> cinema *before* being a positive hero (politically) of the working class. Bourgeois ideology is
> on the screen and in the theater. Otherwise said, the error of modernist cinema is to believe
> that some ideologies hardly acceptable to the bourgeoisie are going to make their films shift
> completely to another camp, when in fact, the combat takes place on a scene already marked,
> already situated, and has been lost a long time ago.[8]

Again the message is clear. Good intentions do not make for a politically
effective film; the form of a film can defeat its presumably revolutionary
content.

In 1977, Serge Toubiana continues many of these preoccupations in
writing a set of essays in which he discusses the place of the spectator in left
wing fiction films. Toubiana's immediate topic for the essays is Yves Boisset's
1977 film LE JUGE FAYARD DIT "LE SHERIFF," a film about corruption
in the French legal system. The movie falls into the category of what Toubiana
calls the "denunciation film," popular in France and Italy at the time.[9]

Toubiana argues that any fictional film always presupposes a "virgin
spectator," one who is willing to forget what he thinks he knows and is ready to
be educated, to accept what the film gives. The characteristic of many of these
denunciation films is the inclusion in the film of a character who is an
investigator of one sort or another—a cop, a journalist, a judge—with whom
the audience can share a desire both for knowledge and for political change.
The difficulty is that the referents in real life (the historical facts or real
situations that inspired the movie) are too often used to support the credibility
of a fiction in which these fantasy desires can be satisfied. Thus, the
fictionalized reality encourages the spectator to lose his or her memory of
political reality, even while it may exploit traces of that memory through
stereotyping and the familiar situations of the Hollywood narrative.[10]

The leftist film becomes caught between identification with the good hero (Toubiana uses the word *investissement*), which involves it then in the mechanics of traditional cinematic fascination, and the denunciation of some aspect of society, which by its nature requires distance and critical thought. The result is usually a fictionalized political discourse about a politics that doesn't really exist.[11]

Toubiana begins to conclude by discussing Brecht, arguing that in the Brechtian theater there is also the presupposition of a spectator who is not yet politically educated or aware, who will be shaken into awareness by the strong dramatization of a scene. In the Brechtian theater the spectator is a member of an acknowledged audience. In film the audience is far more anonymous, and there is the opportunity for "bad desire," i.e., for a "desire for that which lets you know nothing, the desire for blindness typical of all audience activity."[12]

Toubiana sees as the result: "the denunciation cinema can only fail in fleeing the movie mechanism, can only confirm already understood discourse, discourse already produced and transmitted by other institutions." It is a message shared by all four of these articles and one we will see repeated even further, with endless variations, in many articles to be treated in the pages to come.[13]

New Approaches to Film History

One of the features of the new, politicized *Cahiers* was, rather predictably, a revision of its approaches to the history of film. Where the pre-1968 *Cahiers* was eclectic and catholic in its tastes, *Cahiers* after the events of May tended to focus on isolated aspects of film history in far more depth. Perhaps the most noteworthy trend is a definite comprehensive interest in the silent Russian masters; the late 1960's and 1970's witnessed the production of an even greater number of texts on the subject, texts dealing not only with Eisenstein but with many of the lesser figures as well, such as Dziga-Vertov, Michael Romm, the FEKS group, not to mention a special, oversized number of the magazine devoted exclusively to Russia's film theory and practice in the 1920's.[14] Such an interest is clear and logical within *Cahiers'* theoretical framework: Russian films of the 1920's are among the few in the Western world produced under a political system approaching one that *Cahiers* would approve. If the content of a work is dictated by its means of production, these works should be very instructive both for their forms and their content. Similarly, it is hardly surprising that *Cahiers* in the 1970's should publish French translations of previously unavailable writings by Brecht, e.g., his working diary for his period in Hollywood.[15]

Nonetheless, apart from the Russian cinema, historical writing in *Cahiers* became somewhat less frequent. Let us therefore consider merely three significant examples of how *Cahiers'* new theoretical framework begins toward 1970 to be applied to aspects of film history: *Cahiers'* special number on Dreyer, published in December of 1968, its collective text on Renoir's LA VIE EST A NOUS (1936) and its collective text on John Ford's YOUNG MR. LINCOLN (1939).

Published so soon after May 1968, the special issue on Dreyer has the look of the old *Cahiers,* containing appreciations of each Dreyer film, many photographs, and a generally "cinephilic" quality. But there is evidence in much of the writing of the new direction *Cahiers* is about to take. For example, one of the first texts is by Jean-Marie Straub, a rigorously Marxist-Leninist director whom *Cahiers* had begun to champion and would continue to champion, particularly with the release of his film OTHON. Straub's article indicates a direct link between himself and Dreyer (and indeed, both men have produced ascetic, formally rigorous works). Straub acknowledges a superficial idealism in Dreyer's work but nonetheless praises the director's ferocity toward the bourgeois world, his use of direct sound (one of the key elements, also, in Straub's work for its rejection of what might be called aural representation), his rejection of realistic forms, and his close acknowledgment of the union of form to content.[16]

The other two significant articles in the collection are both by Jean-Louis Comolli, the *Cahiers* writer who in this period most consistently suggests the Marxist direction that the publication is to take. In both cases, the articles represent an attempt on Comolli's part to come to terms with Dreyer's consistent use of spiritual issues in his work. Thus in "Rhétorique de la terreur," Comolli praises Dreyer for his presentations of spiritual issues in material terms; his films *materialize* his themes and deal as much with social misunderstanding as with spiritualism.[17] Similarly, Comolli's discussion of Dreyer's LEAVES FROM SATAN'S NOTEBOOK (a 1921 film modelled largely on Griffith's INTOLERANCE, made five years earlier, which contains an episode that is superficially pro-white, anti-red with regard to the Russian revolution) defends the film against charges that it is reactionary on the grounds that the villainous red character is implicitly criticized for *betraying* the revolution.[18] To this reader, Comolli's defenses of Dreyer occasionally sound like rationalizations attempting to fit Dreyer into a politically oriented system. What is more important, however, is not so much whether Dreyer fits into the system as the fact that Comolli attempts to fit him in.

This defense of Dreyer is perhaps one of the most significant links between the old and new *Cahiers.* What the old *Cahiers* admired in Carl Dreyer's films is the same studied attention to form that attracts the new *Cahiers.* It puts in relief the relation between the two: that an idealist film theory will naturally be based on ideal forms, but any materialist film theory must also be based on forms, in their material manifestations.

A link to the old *Cahiers,* albeit a far more tentative one, may be found in its collective assessment of Jean Renoir's LA VIE EST A NOUS, which enjoyed a re-release in France around the end of 1969.[19] LA VIE EST A NOUS was a film commissioned by the French Communist Party in the 1930's and was hence financed outside of normal commercial, capitalist channels. Made by a collective group headed by Renoir, which included many notable people in the French film industry, it was used to generate support for the Party in the elections to be held in 1936.

William Guynn has pointed out that this article, "LA VIE EST A NOUS, militant film," appeared at a moment when *Cahiers* in its political thinking was looking to the French Communist Party for leadership. Guynn notes that by the end of 1971, some twenty-one months after the article appeared, the magazine repudiated it for its uncritical following of the French Communist Party line. While Guynn himself also criticizes it for its political superficiality and lack of genuine critical analysis, the piece is nonetheless a major point in *Cahiers du Cinéma*'s development.[20]

A collective effort by Pascal Bonitzer, Jean-Louis Comolli, Serge Daney, Jean Narboni and Jean-Pierre Oudart, the article attacks the way in which other critics had greeted the reissue of the film: the invariable response was to ignore the film's political discourse and to talk about it either as a Renoir film, from an auteurist standpoint (and see warmth and personal, Renoir-like expression in it) or from an empiricist standpoint (to talk about it as being, for example, well constructed). In other words, the bourgeois critics ignored its political message.[21]

The *Cahiers* collective hardly discounts Renoir's contribution to the work, but they reject a completely auteurist approach and go into a fairly elaborate historical study of the influences to be found in the film's making. (They underline, for example, how one of the collaborators was Karl Koch, who had worked with Brecht, and the film's similarities to Brecht's KUHLE WAMPE, which was released in Paris in October of 1932.) Nonetheless, the authors also emphasize certain ways in which LA VIE EST A NOUS is parallel to Renoir's other work of the period, such as MADAME BOVARY (1934), TONI (1934), and THE CRIME OF M. LANGE (1935), particularly in Renoir's tendency to divide the film into units that complement one another in dialectical fashion.[22]

What the critics find most praiseworthy is the way in which the film is a true political discourse on the situation in France at the time, treating the unfair division of wealth in France, the menace of French fascism and European fascism in general, the position of the Communist Party as the only answer to this situation, with what becomes a double function: to be documentary and didactic. Cited as even more praiseworthy for *Cahiers* is the film's form. The writers see two levels of discourse in LA VIE EST A NOUS, one being general (the presentation of an overview of the historical-social situation of the moment), the other being specific (the demonstration of this general discourse in a series of "exemplary scenes").[23]

The article's authors write of this structure:

> The articulation of these two methods, which regulate LA VIE EST A NOUS as a political discourse, fill exactly the condition of every militant film: to propagate one political signified, a single-minded message, and yet above all escape what is generally fatal to the militant film about this single-mindedness—of being only a transparent enunciation of this one political signified: a stumbling block for all political discourse not to think of its own process of exposition—to the extent that the interrelation of the two methods produces a complex reading of that one political signified. Instead of being only its statement *(enoncé)*, it reflects upon the conditions of its enunciation: it poses not the question of its meaning (given at the very beginning of the film, one and unalterable), but that of its "effects of meaning," that is to say of interference, in the filmic process of the production of meaning, of the question of the receiver of the message.[24]

Thus, LA VIE EST A NOUS is seen as rejecting representation and providing an alternative to it. The film is constructed to make one conscious of the ways in which it is producing its message, so it cannot possibly deceive. Not only the content but the form is politically correct. The audience is informed not only of the end points of the argument but of the process of the argument itself and can therefore be maintained as an *active* audience.

The method used by the film, of mixing documentary and restaged, fictional materials, also receives praise. *Cahiers'* writers see in the work a joining of two movements in the militant film, the mixing of the documentary line (which comes out of Dziga-Vertov) with the use of fiction and representation for political analysis (which comes out of KUHLE WAMPE). This mixture is historically important for it is one of the first and is particularly valuable because the film alternates the two in a dialectical form which deconstructs, in effect, two traditional filmic structures. As in the plays of Brecht, the techniques of the discourse comment on their own nature. The *Cahiers* critics describe the process: "first the introduction of the fiction deconstructs the documentary, subverts it and denounces it as a trick; then the fiction . . . reinvests the documentary shots with meaning (then again connoting them as fictional) and gives them back their value as documents: no longer signs of an ideological fiction, but elements of a true political discourse, which *cancels* discourse of bourgeois propaganda, that is to say crosses it out and redirects it."[25] From this, the *Cahiers* authors conclude that the film is advanced and praiseworthy for following the Leninist ideal of not denying the methods of bourgeois culture but criticizing them and deconstructing them. By taking conventionalized forms and manipulating them, LA VIE EST A NOUS at once comments on those forms and provides an alternative to them. The film becomes a denunciation of the manipulative techniques of the conventional propaganda film.

The article concludes with some criticisms of the work's efficacy as a militant film, of some scenes that are not as effective as they might be. But this treatment of the work is particularly instructive, for it is one of the rare cases in which the new *Cahiers* provides positive criticism of a work, pointing to a practical example of a film which does provide an alternative to bourgeois forms.

Cahiers' text on YOUNG MR. LINCOLN is perhaps one of their most important, for in it the editors attempt to establish a policy toward the older, classic cinema. Their avowed aim is to provide a "reading" of the work, that is, a discussion of the film in relation to the social and cultural codes which produce it. The writers define this attempt in part by what it is not. They claim to offer neither a commentary, an interpretation, a treatment of the work as a closed structure (which would be the technique of a certain branch of semiology), nor an ideological "demystification which disposes of the film in a moralist way" (which would be the method of *Cinéthique*).[26]

The basis for the *Cahiers* reading is the film's mixture of sex and politics, the use of subconsciously sexual imagery and situations to express a political message. To the *Cahiers* critics, this link is the key to the reading:

> the double repression—politics and eroticism—which our reading will bring out (a repression which cannot be indicated once and for all and left at that but rather has to be written into the constantly renewed process of repression) allows the answer to be deduced; and this is an answer without the two discourses of overdetermination, the Marxist and the Freudian.[27]

Thus, the authors state directly one of the primary themes to be found repeated in the new *Cahiers*, that the political repressiveness of the classical cinema is as often as not linked to its underlying sexuality.

The authors provide several long sections on what they see as some of the historically determining factors at work in YOUNG MR. LINCOLN, descriptions of both the state of Hollywood and the U.S. in the 1938-39 period, the political leanings of both 20th Century Fox and Darryl F. Zanuck, and the roots of YOUNG MR. LINCOLN in other works of literature and film. In looking for the film's ideological significance, however, the *Cahiers* critics repeat that they do not wish an ideological simplification of it. They write:

> Our work, on the contrary, will consist in activating this network in its complexity, where philosophical assumptions (idealism, theologism), political determinations (republicanism, capitalism) and the relatively autonomous aesthetic process (characters, cinematic signifiers, narrative mode) specific to Ford's writing, intervene simultaneously. If our work, which will necessarily be held to the linear sequentiality of the discourse, should isolate the orders of determination interlocking in the film, it will always be in the perspective of their relations: it therefore demands a recurrent reading, on all levels.[28]

Thus, the article is built around a method which takes each major scene or sequence of the film and analyzes it to give the main determination of the scene and to indicate the secondary determinants at work. To give an example, the analysis of the first scene of the film, in which Lincoln is seen first running for public office and giving a speech against corruption in politics, is given a primary function of presenting Lincoln as a candidate (reflecting his eventual Republican party candidacy for President, which in turn would be reflective of the then forthcoming 1940 elections in the United States). At the same time, however, the speech against corrupt politicians is described as having the function of moving the film's discourse onto an idealist level: morality takes precedence over political considerations, and this morality becomes the "seed," as it were, of Lincoln's greatness, a greatness which is suggested to have overtones of predestination. The *Cahiers* commentators observe:

> But this very *repression* of politics, on which the ideological undertaking of the film is based, is itself *a direct result* of political assumptions (the eternal false idealist debate between morality and politics: Descartes versus Machiavelli) and at the level of its redemption by the spectator, this repression is not without consequences of an equally political nature. We know that the ideology of American Capitalism (and the Republican Party which traditionally represents it) is to assert its divine right, to conceptualize it in terms of permanence, naturalism and even biology...and to extol it as a universal Good and Power.... The seeds of Lincoln's future were already sown in his youth—the future of America (its eternal values) is already written into Lincoln's moral virtues, which include the Republican Party and Capitalism.[29]

By this method, any given scene is made to be a nexus of political, philosophical, aesthetic, and, in the subsequent sections, psychological considerations. The writers offer a fairly detailed comprehensive analysis of the film, often in the sexual terms of Lacanian psychology, but its goal is always to see the specific signifiers which give meaning to the work.

This type of approach to early films is carried out subsequently in texts on von Sternberg's MOROCCO (1930),[30] and Cukor's SYLVIA SCARLETT (1935),[31] but consideration of them is not necessary to understand the type of methodology adopted. Such studies are all but an end point in the notion of *lecture*. They establish a particular mode of reading as representative of the *Cahiers* line of thought (a mode which is situated somewhere between the empiricism of semiology and the extreme radical politics of *Cinéthique*). What is perhaps more important is that *Cahiers* begins to develop a theory or an approach to film history, one which has yet to be fully exploited or systematized but one which is both methodologically and philosophically provocative.

Approaches to the Historical Film

One of the principles of Marxist thought is that history can be approached scientifically, and the study of history is one of the basic studies of Marxism. Thus, Marxist film critics such as the ones at *Cahiers du Cinéma* would see their interest in a film like YOUNG MR. LINCOLN as a scientific pursuit, as an attempt to see a filmic work as the product of certain definite social forces. What is also of key interest to the *Cahiers* theorists, however, particularly as they approach the mid-1970's, is to find a way to deal with the historical film, that is, the film that takes history as its subject. As we have noted, too, in the late 1970's Jean-Louis Comolli becomes particularly preoccupied with the theoretical questions surrounding the historical film.

The critics for *Cahiers* ask, in effect, these questions: if history is a science, how can one make the historical film scientific rather than ideological? If history is ideology, how can one make the historical film ideologically correct? Here perhaps more than with any other genre or type of critique, the *Cahiers* critics tend to go directly to Brecht for their answers, for their solutions to the problem.

There are two essential groups of writing that summarize and embody *Cahiers'* approach to this issue in a practical way. The first is a pair of articles about a film by René Allio, LES CAMISARDS, an historical film dealing with Protestant revolts in the eighteenth century in the South of France. The second group consists of writings about what the French call *la mode rétro*, referring to the interest in the mid-1970's in films with period themes about the recent past, i.e., the 1920's, 1930's, and 1940's and particularly with the subject of fascism and the Nazi occupation of France. Let us consider each set of writings in turn.

It is easy to understand *Cahiers du Cinema*'s interest in LES CAMISARDS. As mentioned earlier, its director, René Allio, had been well known for his highly Brechtian work on the French stage with Roger Planchon and for THE SHAMELESS OLD LADY, a film adaptation of a short story by Brecht. A Brechtian treatment of a subject dealing with popular revolution would approach one of *Cahiers'* ideals for the kind of film that could be made under a new, radical political aesthetic.

Jacques Aumont immediately praises the work for "a will to show history here as a movement and opposition of social forces and no longer (what almost always is done by the Hollywood cinema and its descendants) as a succession of striking actions or 'historic' words that can be assigned to 'great men'—to film history *against* identification with the heroes that summarize it."[32] Aumont puts himself in immediate acknowledged agreement with François Regnault (author of the second essay on LES CAMISARDS) that the Allio film offers a definite alternative to the *péplum* cape-and-sword films of other eras but wishes to counterbalance the unconditional assertions of Regnault's article with the conclusion that, although the Allio film is correct in its intentions, it is far more questionable in its achievements.[33]

Aumont immediately focuses attention on the film's costuming, as representing the way in which it seeks to achieve its goals. He discusses the way in which Allio intentionally uses two different types of costumes for the nobles and for the camisards. Although both are modelled on historical fact, those of the former were conceived in their entirety, done from models or taken from previous plays; those of the latter were made from more modern materials and treated with greater liberty. Aumont postulates that we can consider two functions of costuming in the historical film. The first function is archeological and represents a desire for authenticity used to support the film's realistic illusion. The second he calls a semantic function, and it can be seen in Allio's attempts to make the rebels' costumes appear natural, spontaneous, even hippie-like, the nobles' to seem artificial and repressed.[34]

Aumont sees the use of this semantic function as representing Brecht's notion of the social gest, i.e., the exterior expression of the conflicts of a society in a work. (Aumont cites Barthes' essay about Brecht and theater costuming, "The Diseases of Costume," as well.[35]) He offers other examples of the social gest in the actors' gestures, the language they use, and many other small touches in the film. All of this work constitutes a way of reemphasizing the central message of the movie, the social conflict at its roots; the form relates to this as much as the content. In Aumont's words, "two 'ideological communities' struggle on the screen, that is to say not only in the fiction, they encounter one another only to affront one another, but they even struggle for possession of the image, which can be to them only alternatively consecrated, the encounter on the screen having for a function the production of conflict, thus the emptying of the screen."[36]

Aumont also discusses the other social determinations present in the film, its analysis of an historical situation—the feudal mode of production and taxation; the class hatred which feeds the revolt; religious ideology—but then proceeds to suggest what he sees as the reasons for the movie's failings. He finds LES CAMISARDS too intent on illustrating the ideas of the scenario, in such a way that there are two readings possible for the film: the first, what Aumont calls a "metaphoric reading," sees the film as a general model for all such class conflicts, all forms of guerilla warfare that are similarly motivated. To Aumont, the film does not present a *contradiction* (in its way of presenting characters and their acting) between what is acted in the film and what seems lived, but only an alternation. What results is a fable, something which can be generalized into a "universal" message, which is exactly what Brecht sought to avoid. The film comes too close to "putting in the same bag all the struggles of liberation without looking too closely to specify the terms of these more or less desperate struggles."[37]

On the other side of the issue, Aumont sees another reading in which "nothing exists on the screen but the most scrupulous, most exact reconstruction of an episode of history." This is also a level on which the film, to Aumont, does not hold up, and he sees in the film "a hesitation between impossible archeological exactitude and modern dress." Similarly, Aumont sees Allio's use of compositions and images out of seventeenth-century painting as suggesting an atemporal and non-historical ideology that has little to do with the materialist ideas the film seems to be advocating.[38]

It is in its historical scrupulousness that the film reveals what Aumont calls an attempt to create a "referential illusion," despite the movie's attempt to see political processes in more abstract terms. Aumont writes:

> Everything takes place, in summary, as if each of the signifiers in the film corresponded to two signifieds: one signified strongly abstract, one referential signifier working to guarantee the first without making it any more concrete. Two signifieds supporting one another, one returning to the other in a tautological game—so the film, condemned to producing independently only one or the other, or one and the other at the same time, but never playing one over the other or against the other.[39]

For Aumont, LES CAMISARDS is a film whose intentions (and, to a certain extent, whose methods) are praiseworthy but which has still fallen into the dominant ideological trap of treating an historical subject not as a product of specific forces, but as a specific event which has the universal implications that Brecht so strenuously objected to. It is exactly what Brecht warned against, that is, the use of naturalism to create the effect of specificity, whereby the result is the substitution of idealist universals for generalities about the scientific effect of social and economic forces on a given society.

Aumont's piece is intended as something of a response to the article which follows it by François Regnault. (The seeming reverse order of the two is used, one presumes, to specify the priority of Aumont's views as those of *Cahiers'* editorial staff in general.) Regnault contrasts the Allio work to the *péplum* film, the usual historical film which, he asserts, converts history into drama in such a way that it becomes impossible for us to see either social forces or ourselves in it. Regnault's article is something of a small history of cinema, for he contrasts to the *péplum* film two alternatives which are themselves opposed forms of the true epic (in the Brechtian sense of the word). Regnault would see this double cinematic expression in, on the one hand, the films of Preminger or INTOLERANCE (to give its Hegelian form), or, on the other, in Eisenstein (the Marxist tradition).[40]

Regnault sees LES CAMISARDS as coming genuinely out of neither the *péplum* nor the epic tradition but rather out of a French tradition of historical annals. He interprets the film in somewhat the same manner as Aumont, maintaining that there is an effect of distanciation but also an attention to detail that makes the film seem present to us. He writes:

The concentration of the fable into episodes at once random and dense permits us to obtain from LES CAMISARDS a realism of forces (and not of things), which is at once an archeological reconstitution (impossible, and infinite, or sterile, because when everything, costumes, objects, words, is finally exact, it still lacks movement, projection, hope) and the epic vision of the world (of which an enlarging winds up producing an effect of density, of the game being worked out in advance in a mythic figure). What is historical first with Allio is not so much a basin, a gun, a livery, a landscape; it is the relationship that one has with them: in that he comes out of Brecht and the practice of a theater where one never conceives of furniture and accessories in anything other than their relationship to the actor, in contrast to the cinema, where the actor often arrives when the archeologist is gone.[41]

Thus, Regnault argues, LES CAMISARDS is historically genuine in its treatment of specific actions and forces. While his interpretation of the film may not be in agreement with the more official *Cahiers* reaction, both articles share a common ground in analyzing the film: they seek to approach it on a materialist basis. The presentation of history as the product of material forces is the ever-emphasized goal. Both see LES CAMISARDS as an important film for its attempt to reach this goal.

A far more theoretical approach to the problem of the historical film is presented by Pascal Kané in his article, "Cinéma et Histoire: L'effet d'étrangeté." To Kané, one of the central problems of the historical film is that the remoteness of the epochs that are treated leads to an alienation effect (in Brechtian terms), a strangeness that tends to increase as the period becomes more distant. Thus, the central problem with the historical film is to maintain an objectivity toward what is being presented, to use this strangeness for understanding.[42]

To demonstrate his point, Kané discusses two stills from two films, the first from Rossellini's THE RISE OF LOUIS XIV (1966), the second from Pier Paolo Pasolini's 1001 NIGHTS (1974). In the former, which Kané very much prefers, every element of the *mise en scène* is significant in that it presents some piece of information which adds to the economic, social, or historic context of the film: the actors are not privileged in the frame but are linked to their surroundings as men in an historical context. In the Pasolini still, however, most of the economic, social, and historic information is removed from the frame: the emphasis is on the characters and on their place in a narrative. Put differently, in Rossellini, the world is presented as an historical extension of the world with which the viewer is familiar; in Pasolini, an indefinite historical past is used to create a world unto itself, a world that does not, therefore, refer to the real world.[43]

To Kané, the notion of "strangeness" is linked to the notion of *lecture* which we have discussed earlier. The first type of film, such as Rossellini's, requires a more careful *lecture* (participation) from the viewer. At the same time however, it is somewhat contradictory, for the notion of political signification implies an understanding of political forces which is seemingly at odds with the idea of strangeness. Kané writes: "But in this case, this production of the signified, that is to say the creation of a space for reading in the film, is it not incompatible with the very strangeness which, we have seen, is often only the product of an inadequacy of reading (either by a lack of knowledge, or because pleasure has supplanted reading) and not yet a complete fact?"[44]

The resolution of the problem is presented by Kané in the notion of the social gest, found, of course, in the theorization of Brecht. Kané argues that the social gest is simply a representation of social relationships offered to the viewer for evaluation: "the gesture will not illustrate but on the contrary will render unusual the process represented." This process of making strange creates a "space for reading" by the viewer. Rather than illustrate, the social gest makes the viewer conscious of the way it produces a meaning or sense.[45]

Kané gives an example from Renoir's LA MARSEILLAISE (1938) of a scene in which Louis XVI eats tomatoes for the first time while the Parisians besiege the palace. In this scene, Kané sees several determinations, including an historical determination (the beginning of the tomato's use in cuisine) and a narrative function (the King is eating alone because the revolution is underway). The effect is unexpected—the use of the tomato distances the effect of the presentation of history.[46]

Kané tries to draw some conclusions about the *Verfremdungseffekt*. He discusses the problem in translating the term into French. "Distancing" suggests a kind of joylessness and "false mastery of the subject" to Kané; "strangeness" suggests simply a new technique of fascination. The true sense of the word, Kané suggests, emerges only by combining the two ideas. He writes: "Thus, there is a necessity today to think of the two aspects: to be able to offer the represented scene to the spectator but to inscribe at the heart of the scene the strangeness, the unexpected, in terms where are marked at once the resistance of the material to representation and a dream-like presence which cannot be mastered."[47]

The *Cahiers* author concludes by asserting the need for such Brechtian thinking amid the trend for films of the *mode rétro* genre, films which make use of history for its effects of fascination rather than for real historical analysis. Kané's main argument is that the historical film offers opportunities to use Brechtian forms, because by their nature they have qualities which tend to be "distanced" or "strange." The difficulty is, as he has said, in the prevention of this quality from becoming merely a different kind of filmic representation that avoids such analysis in the search for pure pleasure. The historical image must offer itself to be read but at the same time contain elements of surprise which produce a desire to read it.[48]

The trend towards films dealing with fascism and sexual perversion (in particular Luchino Visconti's THE DAMNED, 1969, and Liliana Cavani's

THE NIGHT PORTER) results in a *Cahiers* text by Bernard Sichère examining these films and their implications. Sichère's text takes its title, "La bête et le militant," from a quotation from Brecht, where the German playwright calls upon intellectuals to be like beasts toward fascism, to engage in "a writing which kills." Thus, Sichère takes as his goal the development of a proper militant attitude toward the films in question. He calls for analysis of these films that does not simply accept their equation of Naziism to sexual perversion nor deny it but dissect the relationship between Naziism, history, and sexuality.[49]

Sichère sees a need "to assign a place to fascism there where it is, politically, and to denounce it *politically.*" The task for the intellectual also is to discover the ways in which fascism works its way into the bourgeois, intellectual, and popular consciousness, the way in which it becomes a part of the consciousness of a culture. Again, Sichère finds the key in Brecht and looks to the tools of historical materialism (used by Brecht) and psychoanalysis (aided, basically, by the new *Cahiers* theories).[50]

The philosophical foundations of fascism, he asserts, are to be found in bourgeois morality. In terms of the newer standards of morality, however, sexuality has become the religion of the petty bourgeoisie. The problem (presented in outline form) with the films is that they present the relationships between fascism and sexuality in religious terms that become appealing to this new morality, mysticizing both fascism and love, making the revolutionary standpoint inhuman, the reactionary one exciting. The dialectic is always an idealist one of good/evil rather than a political one. By presenting fascism on these terms, it ignores the true nature and real practices of Naziism, which are mainly economic and involved with business trusts, exploitation of the masses, and profits.[51]

By contrast, Sichère finds an alternative in Brecht and then proceeds to summarize Brechtian theory in a paragraph that is instructive, for it indicates the way in which Brecht is here not at all used as a password or way to provide an instant politicized context but rather as a part of Sichère's precisely worked out arguments about the Visconti and Cavani films:

> The theater, for Brecht, must at once fascinate, that is to say exhibit images, tableaux where pleasure is attained, and to deconstruct them by introducing into them a perturbing corrupting element, by showing how they form themselves, what they support, by introducing a disavowal of the tableau beginning with this other regard which is political conscience itself. From which the pedagogical function of such a theater which aims to produce an awakening of political consciousness, and first with the actor himself, whom few current directors even care about.... First with the actor, then with the spectator, invited to participate in the fascination-parody of the actor in his multiple playing, not psychological, but explosive, not fascinating but in alternation, aiming to make the tableau he presents work at once from the interior (by his acting) and from the exterior (in relation to the critical regard of the spectator). The actor who plays Arturo Ui is not Arturo Ui, he is not even

Hitler, he is someone who is coming to expose the lie, the trickery on which is constructed the "Ui effect" or the "Hitler effect," and in the same blow the lie of the theater and the bourgeois play, which demands complicity and not criticism, passivity and not intelligence. To deconstruct the bourgeois or fascist imagination is to show at one time by what proceeding it inscribes itself in consciousness and subjectivity, and what really supports it.[52]

The above paragraph puts in relief clearly Sichère's objections to the Cavani and Visconti films as he opposes their methods to Brecht. "But Visconti, Cavani... refuse such an ironic and deconstructing look which makes appear the accessory fascination effect which they need (the effect of perversion with which their discourse has no place)." Sichère points to the use of flashbacks in THE NIGHT PORTER. Rather than use one set of images to comment on another, the two reflect each other, indicate the same thing, that there is an eternal, non-historic reality which has nothing to do with societal contradictions and change, in other words an eternal psychology. (Sichère in turn links this to the notion of Lacanian psychology of the Other, but this is something of a subsidiary issue to this discussion.) Perversion becomes an eternal truth. He draws the following syllogism: if Naziism equals perversion, and perversion equals *l'amour fou,* then Naziism equals *l'amour fou.* What is ignored is the realization that the kind of sado-masochistic sexuality presented by the film is really a reflection of certain economic relationships: a master/slave form is an economically dictated form. The films become, subconsciously, justifications for capitalist oppression.[53]

Sichère then returns to the place of the intellectual toward these fascist elements he finds in the culture. He cites the case of Georges Bataille, the surrealist-communist writer, as an example of the typical intellectual stance of being simultaneously critical of and fascinated by fascism. He criticizes the usual stance of the intellectual and artist of putting himself apart from the people, the masses. The making of sexuality the religion of the petite bourgeoisie is as much the responsibility of the intellectuals as anyone else, and they need to take responsibility for it and find alternatives. Sichère would conclude that only through the intellectual's understanding of the cultural relationship between political repression and bourgeois sexuality can he escape being implicated in the repressive system.[54]

As the 1970's advance, the *Cahiers* critics find a number of films about the Nazi era which they do admire, among them Joseph Losey's M. KLEIN (1976), Rainer Werner Fassbinder's LILI MARLEEN (1981), and above all Hans-Jürgen Syberberg's HITLER, A FILM OF GERMANY (1978). In all three cases, however, they praise the deliberate artificiality of the films, the purposeful avoidance of realism in the presentation of the epoch.

In writing about M. KLEIN, Losey's film about an Aryan who is mistaken for a Jew during the occupation, Jean-Loup Rivière answers those critics who object to the film's mixture of history with a supposedly "metaphysical fiction."

He instead praises the film for being a psychoanalytic study of the nature of racism. In talking about the film's structure, he writes:

> History is not a decor or a context, it is the equivalent of the fiction; if the two meet at the end, they have stayed separate throughout the film, like opposites, each one interrogating, interpreting the other. History is thus presented as what it is, fragments of images and texts, sifted-through shreds of forgotten objects, a discourse full of death.[55]

Rivière praises Losey's use of scenes that document specific historical details of the period, precisely because he presents them as fragments that remain detached from and in alternation with the fiction of the film.[56]

Louis Skorecki defends the deliberate use of a television spy series structure in LILI MARLEEN, about a singer who becomes a pin-up for the Nazi troops even while she helps her Jewish lover smuggle anti-Nazi propaganda photographs out of the country. Skorecki argues that a television series like HOLOCAUST (1979), by fictionalizing the Holocaust and seeking identification with the persecuted Jews, risks creating the underlying impression that this suffering was simply a fiction.[57] He writes: "To learn the truth by the bias of fiction, is it not to fictionalize, to dream, and in the long run to doubt?" Rather, he sees LILI MARLEEN as a Brechtian film in its refusal to lead the viewer to predetermined answers or judgments about the film's character—particularly the singer, who steadfastly refuses, throughout her experiences, any genuine awakening of political awareness. For Skorecki, "each audience member, manipulated, put into the scene, must accept being at war with himself, split between emotion and reflection, free." The film's stylizations and mixtures of genres, rather than presenting a realist "truth," serve to perplex the audience, to cause it to think about the historical realities.[58]

The film which for the *Cahiers du Cinéma* critics most completely confronts the issues involved in the *mode rétro* trend, however, is Hans-Jürgen Syberberg's HITLER. On its release, several critics discuss the movie in the magazine, including Serge Daney, Pascal Bonitzer, Jean-Louis Comolli and François Géré.[59] The article most relevant to Brechtian theory, however, is Jean-Pierre Oudart's.

Oudart begins his discussion of the movie by describing two different ways we remember films: some produce novelistic, dream-like memories, others are documentaries that we don't remember as dream-like at all. He argues that newsreel footage of Nazi rallies, while documentary, still holds a strong fascination and that there is a type of "dogmatic leftist" who seeks almost superstitiously to suppress this fascination.[60]

Oudart repeats the argument made by Comolli and Géré that German national socialism was a kind of *mise en scène*. Syberberg, in his seven-hour study of fascist imagery, allows the audience to enjoy this *mise en scène* of national socialism, even while we can also understand and critique it. He argues that Syberberg's method is the opposite of Godard's in that Syberberg accepts the dream-like fascination that the film medium can provide, even while analyzing the relationship between the cinema and the Hitler phenomenon. Like Godard, who in Oudart's eyes is a kind of end point in dogmatic leftist filmmaking, Syberberg does show aspects of the apparatus of cinema, with magic lantern and other illusionist effects playing a major part in the film.[61]

Oudart links Syberberg to the cinema of Méliès and magic, by which the audience is enchanted, even while it knows the magician is simply performing tricks. He compares Syberberg's cinema to Leni Riefenstahl's, writing: "HITLER is thus Méliès opposed to Leni Riefenstahl, magic opposed to religion. Little belief-producing effects opposed to big ones."[62] Oudart continues:

> Difficult to react to, HITLER is not a film on which one can take a position. It torments us, makes us stumble over our words in talking about its levels of symbolic, aesthetic and historical memory which produce the referent—Hitler, fascism, between yesterday and today—like the putting into action the positions of these differing memories.[63]

One cannot help but ask whether in Syberberg's combination of symbolic, aesthetic, and historical memories might be found something of the kind of analysis Sichère finds lacking in THE NIGHT PORTER.

Following its politicization, *Cahiers du Cinéma*'s position on the historical movie is that it must always be seen in the light of history as a science, of social and economic material relations. An historical film is praiseworthy to the extent that it articulates the material and cultural realities by which history is structured. The model frequently invoked here is that of Brecht, who sees as a repression of this articulation the traditional elements of narrative, thoughtless identification and fascination, and naturalism. The *Cahiers* critics praise those films that also acknowledge how they are dealing with their historical materials—not as rigid, archeological reconstructions of the past but as thoughtful discourses about it. They argue that the contradictions which make up society can best be dramatized by the use of social gests, which render representations of them concrete, material, readable, and surprising.

9

Key Films and Their Commentaries

A major change in *Cahiers du Cinéma* in the early 1970's is the magazine's eagerness to devote attention to films that are overtly politicized. We can find in the magazine a stream of commentaries about both radical films of which the *Cahiers* critics approve and films which in the magazine's editorial viewpoint do not live up to their left wing intentions. Thus, one may see in the post-1968 *Cahiers* a shift to the left not only in the modes of argument practiced but in the films which the periodical chooses to ignore or quickly dismiss. Where the *Cahiers* writers of the 1950's are very content to talk about nominally apolitical works, those of the 1970's—particularly the early 1970's—are more likely to find such movies unimportant or not worth their effort to discuss. Indeed, the films that the magazine seems more eager to criticize negatively are not those that ignore political issues; they are those which are well-meaning but which defeat their political intentions with supposedly reactionary forms.

In this chapter, let us consider *Cahiers du Cinéma*'s reaction to works by three filmmakers: Costa-Gavras, Jean-Marie Straub, and Robert Kramer. All are deliberately political filmmakers whose works become important subjects for *Cahiers'* post-Brechtian film criticism. Let us conclude the chapter with a discussion of the magazine's extensive treatment of Jean-Luc Godard's TOUT VA BIEN and Marin Karmitz's COUP POUR COUP (1971), two movies that were released almost simultaneously. Both deal with labor unrest, and the magazine's comparison of them is one of its major political statements.

Costa-Gavras

The films of Costa-Gavras are of particular importance to *Cahiers du Cinéma* in defining its position toward political filmmaking in the early 1970's. Costa-Gavras could be considered the most importantly commercial political filmmaker of this period, for films like Z, THE CONFESSION (1970) and STATE OF SIEGE (1973). Z, a portrayal of the famous Lambrakis case in Greece, involving the murder of a member of the Greek parliament, might even be considered the film which gave commercial potency to the treatment of leftist themes in the French cinema. The Greek-born director's work becomes the magazine's prime negative example in taking its stands.

In his review of Z, Jean Narboni points to the unanimity with which the film had been received by the press and by the public (which appears to be the same for both the theaters on the Champs-Elysées and those of the Latin Quarter). Narboni contrasts this to the popular films of Luis Buñuel (which tend to be considered as *both* blasphemous and Christian, atheistic and believing, etc.) and finds the unanimity of Z's reception implicitly incriminating, for it indicates that the film cannot possibly be making a genuinely political statement. If it were, at least some major elements of the population would be offended. Narboni writes:

> There is no such thing in Z [as in Buñuel], for which they are praising the clarity, the single level of reading, where the style of reading, provided and practiced, is the same *for all*. It is thus, that such a film touches in those who approve something which goes beyond their political choices, something more profound, less "narrow," which would be the "human," the "sense of justice," the "essential honesty in every man." That it puts itself in the territory of moral categories, for which we are going to reproach it most violently.[1]

At the roots of Narboni's critique of the film is this observation that the work presents its arguments on moral grounds rather than material, social, or political ones. Z ignores, Narboni would say, social structures, and he laughs at those critics who have treated it as though it were a serious analysis of a political situation. He faults the simplistic nature of the film's apparent political arguments.[2]

Narboni attacks the film stylistically as well. He sees the work's supposed semi-documentary style as being composed largely of flashy effects. He complains about the caricaturing of the villains in the film, seeing in it stereotyping of the worst sort, since by it, Narboni argues, the movie has "defined neither an object of study nor the means to produce it."[3] In a footnote he discusses the fact that the movie never makes direct mention of Greece or the name Lambrakis, thus rendering the film abstract and allegorical i.e., one of what Marx would call the "bad" sort of abstractions. The author provides an example of a scene which summarizes the movie for him. In the book and film, one of the generals receives a phone call from a journalist who asks him if, like Dreyfus, he is going to defend his innocence. In the book, the general merely hangs up on him; in the film, he shouts "Dreyfus was guilty!" The latter produces laughs in the theater. Narboni clearly faults Z for making its political arguments so obvious and audience pleasing that they produce no genuine thought on the part of the viewer.[4]

With the appearance of Costa-Gavras' THE CONFESSION, about Stalinist purges in Czechoslovakia in 1945, *Cahiers* critic Jean-Louis Comolli takes the opportunity to treat general issues of film and politics as they apply to the Costa-Gavras film. Comolli structures his review of the work in the form of fifteen propositions about politics and film, and his fifteen points are well worth recapitulating in this context:

1. Comolli sees as his task not only the treatment of films and their ideologies but also their effects on audiences and critics. The film creates its readings, and THE CONFESSION, by all of its inconsistencies, raises a whole set of questions around the relationship of politics to film.[5]

2. Like many films, THE CONFESSION is in the forefront of the dominant ideology but puts up a smokescreen to hide its ideological operations; in no way does it try to subvert socio-cultural standards.[6]

3. Because it is a film which in no way indicates the way in which it is supposed to be read, its meaning may ultimately be assigned to the sum total of its *lectures.*[7]

4. Every political film must be political on the level of its material nature, the way in which it is written or formulated. Comolli quotes Brechtian theorist Walter Benjamin:

> The tendency of a work can be politically correct only if it is literarily correct. That is so say that the political tendency includes the literary one. . . . Instead of asking: what is the position of a work with regard to the relationships of production of a given epoch? Does it agree with them, is it reactionary or does it aspire to their transformation, is it revolutionary?—instead of this question, or at least *before* the latter, I would like to propose another. Before asking myself: what is the position of a literary work with regard to the production relations of an epoch? I would like to ask: what is its place in these same relations? This question aims directly at the function which the work fulfills in the midst of the production relations of an epoch. Put otherwise, it aims directly at the literary technique of works. . . . An author who teaches nothing to writers teaches nothing to anyone.[8]

5. THE CONFESSION's political discourse reduces itself to its "content" or "message." "The question of its political consistency is raised by its cinematographic inconsistency." THE CONFESSION in no way questions its historical existence, i.e., the means of production whereby it was made.[9]

6. A proposition in the form of a question: how can a film avoid supporting the dominant ideology if it reproduces the styles and the themes of the dominant ideology?[10]

7. The profit motive of the commercial cinema assures the reproduction and functioning of the standard forms of cinematic expression.[11]

8. The profit motive of the film is reflected in its political discourse.[12]

9. Films operate under a double articulation: "the principal articulation (masked, automated) = reproduction of the conditions of domination of the ideology, that is to say of the norms and economic and aesthetic-cultural codes by which it installs and inculcates itself; secondary articulation (declared, contingent) = transmission (as an accomplice *or* critic) of a certain number of ideological themes."[13]

10. "One suddenly sees that if the work of the film does not relate to its principal articulation to make of it a *principal contradiction,* even if its political discourse contradicts the themes of the dominant ideology, *this contradiction remains secondary* and is not sufficient to become concerned with the process of reproduction of the modes of inculcation of the dominant ideology nor, thus, in fact, of ideological themes which are the effects of it."[14]

Here Comolli calls into question those critics who could see neither the covert political implications of Jean-Marie Straub's OTHON (a film whose problematic nature is related to the methods of expressing the discourse rather than to the direct discourse itself) nor the more overt political implications of THE CONFESSION. He concludes that the critics have accepted the program which the film has provided for them rather than *reading* it.[15]

11. Identification with the central character in THE CONFESSION is achieved by illusionist techniques, the artificial techniques creating the effect of reality.[16]

12. The spectator is put into a position of an accomplice rather than a reader; the film puts the spectator in the role of the hero. It encourages a kind of voyeurism toward the torture it portrays, even while the viewer is co-experiencing that torture. It presents the horrors of Stalinism as spectacle.[17]

13. The film's ultimate message is tautological: by the images we see the horror of Stalinism, so we know that Stalinism is horrible. (This point follows from the Marxist critique of empiricism.) In the book, Comolli points out in contrast, there was not only the presentation of the horrors of Stalinism but a certain degree of reflection on them. There is no *analysis* of Stalinism in the film; it becomes a succession of political fantasies.[18]

14. The "political" readings by the critics are also tautological and only confirm the theses provided to the critics by the film.[19]

15. It is the dominant ideology that "fills up the holes," as it were, that supplies the answers to the unanswered questions in the film. Comolli concludes his article by calling for a rethinking of the standard notions about the practice of political cinema, so that it can be "drawn out of the mire" of the dominant ideology.[20]

Thus, Comolli's article is theoretical and a summary and restatement of most of the arguments to be found elsewhere in *Cahiers,* but it is a statement linked to one specific example which crystallizes many of the problems inherent in a politicized cinema which is produced under a capitalist system. Comolli's main thesis reflects that central argument of Brecht—that the means whereby a film is produced have a profound effect on its content.

Several years later, in 1973, Pascal Bonitzer and Serge Toubiana analyze Costa-Gavras' STATE OF SEIGE as a political *act.* Their tone begins far more softly than those previous reviews of Costa-Gavras' films, and they reflect upon the earlier works, noting that although they make use of conventional film forms, Z did introduce an officially political tone into the French cinema which has not been without positive aspects. Similarly, STATE OF SIEGE may be praised if only for the fact that films which explicitly denounce American imperialism are rare.[21]

Bonitzer and Toubiana are somewhat more hesitant when they talk about the forms employed by the picture. They contrast the moral, sentimental attitudes of the thriller genre with the necessities of political discourse:

> The thriller, the adventure film, the "action" film, are *culinary* genres, to take over the terminology of Brecht. One consumes here physical violence and fascist behavior. Now only the mentally retarded can still believe that the real referents which permit the accreditation of the violence in question are found in a pre-war style underworld, with gangsters in felt hats: it makes more money from the point of view of the production to talk of the mafia, or of the more frightful violences which are in the territory of anti-imperialist struggles, struggles against repression, etc. Only, in the last case, one enters into the ambiguity: one is more or less obligated to take "innocent" violence slanted by a political discourse. To the extent that the violence is that of the underworld it relates to morality, a discourse ideologically perfectly adaptable to the "culinary" genres. Morality is sentimental; it makes the subjectivity of the viewer play emotionally; it structures the pleasure and gives it its weight of humanity. Political discourse is something else: it refrains from freeing the viewers from responsibility for their attitudes, brings them back to a non-evident, conscious taking of sides, it moderates pleasure by proposing an earthly reason, a material one, for violence. It strips violence of its tragic, that is to say metaphysical, halo, in relating it to social positions.[22]

Thus, in films like Z or THE CONFESSION, there is always an opposition between violence and non-violence, which could be put into this sentimental, humanist mold. STATE OF SIEGE, on the other hand, has by necessity of its subject to portray two violences, something in common with all films on the class struggle, like POTEMKIN.[23]

It is on this level that Bonitzer and Toubiana fault the film. They see Costa-Gavras as being limited by his pacifism and his humanism, whereby he critiques the Tupomaros, with whom the film deals, for their revolutionary violence. The authors argue that Costa-Gavras is only capable of showing the "what" of imperialist aggression and that he does not understand the "why." If he understood the "why," they continue, his film might actually be able to participate in the popular revolutionary struggles.[24]

Bonitzer and Toubiana argue that Costa-Gavras turns the film's ideological opposition into an aesthetic one and criticize, for example, the casting of a sympathetic actor like Yves Montand as the American oppressor. They argue that in itself it is not necessarily a mistake to make the Montand character sympathetic but rather that those same qualities must be incorporated into the political dialectic of the work. Seen in the light of the systematic oppression, those sympathetic qualities should become repulsive. The authors cite Brecht's character of Master Puntilla: "A man is a man, but that does not prevent him from being an oppressor. And not: An oppressor is an oppressor, but that does not prevent him from being a man."[25]

The *Cahiers* critics trace Costa-Gavras's humanism back to political sources: STATE OF SIEGE is a film that praises democracy and condemns dictatorship, in a manner similar to Z and THE CONFESSION. The contradiction, to them, is that because STATE OF SIEGE is a French film, it implies that imperialism does not exist in France. Commenting against Costa-Gavras' humanism, they cite Brecht's statement that those who would struggle against oppression or torture without struggling against the relationships of property that produce that oppression or torture are like those who enjoy eating their veal but protest against the slaughter of calves. Bonitzer and Toubiana finally challenge Costa-Gavras to make a film on French imperialism and what they call the bourgeois dictatorship in France.[26]

Jean-Marie Straub

The main complaint at *Cahiers* about Costa-Gavras' political films (including his later 1975 production, SPECIAL SECTION[27]), is that their reactionary forms affect their content. A film which reverses the issue, as it were, is Jean-Marie Straub's OTHON, a work for which the emphasis is on form rather than on the specificics, and some attacks on the post-1968 *Cahiers* have paid particular attention to the magazine's defense of the movie.[28] In the film Straub treats the text of the Corneille play as anything but sacred. All of the actors speak French with some sort of foreign accent; Straub mounts the action in modern-day Rome, on location, picking up the sounds of automobiles with the use of direct sound; he often pays more attention to the abstract aural qualities of the actors' deliveries than to the words themselves. All of which has in some quarters been viewed as a desecration of Corneille's verse.

Narboni begins his first paragraphs by talking about the way in which OTHON was received, the way in which the film industry has found nothing to exploit or use in it. The critics, too, are deprived by the film of what ordinarily allows them to function: a subject, a theme, a style, in any of the conventional senses of the words. Narboni sees Straub's use of Corneille's text as the mounting of a play in which the *mise en scène* is not a single illustration of the text but rather a use of language that deals not just with the words or ideas to be expressed but with the physical qualities of the speakers' voices themselves: indeed, the techniques also underline what is musical about the verse play itself, that the rhythmic forms of the language have a meaning and a content in and of themselves.[29]

Narboni's chief point of interest, however, is in the relationship of OTHON to the theater and in turn to the notion of what leftist art should be. He writes:

In fact, it is possible to have an imperfect notion today—in the progressive and irreversible movement of its advance—of the possibility of a general materialist writing [*écriture*] having little to do with what has been thought of as "engaged art" (literature, theater, cinema...) that continues, despite its historically marked failure (theoretical, political) to be perpetuated here and there. This general writing, for which the law was pronounced by Jacques Derrida as *remote reference, to be apart* [*référence écartée, être à l'écart*] (meaning, in its infinite metaphoric circulation, the very foundations of traditional ontology and of mimetology), proceeding by light and decisive *displacements* inside structures that it inhabits to nibble at them and play with them (and not by untimely proclamations of "reversals," which are thus indefinitely prisoners of the same circle), constitutes a mortal danger not only to bourgeois artistic ideology, but also to those who, under cover of progressivism, can only conceive of the Alternative *(Autre)* to lowly naturalism as its banal, formalist inversion. This writing, necessarily linked to the social, historical and political real, provided it does not reflect passively contradictions but is in its turn a producer of contradictions and effects of meaning, is susceptible to taking in charge different signifying practices (of which the cinema is one). Having nothing to do with the unitary myth of total art nor the aspiration toward an absolute art (a synthesis and fusion of all the others), it will insist on the contrary on their distinctive characters and the singularity of their effects of inscription.[30]

Thus Narboni sees as politically positive the act of working with the system of film *écriture*, the deconstruction of the codes of cinema such as Straub practices in OTHON. Such a deconstruction is philosophically materialist because it is a manipulation of the signifiers and makes no effort to presuppose any essential nature to the work of art. It is a formalistic approach, whose argument supposes that if bourgeois art forms reinforce capitalist society, undermining of those forms becomes automatically subversive. This attitude is a link to the formalism previously practiced at *Cahiers*.

Narboni relates Straub's treatment of his subject to three other historical figures in the arts—Eisenstein, Stéphane Mallarmé, and Antonin Artaud. All, he argues, have a common preoccupation with what he calls the *theatrical scene* (something which need not involve, he asserts, only the theater). This notion of the *theatrical scene* involves "making a leap away from representative flattening, spatializing in volume, in scope, expressive linearity, and constituting a material depth (and not an idealist, unifying, totalizing one, such as with the vanishing point and perspective, installing the eye in the center of space.")[31] Thus, in this context, the *theatrical scene* is an alternative to linear perspective, the same ideologically tainted linear perspective that is so criticized in other *Cahiers* articles.

Narboni offers the idea that Straub avoids treating his staging of OTHON as a representation of a preexisting performance, i.e., the film is not a recording of a play. Rather, although the play was obviously not written for the camera, Straub achieves a unity between the verbal and visual levels of the resultant film. Narboni writes about OTHON's being both a staging of the play and its cinematographic transformation, a production of the play that simultaneously subverts the illusion of theatrical space that it creates.[35] Narboni's argument is very similar to that of Comolli in his article on *le direct*. One of the qualities of OTHON is that the presence of the actors and what they do and say is inseparable from the way in which the camera records them. Straub's OTHON exists only for the camera; it is a presentation more than a re-presentation. But it simultaneously acknowledges its relation to the theater.

The *Cahiers* author contrasts this point of view with that of André Bazin, whom he cites as having advocated not films which try to apply cinemato-graphic specificity of setting and technique to theatrical texts but rather those which create their own theatrical universe by emphasizing their theatricality. (These two types of films are in contrast to those purely cinematographic films which are constructed around film's "usual" proclivities for nature.) He sees Straub's film as an almost complete answer to what is the manifest idealism of Bazin's assertions. Narboni argues that Straub superimposes the process of making the representation itself. In other words, OTHON works against the notion that the play has an existence apart from the film, that the film is a mere reproduction of the staged work; in the material presentation that is the film, the two are inseparable. Film is not to be considered, as Bazin would assert, the representation *of something else,* as though that something else would still have existed apart from the moment when it was filmed.[33]

Thus, Narboni argues, the very material structure of OTHON plays against cinematographic illusionism. The sound-track contains much random noise,[34] Straub plays with the illusion of depth and its complementary one of two dimensionality, both of which may be found in film; he alternates theatrical and cinematographic constructions. Sound, image and text are all viewed as a totality. The methods employed by Straub work against the passivity of the spectator: the film must be *read.*[35]

From Narboni's article, one may see a view in *Cahiers* that modern, political thinking about film must come from consideration of the nature of the theater and the way in which narrative films are theatrical expressions. The recognition of theatricality is a way of acknowledging the means whereby cinematic illusion is produced, of acknowledging the symbolic nature of the film medium, of bringing about an active reading on the part of the viewer. This is entirely compatible with the influence of Brecht; from the position (previously held in *Cahiers* by Louis Marcorelles) that Brecht and the cinema are incompatible because of the anti-theatrical nature of cinema, we reach a resolution of the problem by a condemnation of the supposedly anti-theatrical nature of traditional film language.

In subsequent years *Cahiers du Cinéma* continues to champion the films of Jean-Marie Straub and his wife Danièle Huillet, such as INTRODUCTION TO ARNOLD SCHOENBERG'S "ACCOMPANIMENT FOR A CINE-MATOGRAPHIC SCENE" (1975), FORTINI/CANI (1977) and DALLA NUBE ALLA RESISTENZA (1979). The magazine's commentaries continue in the lines of argument raised by Narboni above.[36]

One may consider, for example, Narboni's later reaction to FORTINI/ CANI, a film consisting largely of the Italian Marxist author, Franco Fortini, reading aloud from his book *I Cani Del Sinai,* a text about the Arab-Israeli war of June 1967. Narboni praises Straub and Huillet's method of recording Fortini's reading spontaneously, without rehearsal or preparation, and Straub's horror at the suggestion that he announce who it is who is reading from the book. Rather, Narboni affirms Straub's assertion that the film should be considered fictional rather than a documentary. For Narboni, FORTINI/ CANI calls into question the whole relation of the film to its audience. He writes:

> One sees very well the modern reflection on writing, on the text, that one can draw from it: the author as product of his book rather than source, the text coming back to the father at the end of the road, the reversibility of the writer and the reader. There is also here the intransigent Brechtianism of Straub, the disjunction between the character and the actor, the distance of the actor from what he offers, the citing rather than the expression of the text.[37]

We will return to Straub in Chapter 11 to discuss Jean-Claude Biette's reaction to Straub and Huillet's most recent film, TROP TOT, TROP TARD (1982). What is most important about the magazine's attachment to the work of Straub and Huillet is the extreme dominance of questions of form in the filmmakers' work and the necessity they feel to suggest, in the manner of Brecht, the process whereby they have done their work.

Robert Kramer

The release of Robert Kramer's American film, ICE, made in 1969 (a film about an underground revolution in a fascistic dictatorship in the United States), provides *Cahiers du Cinéma*'s editors with a work that they clearly find provocative and worthy of discussion, but about which they differ in opinion. Late in 1970, *Cahiers* runs a collective discussion on the film with most of its editorial staff participating. While all the members treat the film with respect, there is a tone of uncertainty and disagreement about the success and nature of the movie's achievements. On the level of political analysis, for example, while Jean-André Fieschi accuses the work of having no real analysis of the economics and politics of American capitalism, Sylvie Pierre disagrees, saying that the work indeed does account for the social determinants of what it shows.[38] ICE is clearly a problematic film for *Cahiers,* one which in general its critics admire but one which they have difficulty classifying or placing easily in their theoretical schema.

Cahiers' preoccupations with ICE center around two basic aspects of the film: what they term its "cinephilic" qualities and its use of realism and the conventions of *cinéma vérité.* To treat the former first, Jean-André Fieschi sees in ICE several roots in the history of cinema: the film relates back to the first DR. MABUSE films of Fritz Lang, a certain Lincolnian tradition of Frank Capra, and the French New Wave cinema of ALPHAVILLE (Godard) and PARIS NOUS APPARTIENT (Rivette). There is a certain negative tone to the choice of the word "cinephilic," but in a later paragraph, Jean Narboni defends Kramer's use of cinematographic tradition on much the same grounds that he defends OTHON. He sees Kramer's citing of shots or scenes from the work of American directors, such as Samuel Fuller, Howard Hawks, or Raoul Walsh, as a simultaneous "absorption and destruction, by one text of other texts." By putting these scenes into a new, politicized context, Kramer can comment on and critique the old American cinema.[39] Later in the discussion, when the subject of the film's relationship to the American film, and particularly the *film noir,* is again raised, Pascal Bonitzer talks of the film as a *réecriture* (a rewriting) of the signifier, which in itself is viewed as a political gesture.[40] ICE's transformation of the American cinema, its use of the forms of that cinema to politically beneficial ends, is praised and seen as one of its more significant accomplishments.

The second area of discussion, that of realism and *cinéma vérité,* is far more complex, and indeed it relates to the whole issue, so dear to the *Cahiers* critics, of the political implications of film form. Jean-Louis Comolli emphasizes one of the underlying messages in much *Cahiers* criticism, that the superficial political message in the film is not necessarily its whole political message, and affirms that ICE must be treated for the whole of its political statement, which is not just the sum of each individual political idea expressed in it. As if in explication of this statement, Comolli continues in a later paragraph to discuss how ICE may be read (again the notion of *lecture*) on two levels, the first analyzing the film's "effects of reality," its "hyper-realist, documentary, 'lived' style," and a second level which is clearly fictional, dealing with a war in Mexico and an American revolutionary movement, an unreal, projected situation. What is important for Comolli, however, is the co-presence of these two aspects. He states: "The realism, here, thus serves literally to actualize the dream, to compensate—and thus more or less to designate and criticize—the lack of reality of the situations and political acts filmed."[41]

Pascal Bonitzer reaffirms Comolli's statement by talking of the ways in which the documentary aspects of the film are undermined by other means, namely, a) the frustrating discontinuity of the montage and the narration; b) "the disconnected, floating, dream-like character of certain episodes;" c) the insertion of sequences that have no narrative function. In addition, the use of a Mexican war rather than a Vietnamese war is seen as a positive step toward removing the film from immediate identification or emotional response toward a more intellectual awareness of the meaning of the metaphor, "to oblige the viewer to weave a reading, to tie up the strings, to observe the gaps, the blanks, the holes in the ideological and scriptural path of ICE."[42]

Thus, the emphasis on much of the *Cahiers* critics' praise for the Kramer film lies in the way in which it provokes an audience to active thought. Comolli argues that the film is so completely organized around a principle of discontinuity that it has to be read to be understood.[43] Jean-André Fieschi sees the film as a "documentary on a fiction," dealing with the reversal of these processes (of documentary and fiction) that has been suggested as politically expedient by so much other *Cahiers* writing. It is therefore not surprising when Jean Narboni raises the question of Brecht and his place in ICE's structure. He sees ICE as providing an alternative to the old-fashioned use of realism to produce a sense of "lived" reality, the usual use of *cinéma direct* to render the workings of a narrative believable. Narboni discusses the way in which the narrative elements of ICE remain dictated by the political and social realities established by the movie. The film does not make use of arbitrary effects merely to cement its impression of reality. Rather, the effect of reality in ICE is seen as growing out of the attempt to anchor the narrative into a system of political cause and effect, giving the reasons why each event exists under such a system. ICE becomes praiseworthy to the extent that it contains a true political discourse, and its form is praiseworthy, despite its use of superficial realism, to the extent that it allows this discourse to show through. Jean-André Fieschi offers an example of this technique in the film. In the scene where drugs are taken, the film presents not just the phenomenon of the drug taking, but the reasons, in the economic system, why they are being taken.[44] A political discourse structures the narrative.

Cahiers du Cinéma's round-table on ICE remains one of its landmark texts. Serge Daney has commented that the discussion marks a point of radicalization for the magazine, a point at which it withdrew its support for the French Communist Party in favor of alternative leftist policies.[45] In its subsequent issues the magazine continues to support Kramer's cinematic efforts, calling him the American *cinéaste* "with whom a permanent dialogue can function . . . taking off from the two great questions of the moment: Cinema (Art) and Politics (militant discourse, the experiences of living and struggling)." The magazine asserts that it is Kramer's interest in *écriture,* the "writing" of a film in both images and words, the creation of a new, militant cinematic practice, that its critics relate to so well.[46]

At the time of the release of MILESTONES (1975), Kramer's three-and-a-half hour semi-documentary study of how militant American leftists of the 1960's were adjusting to the 1970's, *Cahiers* published another round-table discussion of the new film. Much of the discussion deals with specifically political issues—the differences between the European and American lefts, the need for extended, patient commitment to militant causes, the situation of American minority groups. The *Cahiers* commentators do finish their discussion with some important statements about the film's structural and aesthetic qualities.

As with ICE, the critics talk about a certain difficulty with following the film, with its multitude of characters, many of whom are unrelated to one another in any narrative sense. Thérèse Giraud discusses the way in which the film has no referential discourse; that is, there is no sense of cause and effect between the episodes of the film. Rather, the film is a kind of lesson that requires us to listen carefully to what the characters say and do, to make our own connections between what we see, to understand those relationships that exist beneath the surface of its disconnected narrative.[47]

Several of the critics note the film's superficial similarities to movies of the *cinéma vérité* movement but emphasize its important differences, particularly in the way it avoids "intimism," i.e., the sense that the camera is capturing something internal about the people it presents. Jean Narboni sees the film as one which takes material that is photographed in a *cinéma vérité* style and structures it architecturally or musically to produce a film comparable to Dreyer, Godard, or Mizoguchi in its formal qualities. As with ICE, the use of *cinéma direct* techniques would go beyond mere naturalism. Pascal Bonitzer describes it as a film where "one takes at once both the accidents of life as the camera records them, and a job of editing which musicalizes the material and gives it a much larger and much more collective vision in drawing together very diverse things, heterogeneous spaces, places and peoples."[48] The movie would acknowledge its restructuring of reality to make a point.

The *Cahiers du Cinéma* critics seem ultimately most impressed with the way the film sees militant activity as a collective activity and the way it reflects a kind of collective voice of the American left. Serge Toubiana's comments conclude the round-table. He says:

> One asks oneself a bit what one is doing in a movie house looking at such a film and suddenly feels a need to look for others with whom one can form a collective to say how one is going to incorporate the film into one's life, how one will share it, how one will define one's personal relation to its ideas to make them live, one's relation to the collective one is in; one has a need to form a collective of spectators who will use the film. It's a film which disturbs our passive position as individual spectators.[49]

One can only be struck by the Brechtian nature of this result Toubiana describes.

Other critics, such as Serge Daney and Jean-Pierre Oudart, also praise MILESTONES in the magazine, in more formally written pieces of criticism.[50] We can see in *Cahiers'* championing of Robert Kramer, who works outside the usual commercial system of production, praise for a filmmaker who not only treats political subjects in his film but who attempts to change the form of his cinema as well. The magazine's critics admire Kramer's use of a dialectical structure (between documentary style technique and the contrivances of his fictions) and his creation of narratives that require an active, participating, reading audience.

TOUT VA BIEN and COUP POUR COUP

There is one text which might be considered the major work of practical criticism by *Cahiers du Cinéma* in the early 1970's: that is the collective critique, written by a group of critics who called themselves *"le groupe Lou Sin d'intervention idéologique,"* which compares two French films of the period, Martin Karmitz's COUP POUR COUP and Jean-Luc Godard's TOUT VA BIEN. The choice of films is hardly arbitrary. The two works were released in Paris at almost exactly the same time, and both deal with workers' strikes and the sequestration of employers. Both works think themselves to be radically leftist, even Maoist. The Karmitz film was shot with a group of workers themselves; shooting was done simultaneously with camera and videotape, so that workers could critique the material as it was shot. Godard's film is his first since 1968 made with both stars (Yves Montand and Jane Fonda) and a fairly conventional narrative; Godard claims to have modelled the film after Bertolt Brecht's famous text on *The Rise and Fall of the City of Mahagony,* in which he outlines the differences between dramatic theater and epic theater.

While the *Cahiers* discussion of COUP POUR COUP and TOUT VA BIEN is practically oriented toward dissecting the two specific films, it also has a heavily theoretical side, like so much of the work from this period. What becomes particularly remarkable about this text is that it is a balance of theory and practice, using each to enlighten the other. Because of the similarities in theme and aim in the Godard and Karmitz films, they are natural films for comparison. The *Cahiers* critics write in their introduction to the analysis that the two films are "examples of cinematographic practices exerting themselves to go beyond the problematic of the 'progressive' or 'engaged' film, to take part explicitly in the revolutionary struggles being carried on today in France by the proletariat and its allies, and thus to trace, between them and the rest of current production, a radically different line of demarcation." They see their task as trying to see if the films really do achieve their goal of aiding in the political and cultural struggles of the workers, from the point of view of the Marxist-Leninist position they have adopted.[51] The simultaneous appearance of COUP POUR COUP and TOUT VA BIEN provides *Cahiers* with a perfect opportunity to articulate concretely its new positions, to demonstrate how many of its theoretical stances may actually be applied to specific examples of film criticism.

In the first section of the analysis, entitled "COUP POUR COUP, à la remorque du révisionisme," the critics attempt to analyze the Karmitz film, going back to its erroneous philosophical assumptions which are basically, they assert, empiricist assumptions. That is, they claim that the film makes the old empiricist error, that of assuming that one only need look at reality to understand the truth. To the *Groupe Lou Sin,* one must argue:

Karmitz and his comrades have fallen into the basket: they have thought they were producing a true understanding of a precise situation, in contenting themselves with a passive reflection, organized under the form of a "reconstruction." For them, it was simply a matter of reproducing the postulates of sensory perception, the workers "reliving" their experience under the camera eye, without submitting them to a true task (to know the balance sheet of Communist struggles, permitting a reflection of their essence, their internal laws), instead of a *bricolage-assemblage* of informational elements organized in a supposed "model."[52]

The *Cahiers* critics assert that what is needed in a film is an understanding of social, political, and economic *processes* and that those processes cannot be seen merely through the observation of reality.

What is even worse, however, is the passivity of the empirical approach, the lack of willingness to seek to transform what is observed, the contentedness merely to recognize it. The film's intention of giving a voice to the workers is found to be politically dubious in itself, without a strong Marxist-Leninist theoretical base to give direction to the process. Thus, on the most initial, primary level, the film fails to make the conceptual leap from empiricism to dialectical materialism.[53]

Cahiers' assessment is also critical of COUP POUR COUP on directly political levels as well. While both COUP POUR COUP and TOUT VA BIEN thematically treat the break with revisionist Communism, the *Cahiers* commentators see Karmitz's treatment of the problem to be erroneous for submitting to two essential illusions which turn his position, which seeks to be anti-revisionist, into a revisionist one. First, he sees the struggle as purely an economic one, as a struggle between workers and bosses and not a struggle against a bourgeois state. Second, the assumption that the workers can achieve everything without political, theoretical direction is a position which turns into "ultra-democratism" and "bureaucratism." In the end, COUP POUR COUP is ruled by a position which is described as "anarcho-unionism," which, unguided by genuine Marxist theory, becomes only a sub-genre of revisionism.[54]

The arguments continue in a second section, "Deux lignes, deux voies," which discusses further the approach of COUP POUR COUP. *Cahiers* does credit the Karmitz film with some significant achievements. The authors admit that the film does at least show the working class, the places where the workers work, the class hatred that they feel, and concrete evidence of exploitation.[55] Nonetheless, they insist on denouncing the movie's "illusions and errors."

The attempt to give a voice to the workers, for example, is a notion which they criticize in Karmitz as "an ultra-democratic delirium." The *Cahiers* critics contrast the two possible uses of videotape in the shooting of such a film. On the one hand, it can be used to criticize the process of making the film *politically* (which would be the correct use), to enable it to take a clear political line. On the other hand, it can be used at the service of perfecting the film's realism, a use which they argue can only end up in service of a bourgeois ideology, allowing for the film to be judged not on the basis of its political thought but on whether it seems true to life.[56]

In keeping with the interest in the new *Cahiers* in the way in which critics receive films as an index of their meaning, the article cites a review in *Cinéma 72* by Gaston Haustrate. Haustrate is very favorable to the film, but the *Cahiers* writers attempt to show how he has been taken in by its underlying ideology. The *Cinéma 72* critic talks about "very strong moments of absolute truth which shoot through the screen," the parts of the film which seem "captured" and those which seem directed and manipulated and particularly a scene in which a young worker asks an old one about the days of 1936. Haustrate notes that it is less the content of the questions and answers than the sense of the natural and the truth of the moment that is important about the scene. The *Cahiers* article uses these observations to point to the way in which Karmitz builds an ambiguous, idealist, and ultimately non-political discourse out of his material.[57]

While the writers repeat their assertion that the content of COUP POUR COUP is just, that it shows the bourgeoisie things that that class does not want to look at, they argue that it does not go beyond that. What the bourgeoisie does not want in its art, they claim, is politics. So the argument continues:

> The bourgeoisie does not like it when one calls to mind that reality (social practice) is political, where by contrast it adores a fiction which obeys, to critique it, the norms of the ideology of the real which it has instituted in the arts: before being political, the "reality" is the expression, the reflection or the object of an individual sensibility, reality is life, reality is alive, it is *thus* lived, conforming to individualist, anti-dialectical philosophy which can imagine "life" only as function of a subject "gifted with interiority," conforming to an idealism which makes reality depend on "consciousness," conforming to a bourgeois humanism which makes "Man" the center of everything.[58]

For these notions, the article substitutes those of the *Groupe Dziga-Vertov*, emphasizing the need to make political films politically, to let the political considerations of the film dictate how it will be made. Thus, the kinds of purely technical decisions which Karmitz makes become politically questionable: the use of ellipses and a style of editing founded on direct cutting to continue a line of action is seen as a repression of political reflection, for it allows no time for thought by the viewer. The work uses a filmic style that is derived from the American cinema (e.g., Kazan, Vidor, Biberman), the classic, "transparent" cinema. By presenting the film as a closed discourse and not discussing how the making of the film itself enters into the political process, Karmitz avoids any genuine political comment on the film's own place in the struggle. The *Cahiers* article asks in its last paragraph the question that it has been asking throughout the 1970's: "can one make a revolutionary film without criticizing bourgeois representation?"[59]

The third section of the *Cahiers* article, "Critical realism, critique of realism," finally begins to compare COUP POUR COUP to the admired film, TOUT VA BIEN. Again, the intense criticism directed toward COUP POUR COUP is tempered by a realization of some of its advances: both films are cited as dealing with genuine problems of social structure and not only superficially political issues, i.e., they deal with the relationship of the means of economic production to a capitalist society in general. Both works seek to make certain theoretical points from Marxist-Leninist thought. The critics prefer, however, the Godard film's willingness to acknowledge the personal intervention of the filmmaker; the film speaks mainly for the filmmakers. Paradoxically, this admission allows the film to speak for the masses more effectively, for unlike COUP POUR COUP, it does not falsely pretend to be speaking for them.[60]

The *Cahiers* critics discuss the reports, for example, that in COUP POUR COUP the workers themselves found that they could play the workers most realistically (and that the few professionals engaged for the film were effective only as bosses and in other such roles—presumably because they themselves were of the same bourgeois class). The *Groupe Lou Sin* finds this assumption to be reproducing the very social structure that the film is attacking. By locking itself into a structure in which the representation must look authentic and real, it is locking itself into the very structure of oppression that is at the heart of the problem.[61]

In contrast to this, the authors present the use of actors in TOUT VA BIEN as exemplary. The need to make the film with a big budget required the hiring of Yves Montand and Jane Fonda. Faced with the problem of presenting workers on the screen, Godard and Gorin rejected the notion of having stars play them and, deciding that real workers (overly influenced by the cinema) would play themselves in the manner of Jean Gabin, chose to have real, exploited actors play the oppressed, exploited workers. Montand was not used to play a worker precisely *because* he could do it too well; he would reproduce the popular conceptions of a worker, conceptions which themselves are the result of capitalist ideology.[62]

It was Godard and Gorin's intention to underline all of the contradictions about the use of actors in a film ("Contradictions between the economy of the film and the politics of its author, contradictions between secondary players and stars, contradictions between the real social status of the actors and the social role—the persona—assigned to them by the fiction").[63] Where COUP POUR COUP wishes to efface the role of the bourgeois intellectual in the class struggle (by its avoidance of actors, its emphasis on the superficial qualities of workers), TOUT VA BIEN, being made by bourgeois intellectuals, seeks to discover and discuss the place of this class of people in the revolution. This, in turn, allows TOUT VA BIEN to analyze issues completely bypassed in COUP POUR COUP, like the real nature of revisionism or the influence of the bourgeoisie on the working classes.[64]

The *Cahiers* article again repeats its familiar message: that the Karmitz film makes use of the same cultural standards, the same ideological tools of the bourgeoisie, rather than attacking bourgeois ideology and culture within the film through the use of a materialist, Brechtian conception of cinema. The critics emphasize that it is not a question of form to the extent that notions of structuring a plot and characters are really conceptions of content. They assert further that themes and messages alone do not make for the film's political content, pointing to a scene in TOUT VA BIEN in which Jane Fonda voices what they consider to be some erroneous political opinions. They admit that the position should be criticized and should have been criticized by the film; but the technique of TOUT VA BIEN presents this point of view in such a way that it can be criticized by the audience. Despite the presence of an incorrect analysis, the work is still correct in its process, which is the main, important point.[65]

TOUT VA BIEN thus becomes praiseworthy because the strike it presents is explicitly exemplary, that is, a "crystallization, a condensed reflection of forces and contradictory positions which confront each other on the scene of the class struggle today in France." In addition, the place of the viewer is always considered; the audience is constantly being questioned by pseudo-inter-viewers, who serve as a direct challenge to the audience, presenting for its consideration a variety of opposing and contradictory political discourses.[66]

The opposite, again, is found to be the case in COUP POUR COUP. The strike in question is not presented as explicitly exemplary, and the film's discourse therefore runs contrary to the work's avowed Maoism. It is not presented as a strike having a certain historical significance but as a single event, and, what is worse, a subjective event, with an accent on "affectivity and the outcome" rather than on "the process and the logic" of the events presented. COUP POUR COUP becomes, therefore, a film "without directly political effects."[67]

Thus, the *Cahiers* article contains criticisms of the Karmitz work's treatment of unionism and revisionism for the lack of specific references (which name names and unions) to real political organizations; the assumption that the names do not need to be given implies further that the film is made for a predetermined audience of people already converted or sympathetic. The film treats revisionism in terms of certain people outside the working class, rather than as a stance or an ideology which is a part of it, and implies that the spontaneous rebellion of the workers can overcome the revisionism without the development of an alternative theoretical line. The lack of exemplarity is achieved by the film's techniques:

Effects of the real, yes, but with the real itself completely indeterminate; it is that the Boursac factory is not like the Salumi factory of TOUT VA BIEN, an explicit metaphor of the state of struggles (against the management, against revisionism) today in France but a shameful metonymy, all poisoned with the lived, naturalism, sensualism, all in the shade of the myth of expression: "The purpose of BLOW FOR BLOW is not to engage in a type of abstract debate on the theme 'for or against unionism.'"[68]

The Karmitz movie thus may be seen as coming directly out of the Bazinian ideal (an idealist ideal) of respecting reality, of not intervening in it, of presenting it unaltered.

Many of the criticisms in the latter paragraphs of the *Cahiers* article center around the question of whether the strike being shown in COUP POUR COUP is intended to be modelled around a single real event or to present a typical strike. Although there are similarities between events portrayed in the strike and a particular real instance, because these are left indefinite, the film's political message is left indefinite. Similarly, in scenes where some local peasants perform actions to indicate solidarity with the strikers, the audience is never sure whether they are intended to be individual actions or they represent the actions of the class as a whole. "This nebulousness, let us repeat, is not accidental, it is not a break in the working method of the actors, it is a system, a writing style, it is the condition of the film's success." The dramatic effectiveness of COUP POUR COUP depends on this style: to present contradictions (and thus have a real discourse) would be against the dramatic principles of the work.[69]

The text by the *Groupe Lou Sin* on TOUT VA BIEN and COUP POUR COUP breaks little new theoretical ground, but it does represent a kind of culmination of certain preoccupations which had begun to appear in *Cahiers* following 1968. (If one compares it, for example, with the Pascal Bonitzer piece that treats Karmitz's earlier film, CAMARADES, one sees many of the same ideas but treated in greater depth and with a broader scope.)[70] Taking the pieces of *Cahiers* criticism out of chronology, as this study has frequently done, may seem a bit repetitious; in the context of the work that has gone before it and after, however, this particular text is probably the most thorough application of what were then still fairly new theoretical issues at *Cahiers*. There are no examples of criticism comparable to it subsequently, probably because many of the notions articulated in this piece could, in following years, be taken a little more for granted without much need to be restated.

In the months that follow, TOUT VA BIEN remains something of a landmark film. *Cahiers* runs, for example, a detailed analysis of its reception by the critics.[71] It is referred to admiringly in subsequent reviews. The question of its financial lack of success, its inability to reach a major audience, is brought up again in Serge Daney's discussion of another film of Marxist, Brechtian intent, René Allio's RUDE JOURNEE POUR LA REINE (1973). Daney attempts to offer a constructive criticism of the situation. The difficulty with both TOUT VA BIEN and RUDE JOURNEE is that they look at "ideology" (in the Althusserian sense) as something to be escaped in favor of science. To the extent that ideology provides many of the major pleasures of moviegoing, this presents a problem. In other words, the struggle is presented in negative terms: it is always the bourgeois ideology from which one escapes, never the new ideology that must be constructed. In Daney's terms, the new question is "How to combat effectively the dominant ideology if one does not oppose an *other* ideology to it?"[72]

Daney talks of the conventional position of the leftist intellectual toward commercial films, namely, one of taking pleasure in seeing through the ideological devices of these politically repressive forms, a "pleasure at not being fooled." He outlines the goal that the intellectual generally has for the public: "It is necessary, thus, to bring oneself to their aid, demystify the noxious product, introduce the real, the concrete into the scene encumbered by bourgeois mythology, advise the masses against forgetting themselves at the movies, and to demand them on the contrary to find themselves, and their problems there."[73]

Daney sees this as a misdirected approach, since the terms of the masses render the question irrelevant and of little meaning to them. For the act merely of putting a film, image, or advertisement at a distance from oneself is not the way these things are used by the masses. Daney has no clear answer to the problem but suggests rather that the answer is to be found in Lacanian psychology (film as a fulfillment of desires) and in the creation of alternative ideological forms. He ends by suggesting that a politically correct cinema must arise from a politically correct social order.[74]

In summary, then, we see that *Cahiers'* approach to specific films remains largely theoretical, that these films are used to demonstrate the political generalizations raised by their even more abstract writings. The struggle to be found in *Cahiers* against bourgeois ideology in cinema lies in an attempt to recognize where the content of would-be "progressive" films is influenced for the worse by their forms and where the substitution of new forms has resulted in political discourse of an advanced nature. The approach to film represented here builds directly on Brecht. At the same time, however, much of it begins at pre-Brechtian levels of theorization (e.g., the concept of history as a science, the rejection of empiricism in favor of dialectical materialism, the social determination of all forms of ideological expression). Thus, although Brecht is an influence, one gets the impression that some of the same points of discovery might have been made even had he not existed.

While the practical writings in *Cahiers* rarely go beyond the theoretical issues already brought up and developed in the magazine of this period, they provide a needed complement to the theoretical writings. They also demonstrate, if indirectly, how much of this same theory has been employed by filmmakers (e.g., Godard-Gorin in TOUT VA BIEN, Straub in OTHON, Allio in LES CAMISARDS), suggesting a symbiosis between French film theory and production in this period. What the above articles demonstrate is that, if the points of major theoretical concern shift in *Cahiers* between 1968 and 1975, then so do the standards of practical application, both in terms of the kinds of films discussed (almost always with some pretense to political relevance) and the way they are treated (always in terms of their "true" political discourse). After being perhaps the most influential French film magazine of the late 1950's and 1960's, *Cahiers* becomes one of the most theoretically rigorous in the early 1970's; that this rigor should extend to the practical analysis of films was in every way logical.

The Late 1970's and After

One of the problems that *Cahiers du Cinéma* faced as it took on its intensely political stances was the alienation of that presumably large part of its readership that consisted more of moviegoers and film lovers than ideologues and political activists. The early 1970's saw a certain decline in the magazine's circulation, accompanied by a certain irregularity in its appearance. Its format became sober and not conventionally marketable: November 1972, for example, marks the first issue of *Cahiers du Cinéma* to have no photographs. By the mid-1970's the magazine was experiencing significant financial difficulties.[1]

By 1976, however, the magazine had returned to greater regularity in publication, and at the end of 1977 it made a conscious effort to improve the situation by launching a campaign for subscribers and seeking increased working capital. There were also changes in the format and the editorial content of the magazine which suggest a reaching out to a wider readership.[2]

With the February 1978 issue, the magazine moved to a format that featured a return to photographs on the cover and a marked increase in the number of illustrations and stills in each issue. While *Cahiers* maintained its interest in relatively abstract, theoretical writing on film, there were also some new features. A series of interviews with cameramen and other technicians suggested an appeal to those readers interested in the problems and techniques of filmmaking itself. In 1980, partially in response to the popularity of science fiction and fantasy films, *Cahiers* began an elaborate series of articles about special effects in film. Similarly, the magazine greatly expanded its *"Petit Journal de Cinéma,"* a section at the end of each issue devoted to news, short interviews, and production reports—all of interest to regular moviegoers and cinephiles.

There is even evidence of a repudiation of the magazine's more extreme positions from the early 1970's. In early 1981, for example, Sylvie Pierre describes the "dark years" of 1972 to 1975 as "a huge, morose regression in cinephilic understanding."[3] Even Pascal Bonitzer has recently written that the magazine's position in the early 1970's of "putting politics in the commanding post" resulted in a period in which the magazine did not really talk about cinema very much.[4]

All of this points to an apparent attempt by the magazine to come to grips with the inherent contradiction it had produced. On the one hand, those who write for the journal must inevitably do so out of a fundamental love of movies. And movies, especially Hollywood movies, are by and large the product of both capitalist technology and a capitalist production system—both at least in some ways at odds with Marxist political ideals. The renewed *Cahiers du Cinéma* of the late 1970's and the 1980's has been much more unabashedly cinephilic than that of the early 1970's, devoting much more of its space in particular to the discussion of Hollywood movies and filmmakers. We see a return to some of the practices—the writing of "best film" lists, the inclusion of production reports on forthcoming movies—from an earlier era. But the magazine has also tried to understand the political and social nature of its own cinephilia.

Let us divide our discussion of *Cahiers'* most recent developments into four parts. We will deal first with general, theoretical treatments of the problem of cinephilia. Second, we can consider a renewed interest in the actor. Third, we will find in the *Cahiers* of the late 1970's an attempt to get back to its roots. Finally, we will end the chapter with a look at Jean-Claude Biette's comments on TROP TOT, TROP TARD, a 1982 film by Jean-Marie Straub and Danièle Huillet; Biette's remarks almost perfectly encapsulate the attitudes of the magazine as it enters its third decade of publication.

Texts about Cinephilia

Perhaps the most thorough outlining of the issues involved in exploring the nature of cinephilia is in an article by Louis Skorecki, "Contre la nouvelle cinéphilie," which ran in the October 1978 *Cahiers du Cinèma* along with a response by Pascal Kané. Skorecki delves into what one might call the history of cinephilia, in terms of its origins in post-war France (with the film addicts of the Cinémathèque in the 1950's), its development into extreme forms (such as the MacMahoniens of the 1960's), its popularization around May 1968, and its subsequent incorporation into the mainstream of French thinking about film. Skorecki describes the cinephile's pleasure at seeking out and reconsidering obscure movies, a kind of anti-social (and, on a Freudian level, perhaps predominantly homosexual) withdrawal from the cinematic mainstream. He notes the cinephile's obsession with categorizing works, drawing up eccentric lists of preferences, fetishizing "privileged moments" from specific movies. Skorecki pronounces the old cinephilia dead in the contemporary world, precisely because increased public awareness of film has taken away the marginal rebelliousness of the activity. With regular moviegoing and factory-like studio production a thing of the past, we "no longer have cinema, only films."[5]

Skorecki discusses how the notion of the *auteur* has been incorporated into the commercial workings of the film industry, as part of the marketing of films. This all but renders the term meaningless, he argues, for once every director becomes an *auteur,* there is no need to use the label. Likewise filmmakers, having come to think of themselves as *auteurs,* work all the more self-consciously. Skorecki concludes that television today is the domain of the equivalent of yesterday's cinephile—it is culturally disreputable and provides for endless hours of what most would consider a kind of cultural dissipation. Skorecki is asking of *Cahiers*-style cinephilia: where have we come from? where are we going?[6]

Kané's response to Skorecki puts his essay into the context of *Cahiers'* political work from the 1970's. Kané argues that the point of extreme cinephilia is, ultimately, to view works without proper critical perspective. He cites a kind of systematic "anti-Brechtianism" in the MacMahoniens' thought and argues that those filmmakers most commonly cited by the hard core cinephile, such as Jacques Tourneur, are those who most conform to the standard production system and whose works most emphasize the inherent fascinations of that production system. Kané traces the sources of cinephilia back to economics.[7]

Skorecki's ideas are picked up later by Bernard Boland in his discussion of PASSE-MONTAGNE, a French film from 1978 by Jean-François Stévenin, a director whose previous experience had been primarily as an actor. In his review of the Stévenin film, Boland includes an extended discussion of cinephilia in post-Lacanian, psychoanalytic terms. He sees it as arising from a fascination with the filmic image as a visible phallus, a representation of power, a castrating mother who subdues the passive spectator-child. The filmmaker or *auteur* assumes a place of power by working in a medium which by its mechanical nature encourages such passivity and fascination. A Brechtian cinema, to extend Boland's idea, would be one that fights against this mechanism of symbolic castration.[8]

What the French New Wave did for cinema, Boland argues, was to provide for a fantasy of assuming the position of power: the cinephile/film addict, such as Godard or Truffaut, became the director himself. By breaking standard rules of "good" technique, the New Wave filmmakers at once sought to kill the two castrating mothers involved—the classic American cinema and the French "tradition of quality"—only to submit to their own kind of participation in the mechanism. In Boland's words, "the cinema of the New Wave represented a sort of absolute cinephilia: as if the spectator were making the film he saw." By extension, Jean-François, Stévenin, by acting in as well as directing PASSE-MONTAGNE, redoubles this device. He becomes the cinephile director making the film, who, as an actor, is also participating in the fiction, which in turn is about a man who shows another man (in a sense, directs him) the life of a small village in the Jura mountains.[9]

As is often the case in many of these articles, one of Boland's most telling comments is in a footnote. He relates a remark made by Serge Daney arguing that, in contrast to the MacMahoniens, the less extreme auteurist *Cahiers* critics would be somewhat leftist. Where the MacMahoniens would submit completely to the passive pleasure of the film-machine, "condemned to speechlessness and to contemplation," the auteurists, in wanting to make films themselves, introduced elements of discussion, questioning, dialogue, of distance from the films they admire. Out of this latter kind of cinephilia could grow *Cahiers'* more politicized approaches.[10]

Perhaps the most polemical of the new studies of cinephilia—one that suggests a new reconsideration of film theory and a rejection of *Cahiers'* early 1970's viewpoints—is an essay by Jean-Pierre Oudart discussing Stanley Kubrick's A CLOCKWORK ORANGE (1971) and Robert Kramer's MI-LESTONES. Oudart argues that the brilliance of Kubrick and Kramer is in their playing of a dual game—Kubrick by using the fascination of the Hollywood cinema even while criticizing the relations of power which that Hollywood cinema indicates, Kramer by alternating effects of documentary with a highly novelistic narrative structure.[11]

Oudart opposes Kubrick and Kramer to Godard and Straub, mentioning the "unthinking dogmatism" of the latter pair. He decries the leftist position of wanting to deconstruct all effects of reality as a way of taking away the dream-like nature of film. While Oudart admires the careful *écriture* and analytical nature of the Kubrick and Kramer films, he praises their "realism of the imaginary." He rejects "the good old apostles of film-work, who support a dogma of the laborious conception of a cinema attended by suffering spectators, a cinema which makes you work." Instead, Oudart calls for a cinema that permits one "to dream, to fantasize, to listen in on the reverberations of its fiction, to be moved without self-consciousness, without surveillance."[12] He argues, in effect, that the approach of the didactic leftist critics is deadly to cinephilia.

Oudart's polemic represents a definite change of position for a *Cahiers du Cinéma* article. One can surely relate it to Oudart's discussion of Syberberg's HITLER, for there, too, Syberberg argues that political analysis can exist side by side with filmic fascination. While there is no evidence that the magazine as a whole shares at this point in Oudart's contempt for "leftist critic-semiologues," there is clear evidence here of a shift in *Cahiers* toward a more pluralist, less radical editorial policy. It suggests an attempt to synthesize the magazine's former cinephilia with its later leftism.

A New Interest in the Actor

Boland's article on PASSE-MONTAGNE, which we mentioned earlier, also relates to a second preoccupation of the *Cahiers* critics in the late 1970's and early 1980's: a new interest in the place of the actor in the film. Two American filmmakers much admired by the *Cahiers* critics at this time are John Cassavetes and Paul Newman, both directors whose first reputations were made in front of the camera and whose reputations as directors relate very much to the highly charged performances they get from their actors.[13] Boland reflects this interest in actor-directors when he compares PASSE-MON-TAGNE to the films of Paul Newman and Charles Laughton, actors whose directorial efforts make for, in Boland's terms, "the most troubling and unclassifiable films." By emphasizing the work of the actor, these films call attention to that middle ground between the creation of the power-holding director and the unguarded belief of the spectator.[14] This ambiguousness of the actor's place seems to fascinate the *Cahiers* critics.

We see similar ideas expressed in François Regnault's discussion of Robert De Niro's performance in Martin Scorsese's NEW YORK, NEW YORK (1977). Regnault argues that the greater part of critical thought about cinema has involved the elimination of the actor as a real body (such as the actor would be on the stage) either through the breaking up of the image through editing or through working with on-screen and off-screen space. Regnault asserts that the great screen actor is aware of the intervening technologies involved in filmmaking and "plays with the whole of the set, with the camera that looks at him, with the technical end of things, all as though with a musical instrument."[15]

Regnault defends De Niro's performance precisely because it says "See how I like to act." Comparing De Niro to Chaplin, he concludes that what rescues the performance from being mere clowning is:

> the recognition in him [De Niro] by us of this inner jubilation which is sent out from the invisible nature of the actor and to which he adds the humility of visible know-how. It is the jubilation that makes of every great actor a comic actor. What great actor is not comic?[16]

Recalling the great admiration Brecht had for Chaplin, one can see the clear relation to a Brechtian attitude: the ideal actor is not the one who creates a convincing illusion of reality but the one who produces the most pleasure in the comparison of the illusion to reality, in acknowledging how he has helped create the illusion.

Likewise, Serge Le Péron discusses the performances in Alain Tanner's JONAH WHO WILL BE 25 IN THE YEAR 2000 (1977) as one of the ways in which Tanner avoids the pitfalls of naturalism, by playing with a deliberate and recognizable coding of the actors' performances. Each actor or actress has a number to perform, which relates both to a type of character and to that performer's screen image.[17] With both Regnault and Le Peron one can see an attitude toward acting similar to the theories expressed by Jean-Louis Comolli in "Le détour par le direct." Just as, according to Comolli, good *cinéma direct* does not so much record reality as allow for a new reality to be created for the camera, certain films offer a new kind of performer-filmmaker relationship in which the actor is indeed a kind of co-creator of the staged reality that emerges when the film is projected. By the same token, in *Cahiers du Cinéma*'s prizing of the work of John Cassavetes and Robert Kramer, both of whom combine *cinéma direct* techniques with great attention to their performers, we see a link to the attitude found in some of Louis Marcorelles' writings that suggests ways in which a Brechtian treatment of the actor has emerged out of the *cinéma direct* movement. (There is an irony here, of course, in that Cassavetes' background as an actor is that of the New York Actors' Studio, the very school of performance Marcorelles pointedly rejects in the 1950's in favor of a Brechtian acting style. See Chapter 5.) The film shows us reality, but in the process of acting out and recording that reality, it makes that reality strange, comments on it, turns it into a discourse.

A similar consideration of the actor recurs in a theoretical essay by Jean-Louis Comolli called "Un corps en trop." Comolli argues that any fiction film involves "attribution of real bodies to imaginary characters" and that there is always a tension between the reality of the body filmed and the imaginary body of the character portrayed. The latter body must often be a type, depending on the requirements of the narrative. In the historical film, there is a third element providing tension if the actor is playing a person who really existed; then there is an "interference, even a rivalry between the body of the actor and the other, the 'true' body, of which the (historical) disappearance has left traces by images that are other than cinematographic."[18]

Comolli compares two characters in Jean Renoir's 1938 film about the French Revolution, LA MARSEILLAISE: Jean-Joseph Bomier, an historical figure created for the film and played by the actor Edmond Ardisson, and Louis XVI, played by Pierre Renoir. It is clearly harder for the audience to accept Pierre Renoir as Louis XVI because we are aware of the differences between Pierre Renoir's body and Louis XVI's. What Comolli emphasizes, however, is the way in which both Jean and Pierre Renoir do not attempt completely to disguise the problem or hide this case of having the "wrong" body. Rather, they emphasize certain differences, use them to produce something comparable to an estrangement or alienation effect.[19]

All of these texts point to a view of film acting that sees the proper screen performance as being not the one that is seamlessly mimetic, one that cannot be distinguished from reality, but rather the one which shows the illusion being made. The actor is, perhaps, an element of film production that can potentially subvert illusionism, even while providing for the audience's pleasure at seeing illusions being made.

In a short editorial, published in 1981 as part of the magazine's special two-issue survey of the French cinema, the *Cahiers* critics acknowledge, in effect, a certain neglect in the magazine of the actor, particularly during its most politicized period. On the one hand, they argue, the New Wave created a new generation of actors; on the other hand, so many figures in the French cinema associated with *Cahiers du Cinéma*—such as Bresson, Tati, or Rouch—have deemphasized the role of the actor. They cite Godard's TOUT VA BIEN, in which Godard acknowledges in the film having hired Jane Fonda and Yves Montand purely out of economic necessity, as a kind of low point in respect for the actor's contribution to movies.[20] The magazine has entered the 1980's, however, with a renewed interest in these problems of screen performance.

A Return to Origins

One outcome of the new preoccupation with cinephilia at *Cahiers du Cinéma* in the late 1970's has been a kind of return to roots on the part of the magazine. Where writing from the late 1960's and early 1970's suggests that the critics were trying to break with the tradition begun by André Bazin, Eric Rohmer, and François Truffaut, we can perceive in more recent issues of the magazine an increased sense of continuity between the present and past of the journal. In the 1980's we can even see the journal try to revive, in somewhat modified form, certain traditions abandoned after the events of May 1968. *Cahiers du Cinéma*'s special number on the French cinema published in May of 1981 (No. 323-24) prides itself on being the first such issue since 1965. Similarly, in its special issue on the American cinema published in April of 1982, Serge Toubiana, in an introductory editorial, sees the special number as a continuation of a tradition begun with No. 54 of *Cahiers du Cinéma* in 1954 and No. 150-51 from 1963.[21]

The May 1981 *Cahiers du Cinéma* contains numerous reflections on the magazine's history and the simultaneous history of the French cinema, including a short piece by Jacques Doniol-Valcroze on how the journal got its name.[22] The articles particularly emphasize the importance of the French New Wave: there are interviews with Eric Rohmer and Jacques Rivette and even a special one-page appreciation of Claude Chabrol.[23] In more than one article, the authors point out that in 1981 the French cinema is faced with a situation very much comparable to that of the 1950's, whereby a certain "tradition of quality," of rather dull, academic, well-made commercial films has come to dominate the scene. In this context, the more independent work of former New

Wave *cinéastes* like François Truffaut, Eric Rohmer, or Jacques Rivette is valued favorably. In one article, Serge Daney argues that those filmmakers who most successfully worked during the 1970's are those who managed to work independently, like Truffaut or Rohmer, either with their own production companies or with independent-minded producers. Daney sees success in the French cinema as involving escape from the commercial mainstream.[24]

A significant article in this issue is Pascal Bonitzer's "Juste un image." In it, Bonitzer argues that what has unified *Cahiers du Cinéma* throughout its history, in both its early period and during its politicized years, has been its belief in film as an art of images, i.e., the creation of a visually based cinema. Bonitzer here reaffirms the magazine's formalist base and its stance against a cinema that would be academic, based on the visualization of preconceived, written screenplays consisting mainly of dialogue. He writes:

> Everything begins in fact here: ideas must be ideas for *mise en scène* (Truffaut) or ideas about editing (Godard), not ideas about dialogue. The authors of films are not those who write them, but those who direct them. The heart of a film is not in its subject, but in its *mise en scène*.[25]

By this token, Bonitzer finds in Straub and Godard the Hitchcock and Hawks of the 1970's.[26] In an indirect way, Bonitzer articulates the primary thesis of this study, namely, that the formalist preoccupations of the early *Cahiers du Cinéma* created an atmosphere suited to the elaboration of a Brechtian ideal of film.

By the end of the 1970's the critics for *Cahiers du Cinéma* became particularly admiring of the later films of Truffaut and Rohmer, despite these directors' more or less apolitical subject matter. In listing their "best films" for 1981, twelve out of fourteen *Cahiers* critics listed Rohmer's THE AVIATOR'S WIFE. Seven out of fourteen included Truffaut's THE WOMAN NEXT DOOR.[27]

One of the most striking signs of change in this regard was the appearance of François Truffaut in a still from THE GREEN ROOM, a film in which Truffaut also acted, on the cover of the April 1978 issue, No. 287. In the following issue, Pascal Bonitzer calls THE GREEN ROOM "the most beautiful and most profound of Truffaut's films" and "one of the most beautiful French films in recent years." Bonitzer goes on to cite what he calls one of André Bazin's most metaphysical and religious articles, dealing with film as a kind of preservation from death. He praises Truffaut for having exactly the same discourse as Bazin. In Truffaut's adaptation of a story by Henry James of a man who builds a shrine to his dead wife, Bonitzer sees an embodiment of Bazin's ideas about the "eternal re-deaths of cinema."[28]

As the 1970's closed, there were articles praising Truffaut films like THE MAN WHO LOVED WOMEN (1977) and LOVE ON THE RUN (1978), and in September 1980, accompanying the release of THE LAST METRO, *Cahiers du Cinéma* published its first interview with Truffaut in over 13 years.[29] Justifying this, Serge Toubiana writes, contrasting the kind of "golden mean" found in Truffaut to the "outer limits experimentation" that preoccupied *Cahiers du Cinéma* in the 1970's:

> Some will surely not fail to interpret this "return" to Truffaut as a cop-out by *Cahiers*, a sort of final compromise with a *cinéaste* who has "sold out to the system." Too bad for those who will not see that through the line of our questions emerges the idea that for us the seeking of this "golden mean" is perhaps also an "outer limits experiment."[30]

Toubiana goes on to talk of the need to hear what Truffaut has to say about the cinema because of his knowledge and love of it and his professionalism as a craftsman. Ultimately, Toubiana argues that Truffaut's thoughtfulness about film is the most important reason to consider him.[31]

Critics for *Cahiers du Cinéma* have also written a number of articles in praise of the more recent films by Eric Rohmer. Pascal Bonitzer lauds THE MARQUISE VON O (1976) as a superb examination of bourgeois sexuality.[32] François Géré praises PERCEVAL (1979) for the effect of estrangement produced by its mixtures of stylization and specificity.[33] Most remarkable and enlightening, however, is Pascal Bonitzer's evaluation of Rohmer's THE AVIATOR'S WIFE, which Bonitzer calls "one of Rohmer's best films and a majestic lesson in cinema." Bonitzer argues that on an economic plane, THE AVIATOR'S WIFE, which was shot in 16mm, is a throwback to the best qualities of the French New Wave in that Rohmer attempts in the film to make an important, complex, subtle movie with little money, unknown actors, and a spontaneous camera style. In addition, however, Bonitzer praises the film's organization of space, arguing that Rohmer takes conventions and situations from classical dramaturgy and uses them cinematically, providing for "a majestic lesson . . . by the cinema on the theater."[34] The care and precision of Rohmer's *mise en scène* impresses Bonitzer, in much the same way the THE GREEN ROOM's does. Bonitzer praises both Truffaut and Rohmer for their intelligence and analytical skills.

In this sense we see a return by *Cahiers du Cinéma* to its previous formalism. In other articles from the late 1970's and later, critics for the magazine reaffirm a love or respect for directors formerly in the magazine's pantheon during the 1950's and 1960's, such as Carl Dreyer, Kenji Mizoguchi, Samuel Fuller, Jacques Tati, or Roberto Rossellini.[35] T.L. French has noted that the magazine, having rejected the cinema of Jean Rouch in 1971, reacknowledges his genius in 1977.[36]

One may view these developments in two ways. On the one hand, given the fashionableness of the anti-communist "new philosophers" in the France of the late 1970's, it is not hard to imagine a possibly eventual total turnabout of the magazine's formerly Marxist positions. Is not Bonitzer, for example, guilty of exactly what the magazine accused its early founders of: praising certain movies as movies, ignoring their political or ideological content? The most intelligent defense one might make of Bonitzer is that he does discuss their ideological content but in ways that become much more complex, ambiguous, and even contradictory. In certain ways, he has not abandoned certain fundamental assumptions from which we have been working—that the form of a film directly relates to its content and that questions of form and content cannot be separated from the economic system under which a film is made. Understanding how a film like THE GREEN ROOM describes metaphorically the death-mask nature of cinema or how THE AVIATOR'S WIFE treats the nature of classical theater relates ultimately to the political ideology of how our society treats both death and the theater.

If Brechtian criticism in the early *Cahiers* praised certain works for using techniques of estrangement without considering it necessary to talk about the direct political consequences of the work, Bonitzer appears to be assuming a certain level of political awareness in the reader. If the goal of the Brechtian theater is to provide a theater in which spectators can make up their own minds, the goal of the effective post-Brechtian film would be to contain an intelligent discourse and to invite the audience to see how the discourse emerges from the images and sounds in the film. In this respect, one suspects Bonitzer would argue for both THE GREEN ROOM and THE AVIATOR'S WIFE as films which encourage an active, post-Brechtian spectatorship. There is in them, perhaps, the beginnings of a synthesis between the old cinephilic and the new politicized journal.

TROP TOT, TROP TARD

In examining how *Cahiers du Cinéma*'s critical policies have developed in the late 1970's and early 1980's, we have discussed its critics' attempts to reconcile their love of art with their love of politics and the inherent contradiction between cinephilia and political activism. We have seen the magazine's interest in the actor and in those directors who emphasize the actor's presence as a kind of intermediary between the powerful director and passive audience. And we have seen *Cahiers'* critics become, in some ways, preoccupied with their roots and sources.

Within this framework, one of the most striking articles from the early 1980's is Jean-Claude Biette's review of a film by Jean-Marie Straub and Danièle Huillet, TROP TOT, TROP TARD (1982). We have discussed Straub and Huillet's OTHON as the kind of radical cinema that the politicized *Cahiers* defended, and TROP TOT, TROP TARD appears to continue exploring cinematic forms radically opposed to classical narrative. The film consists largely of panning shots of the French countryside contrasted to panning shots of the Egyptian countryside. Over the French footage, the audience hears a voice read a letter by Frederich Engels; over the Egyptian footage is read the postface to Mahmoud Hussein's *The Class Struggle in Egypt*.

Biette's review is particularly provocative because it centers on the three areas we have discussed. It talks about the tension in Straub's work between aesthetics and politics, about the unique place of the actor in the film, and about the roots of the work in the classical cinema formerly idealized by *Cahiers*. Typical of the new *Cahiers* is that Biette's comments on the Straub work are in an issue of the magazine that contains a short tribute by the writer to the films of Allan Dwan, a Hollywood veteran much beloved by the MacMahoniens of *Présence du Cinéma*.[37] There is all but a dialectic internal to the number of the magazine.

In his review, Biette discusses the tendency in all of Straub's work for the director to contrast his political hatreds (for "bankers, lawyers, military men, men of power, agents of repression, and opportunist democrats") with his love for artists (composers such as Bach and Schoenberg, writers such as Brecht, Pavese, and Fortini) on whose writings, musical or literary, Straub based his previous works. There would be a tension throughout Straub's work between their political militancy and their highly formalist, artistic rigor.[38] There is a dialectic, as it were, between their political content and their love of art.

At the center of Straub's filmmaking, Biette sees the director's use of "characters who are, first of all, in the present as experienced by the audience, filmed actors." Biette sees all of Straub's films as recorded traces of mankind's past—in writings, music, attitudes, political actions—enacted by performers whom we can appreciate on an aesthetic level.[39] In this sense, Straub concerns himself with the problem of filming history.

Biette links this approach to the precedent of Jean Renoir, surely the one French movie maker most important to the filmmakers of the New Wave. Biette argues that in his early films, such as CHARLESTON (1927), LA FILLE DE L'EAU (1924), and LA PETITE MARCHANDE D'ALLU-METTES (1928), Renoir develops "that which is most profoundly linked to the present: the living truth of the actor. And the art of the present consists of, in this operation of recording by image (and later by image and sound), those things in the actor which oppose, fight against, resist [the novelistic or the fictional illusion.]" We come to sympathize with the actor and find him aesthetically pleasing even when we participate in Straub's political hatred for what that character may say and do. The actor playing a negative character has an "element of fragility, this dose of mortality that he shares with the 'positive' characters, in the form of bare arms, visible napes of the neck, voices tired from fatigue, faces empty after story-telling, defeated by real life (which is what professional actors can rarely give, under the aesthetic of cinema-art-of-the-present)."[40]

The result is, for Biette, a resolution of Straub's love-hate, past-present tensions. Biette implies that the camera records the "truth" of the Straubian actor's performance in a way perhaps comparable to the truth of the landscapes that also appear in the film. This point of view almost evokes the earlier phenomenology of Bazin or particularly the points of view, mentioned earlier, of Jean Domarchi and Pierre-Richard Bré, who see film art as based on man's physical relationships.[41]

Biette's article synthesizes many of the preoccupations of what one might call the old and the new *Cahiers du Cinéma*—its formalist, phenomenological, and cinephilic tendencies with its leftist political ones. Biette sees TROP TOT, TROP TARD in terms of its cinephilic precedents in Renoir, Griffith, and Chaplin, while discussing the actor in terms of the actor's relation to a seemingly recorded reality.

In conclusion, then, the *Cahiers* of the late 1970's and early 1980's only confirms the sense of continuity between these tendencies in the magazine. More than ever before, the *Cahiers* critics have seemed aware of the discomfort that motivates so much of their writing, which is the same one evident in the Straub-Huillet film: the need to live both politically and cinephilically. If a critic rejects the latter tendency, there is no longer a need for a specially film-oriented journal. One is concerned only with politics. If a critic rejects the former tendency, he denies the movie its relation to the real world.

11

Summary and Conclusions

We have seen five types of writing developed in *Cahiers du Cinéma*, at times in an overlapping manner: first, *Cahiers'* formalist texts; second, its apolitical Brechtian writings; third, its directly politicized Brechtian criticism; fourth, those texts that begin with Brechtian premises but go beyond them to new directions in film theory and critical practice; and fifth, those writings that in various ways synthesize the magazine's earlier formalist and cinephilic tendencies with its later politicization. While the preceding pages have contained a treatment of the relation between *Cahiers* and Brecht under different categorizations, let us summarize this study by regrouping the subjects covered under these five major sub-headings.

Cahiers' Formalist Texts

Cahiers' formalist period, which may be roughly designated as starting with the magazine's inception in the early 1950's and extending through the mid-1960's, can be categorized by the specification of two extreme, radical wings present in the magazine at this time. At one end, there are the rigidly philosophical, Platonist writings of Eric Rohmer, which seek to reduce the beauty of cinema to the underlying, often musical forms which structure great filmic works. At the other extreme are the MacMahoniens, like Michel Mourlet or Jacques Serguine, who see the beauty of film in its presentation of the human figure, i.e., in the physical relationships shown among men and women, be they violent, erotic, or fraternal. For the MacMahoniens, film's glory is in its presentation of the physical gestures of the actor. Most of the writings in *Cahiers* during this period may be placed somewhere between these two wings.

This period in *Cahiers* is not only one of great critical achievement in itself but is also important for the laying of the groundwork for the absorption of Brechtian ideas into the magazine. The following points are important in this regard:

1. Much of this early *Cahiers* writing, particularly before 1960, is couched in philosophical terms and contexts, sometimes Catholic, sometimes Platonist,

sometimes phenomenological. While the idealism of this period is later to become anathema to the materialist *Cahiers* critics of the early 1970's, there are affinities between the two groups, both in the attempt to argue film theory from certain theoretical postulates and in privileging the viewer's rational, intellectual responses over his emotional ones. Similarly, the influence of phenomenology establishes a precedent for viewing a film not as an objective reproduction of reality but as a mediated reality, a discourse on reality.

2. The early *Cahiers* critics establish in the magazine the treatment of form as an integral part of a film's meaning. With a critic like Rohmer, this preoccupation with form grows out of a Platonistic search for the film's essential forms. With the later critics, the forms employed by the work of art are an integral part of their political signification. In both cases, there is an implicit need to make the film a precise object of study. In the early *Cahiers,* this is done by a critic like Godard, for example, trying to see film as a changing set of points on a graph: *mise en scène* becomes the geometric expression of cinematographic ideas. In the later *Cahiers,* this desired scientific approach is achieved first through the influence of an advanced formalist critic like Noël Burch, later through the qualified incorporation of semiological thought into the magazine. The increasing need to see film criticism as a scientific pursuit eventually becomes joined with the Marxist conception of history and social structures as objects for scientific study. The forms of the film are discussed in terms of their social functions.

3. That branch of the early *Cahiers* that sees film as an art based mainly on the presentation of physical relationships among the performers (i.e., the MacMahoniens, primarily) reveals a preoccupation with film as a means of physical rather than psychological expression. While in the early *Cahiers* this involvement with the physical aspects of human behavior is sometimes linked to an underlying spiritualism about the meanings of these gestures, there is also an affinity between this emphasis on the physical, material nature of cinematic acting and Brecht's notion of gestic acting, whereby the actor selectively presents those gestures of a character which indicate his position in a social structure.

4. Like its transformed counterpart, the early *Cahiers* rejects the idea of realism as the only acceptable mode of expression in film. Both see the truth in a film as arising not from its successful imitation of the surface qualities of reality but in the accuracy of its discourse. While in the old *Cahiers* this may again be seen in terms of an expression of underlying spiritual values, in the new *Cahiers* it becomes linked to the Marxist methodological favoring of dialectical materialism over empiricism. In other words, a film is not necessarily good because it convinces the viewer that he is watching a real event. Rather, it must present a logical analysis of real social forces.

5. The early *Cahiers* is interested in the relationship between film and theater, much in evidence in the magazine's early direct interest in Brecht. A critic like Jacques Rivette, however, also suggests a link to Brechtian thought in his admiration for the theater of Denis Diderot (whose similar theories precede Brecht's by several centuries). The use of deliberate theatricality is admired in the later *Cahiers* as a way of avoiding conventional cinematic representation, but precedents for this idea may be found earlier in the magazine.

6. Some of the early *Cahiers* critics, especially the MacMahoniens, admire the work of Joseph Losey, a director whose work on both stage and screen had been influenced by Brecht. Much of *Cahiers'* interest in Brecht may well grow out of its interest in Losey.

In this pre-1968 period, Brecht is in the process of becoming an established figure on the French theater scene. The popularity and fashionablness of the German dramatist in French intellectual circles joins with the above set of influences to make *Cahiers'* first treatments of Brecht and Brechtian thought hardly as surprising or unexpected as they might seem at first glance.

Cahiers' Apolitical Texts on Brecht

In general, *Cahiers'* first approaches to Brecht are due far more to an interest in the notion and techniques of distanciation than they are in the political theory which accompanied their conception. In the magazine's special Brecht number, for example, the editors present an essay by Losey on the use of filmic techniques to Brechtian ends that makes comparatively little mention of Marxist theory. (Similarly, Fereydoun Hoyveda's critique of Losey's film EVA makes no mention of politics whatsoever but rather sees the work as a formalist masterpiece which plays on the viewer's intellectual rather than emotional involvement.) Bernard Dort's essay in the same number of the magazine links Brecht to many of *Cahiers'* established preoccupations, e.g., Chaplin's MONSIEUR VERDOUX, Chabrol's LES BONNES FEMMES, the films of Antonioni.

The critic who writes most about Brecht in *Cahiers* at this time is Louis Marcorelles, who sees in Brechtian acting theory a valuable alternative to standard conceptions of film acting (e.g., the Actors' Studio techniques of Kazan, the mechanical approaches of Hitchcock or Antonioni). For Marcorelles, Brecht also represents a form of socialist art that avoids the academicism of Stalinist socialist realism. On the other hand, the critic also attempts to divorce Brechtian technique from content (as when he sees the Bergman of THE VIRGIN SPRING as practicing a kind of Christian variation of Brechtian theater) and remains skeptical about the applicability of Brecht's theories to the cinema.

Among the films to which the *Cahiers* critics of this time attempt most notably to apply Brecht-related thought are those of two of its former critics, Claude Chabrol and Jean-Luc Godard. In both cases, the films in question are superficially apolitical; rather, they are seen as objective, dispassionate works which require new, more active attitudes on the part of the viewer. *Cahiers* also responds favorably to works it sees as Brechtian from the new Italian cinema and on occasion even discusses films like Billy Wilder's IRMA LA DOUCE and Raoul Walsh's OBJECTIVE BURMA in similar terms.

In summary, therefore, the treatment of Brecht in this period must be seen as incomplete or even distorted. The techniques of his theater are very much admired, as are the accompanying objectivity and detachment, but the magazine is as yet not ready to embrace the philosophy which motivates them.

Politicized Brechtian Criticism

Changes in *Cahiers* begin to become marked around 1966, when essays by Michel Mardore and Jean-Louis Comolli begin to raise political issues and call for the rational, objective, unemotional treatment of economic and social themes in the cinema, while at the same time calling for a detached, critical mode of viewing from the spectator.

After 1968, *Cahiers* begins to adopt certain positions which are close to the political attitudes of Brecht. One of the most important is the treatment of films as commodities, the recognition of their place in the marketplace, and the coordinate rejection of the idealist notion of art. (This attitude is derived in part from the influence of the then-new magazine, *Cinéthique*.) For the new *Cahiers*, the content of a film is invariably affected by the way in which it is to be financed and marketed; a film made through capitalist funding will almost always have an underlying message supportive of bourgeois ideology. In addition, *Cahiers'* criticism begins very adamantly to criticize cinematographic naturalism for most of the same reasons that Brecht rejected theatrical realism, arguing that naturalism inhibits true political discourse. For *Cahiers*, as for Brecht, naturalism becomes a set of conventions which prevent the audience from recognizing itself and specific forces of society in a film.

Much of *Cahiers'* most specifically Brechtian criticism after 1968 occurs with discussions of the *Groupe Dziga-Vertov*, whose 1972 film, TOUT VA BIEN, was made by Jean-Luc Godard using Brecht's notes to *The Rise and Fall of the City of Mahagony* as a model. The goal of the *Groupe*, to "make political films politically," implies a consideration of the economic and political significance of all the elements of the film (since these are, in turn, all economically determined). The cinematographic illusionism inherent in realism is rejected in favor of a form of cinema which prefers to keep the audience totally aware of the nature of the filmic discussion taking place. The release of

TOUT VA BIEN simultaneously with COUP POUR COUP, a film on a similar theme (a strike) made by Marin Karmitz in a realistic, documentary style, proves to be the occasion of a lengthy polemic against the latter film. The *Cahiers* critics argue that the Karmitz film is politically regressive and revisionist precisely because it is formally counter-revolutionary, because it makes use of the techniques of the bourgeois cinema, such as identification and realistic representation.

With similar arguments, *Cahiers* attacks many of what it calls the *films progressistes,* referring to films with leftist leanings which couch their messages in the techniques and narrative structures of the conventional, commercial cinema. Works such as certain French police films of the early 1970's, the movies of Costa-Gavras, and new, politicized Italian films like THE WORKING CLASS GOES TO HEAVEN and THE MATTEI AFFAIR come in for particular attack, and they are analyzed to show the way in which their overtly leftist messages are undercut by their cinematographic methods. By contrast, a genuinely progressive film like LA VIE EST A NOUS, from the 1930's, is analyzed to show how its techniques allow for a revolutionary message to come through.

Directly Brechtian criticism also occurs with discussions of the treatment of historical subjects in films. Pascal Kané writes theoretically about the way in which the inherent staginess of historical topics must be used to create an understanding of the historical and social forces at work in the society presented. Articles on René Allio's LES CAMISARDS attempt to evaluate the success with which the film deliberately applies Brechtian theory to the presentation of an historical situation, through the use of an approach derived from Brecht's notion of the social gest in costuming, acting styles, and the construction of the narrative. Bernard Sichère's review of films of the *mode rétro* genre, such as Luchino Visconti's THE DAMNED or Liliana Cavani's THE NIGHT PORTER, seeks to demonstrate how, without Brechtian techniques, the treatment of the subject of fascism winds up as a glorification of fascism. By contrast, movies like Joseph Losey's M. KLEIN, Rainer Werner Fassbinder's LILI MARLEEN, and Hans-Jürgen Syberberg's HITLER avoid naturalism in treating the Nazi era and so meet with the *Cahiers* critics' approval.

In such articles the *Cahiers* critics advocate not only a stance supportive of Brechtian techniques but a politically Marxist, materialist position as well.

Going Beyond Brecht

The major task of the politicized *Cahiers,* however, is to apply Brechtian theory, devised specifically for the stage, to film. Much of the criticism in *Cahiers* after 1968 represents an elaboration of Brechtian theory to treat specifically cinematic issues. Often the conclusions drawn make no reference to Brecht, but the standards employed are comparable to those of the German dramatist, i.e., the *Cahiers* writers reject realistic cinema, a spectator who is passive and emotionally involved, and any notion of apolitical subject matter. These elaborations of Brecht cover the following areas.

1. *Cahiers* theorists such as Jean-Louis Comolli and Pascal Bonitzer discuss the ways in which almost all the techniques of the conventional narrative cinema have been determined by the capitalist system which gave birth to them. Even linear perspective is criticized as reactionary (for putting the viewer in a physically passive position), as are the notions of "off-screen" space, the traditional use of deep focus described by Bazin, and the concept of the shot as the primary structuring device in film. All contribute to the mystification of the audience regarding the real nature of cinematic communication. Similarly, Jean-Louis Comolli calls for an approach to film history which would discuss "signifying practices," that is, the use of techniques as applied historically in specific contexts rather than the usual history of the cinema as a series of technical innovations. By contrast, Eisensteinian montage is praised as offering an alternative to cinematic illusionism and opposed to the conventional system in which montage is customarily suppressed. And for a period of time, Comolli finds an alternative to traditional cinematic representation in the *cinéma direct* movement. *Cahiers du Cinéma* attempts to rewrite film history and theory.

2. The *Cahiers* of the post-1968 period applies to film theory the post-Freudian psychoanalytic ideas of Jacques Lacan. In this framework, classical cinema becomes particularly pernicious because it reproduces so accurately the Lacanian system whereby the infant develops his sense of self through his proportionately overdeveloped visual faculties. Out of Lacanian psychology grow many of the writings of Jean-Pierre Oudart, who systematizes the code of classical editing into his system of the "suture," whereby the standard structure of shot/reverse-shot creates the false illusion of a total reality on the screen. Such psychoanalytic theorization offers another warning of the extreme passivity of the viewer produced by traditional film forms.

3. Finally, there is the notion of deconstruction, whereby a politically correct film (e.g., Jean-Marie Straub's OTHON, or Robert Kramer's ICE) will borrow elements from traditional, bourgeois art forms, only to manipulate them in such a way that the viewer will be able to perceive their mechanisms. Deconstruction thus exposes the place of these mechanisms in the traditional film and the way in which they ordinarily prevent us from apprehending their place in the economic system which the bourgeois film reinforces. Such a deconstructed film forces the viewer into a position of active reading *(lecture),* whereby he must analyze the information provided and come to a rational judgment.

Merging Politics and Cinephilia

Toward the end of the 1970's *Cahiers du Cinéma* begins to reject the extreme radicalism of some of its post-1968 Marxist positions. The magazine starts a return to some of its older, cinephilic editorial positions, but in the process it also examines and reflects on the nature of this love of movies. Critics like Louis Skorecki, Pascal Kané, and Bernard Boland discuss some of the psychological drives behind the cinephilia that had been so characteristic of the magazine in its early years. Jean-Pierre Oudart directly attacks what he sees as an excessively dogmatic, analytical, demystifying trend in leftist film criticism. To the films of Jean-Marie Straub or Jean-Luc Godard, he prefers those of Stanley Kubrick and Robert Kramer, which he sees as containing both intelligent political discourse and the cinephilic delights of the imaginary.

Parallel to these developments, one can see the emergence of a new interest in the actor and particularly in the way in which the actor can work against complete passivity in the audience. Jean-Louis Comolli examines this question with particular regard to the historical film, using Jean Renoir's LA MARSEILLAISE as a prime example.

The end of the 1970's and the start of the 1980's see *Cahiers du Cinéma* returning somewhat to its heritage in the French New Wave. The magazine praises films by François Truffaut and Eric Rohmer for their cinematic intelligence and for their makers' ability to circumvent the pressures of the commercial system and do work of integrity. Pascal Bonitzer in particular argues for a continuity between the early formalist *Cahiers* and its later politicized transformation. In both, he argues, there is a rejection of a literary, verbally conceived cinema.

If there is a backing off at this time from demanding militant political commitment from all cinema, much writing in the more moderate *Cahiers du Cinéma* still shows the influence of its more fervently Marxist period. Jean-Claude Biette's review of Jean-Marie Straub and Danièle Huillet's TROP TOT, TROP TARD embodies all of the themes of the magazine's most recent period in its treatment of a film that is at once highly political and rigorously formalist. It acknowledges the tension between politics and aesthetics as a fundamental one; it discusses actors as figures who stand somewhere between physical reality and fictional reality in a film; it shows the militant movie's sources in cinematic tradition.

Conclusions

What conclusions can one draw from this succession of five types of writing in *Cahiers du Cinéma?* Let us suggest only three:

1. The transition between the old, formalist *Cahiers* and the later, politicized *Cahiers* is characterized by far more continuity than is immediately apparent. There is no denying that *Cahiers du Cinéma* after 1968 takes positions that are antithetical to those of the magazine in the 1950's. Nonetheless, there is a definite progression in *Cahiers* from ideas that run contrary to those of Brecht, through an apolitical acceptance of Brechtian theory, to the advocacy of a militantly Brechtian cinema. Many of the positions of the early *Cahiers* contain the seeds of what the magazine was to develop into.

2. Bertolt Brecht is the pivotal figure for these changes in *Cahiers du Cinéma.* Undoubtedly, the increased leftist politicization of French culture in the late 1960's would have had some effect anyway on a major French film journal. Brecht, however, becomes the figure to suggest the direction in which the making of a political cinema (and a political film criticism) was to go. So many of the ideas which the later *Cahiers* suggests as radical alternatives to traditional forms operate from assumptions that are close to Brecht even when no mention is made of him. Brecht also becomes a major link between *Cahiers* and other branches of French intellectual thought, particularly through the semiology of Roland Barthes.

3. *Cahiers'* politicized criticism offers a major alternative to conventional film criticism. It has not been the aim of this study to debate the merits of the various *Cahiers* positions, and surely there are countless arguments that might be made against them. What *Cahiers* does demonstrate, however, is that if one begins from materialist premises whereby the various elements of the film medium are seen as economically determined, one may wind up with a far different conception of the place of film in society than is customarily assumed. *Cahiers* presents a challenge to standard film aesthetics, one that demands to be answered before the validity of either type of film criticism is to be taken for granted.

That, one must argue, is the chief value of these developments that have occurred in *Cahiers du Cinéma.* For the authors involved consistently raise the question not so much of what is a good or bad film but why films are made and how they should be made. This consideration of the filmmaker's work, both as a system of *écriture,* as a unique kind of writing, and as something which has a place in the economic and political world, gives a purpose and a significance to the writings produced. It renders them major moral documents in the field of contemporary film theory.

Notes

Chapter 1

1. "Editorial," *Screen,* XVI (Winter, 1975-76), p. 3.

2. François Truffaut, quoted in *Cahiers du Cinéma,* No. 226-27 (janvier-février 1971), p. 121. Maureen Turim uses this statement as an opening comment for her own study of *Cahiers du Cinéma,* discussed below. While early issues of *Cahiers* are given volume numbers, this practice has been discontinued by the magazine in recent years. For the sake of consistency, therefore, all footnotes will give only the number of the individual issue and its date.

3. Peter Cowie, ed., *International Film Guide 1976.* (London: The Tantivy Press; New York: A.S. Barnes & Co., 1976), p. 600.

4. See in particular: Dana Polan, "Brecht and the Politics of Self-Reflexive Cinema," *Jump Cut,* No. 17 (1978), pp. 29-31; essays by Martin Walsh, collected in *The Brechtian Aspect of Radical Cinema* (London: British Film Institute Publishing, 1981); and the special Brecht issue of *Screen,* XVI (Winter, 1975-76). For criticism from the 1980's, see Sylvia Harvey, "Whose Brecht? Memories for the Eighties," *Screen,* XXIII (May-June, 1982), pp. 45-59; Alan Lovell, "Epic Theater and Counter-Cinema's Principles," *Jump Cut,* No. 27 (1982), pp. 64-68.

5. Peter Cowie, ed., *International Film Guide 1982* (London: The Tantivy Press; San Diego and New York: A.S. Barnes & Co., 1982), p. 495.

6. Maureen Turim, "The Aesthetic Becomes Political: A History of Film Criticism in *Cahiers du Cinéma," The Velvet Light Trap,* No. 9 (Summer, 1973), pp. 13-17.

7. T.L. French, ed., *Cahiers du Cinéma* (New York: The Thousand Eyes, 1977).

8. Sylvia Harvey, *May '68 and Film Culture* (London: British Film Institute, 1978).

9. William Guynn, "The Political Program of *Cahiers du Cinéma,* 1969-1977," *Jump Cut,* No. 17 (1978), pp. 32-35.

10. A study in Italian apparently does exist—P.A. Laqua, "Lo spazio cinematografico problema aperte delle teoriche del film," *Cineforum,* No. 114 (May-June, 1972), pp. 71-92—but this author has been unable to consult it. A helpful chronology of events on the French film scene from 1968-1980 appeared as "Chronologie (sélective)," *Cahiers du Cinéma,* No. 323-24 (mai 1981), pp. 23-25.

Chapter 2

1. Bertolt Brecht, *Brecht on Theatre: The Development of an Aesthetic,* ed. and trans. John Willet (New York: Hill and Wang, 1964), pp. 180-81.

2. Ibid., p. 184.

3. Ibid., p. 189.

4. Ibid., pp. 96-97.

5. Ibid., p. 139.

6. Ibid., pp. 104-5.

7. Bertolt Brecht, *Ecrits sur la literature et l'art 1: Sur le cinéma,* textes français de Jean-Louis Lebrave et Jean-Pierre Lefebvre (Paris: L'Arche, 1970), p. 167.

8. Bertolt Brecht, *Brecht on Theatre,* p. 140.

9. Ibid., p. 139.

10. Ibid., p. 71.

11. Ibid.

12. Bertolt Brecht, "Sur le système cinémetographique," *Cahiers du Cinéma,* No. 114 (décembre 1960), pp. 14-20.

13. Bertolt Brecht, *Ecrits sur la literature et l'art 1: Sur le cinéma,* p. 169.

14. Ibid., p. 177.

15. Bertolt Brecht, *Brecht on Theatre,* p. 50.

16. Bertolt Brecht, *Ecrits sur la literature et l'art 1: Sur le cinéma,* p. 183.

17. Bertolt Brecht, *Brecht on Theatre,* p. 37.

18. Bertolt Brecht, "Notes sur l'opera *Grandeur et décadence de la ville de Mahagonny,"* *Cahiers du Cinéma,* No. 238-39 (mai-juin 1972), pp. 28-32.

Chapter 3

1. Maurice Schérer, "Vanité que la peinture," *Cahiers du Cinéma,* No. 3 (juin 1951), p. 24.

2. Eric Rohmer, "Le celluloïd et le marbre, IV: Beau comme la musique," *Cahiers du Cinéma,* no. 52 (novembre 1955), pp. 26-27.

3. Ibid., p. 29.

4. Eric Rohmer, "Le celluloïd et le marbre, III: De la métaphore," *Cahiers du Cinéma,* No. 51 (octobre 1955), p. 6.

5. Richard Roud, "The French Line," *Sight and Sound,* XXIX (Autumn, 1960), pp. 167-71.

6. Maurice Schérer, "A qui la faute?" *Cahiers du Cinéma,* No. 39 (octobre 1954), pp. 6-7.

7. Jacques Rivette, "Lettre sur Rossellini," *Cahiers du Cinéma,* No. 46 (avril 1955), p. 15.

8. Ibid., p. 19.

9. Maurice Schérer, "A qui la faute?", pp. 7-8.

10. Ibid., p. 8.

11. Amédée Ayfre, "Néo-réalisme et phénoménologie," *Cahiers du Cinéma*, No. 17 (novembre 1952), p. 9.

12. Ibid., p. 14.

13. Jacques Rivette, "De l'abjection," *Cahiers du Cinéma*, No. 120 (juin 1961), p. 55.

14. Christian Metz, *Film Language, A Semiotics of the Cinema*, trans. Michael Taylor (New York: Oxford University Press, 1974).

15. "One of the texts that particularly marked me when I was a young reader of the *Cahiers* was a piece by Rivette on Pontecorvo's KAPO. He described a scene in the film, the death of Emmanuelle Riva near the barbed wire. Pontecorvo—at the moment of his character's death—did a camera movement in order to re-frame the face in the corner of the screen and make it a prettier shot. Rivette wrote: the man who did this travelling shot is worthy of the profoundist contempt."—Serge Daney, in T.L. French, ed., *Cahiers du Cinéma* (New York: The Thousand Eyes, 1977), p. 30. *Cahiers* critics seem habitually to refer to this review by Rivette when talking about films that deal with Naziism. See Serge Daney, "L'état-Syberberg," *Cahiers du Cinéma*, No. 292 (septembre 1978), p. 5; and Pascal Kané, "Point de vue," *Cahiers du Cinéma*, No. 301 (juin 1979), p. 13.

16. Jean-Louis Comolli, "Vivre le film," *Cahiers du Cinéma*, No. 141 (mars 1963), pp. 14-29.

17. Jean-Luc Godard, "Review of Astruc's UNE VIE," in Peter Graham, ed., *The New Wave* (Garden City, N.Y.: Doubleday & Co., Inc., 1968), pp. 81-83; also in *Cahiers du Cinéma*, No. 89 (novembre 1958).

18. Jacques Rivette, "La recherche de l'absolu," *Cahiers du Cinéma*, no. 52 (novembre 1955), p. 46.

19. Eric Rohmer, "L'hélice et l'idée," *Cahiers du Cinéma*, No. 93 (mars 1959), p. 50.

20. François Weyergans, "Le verbe treize," *Cahiers du Cinéma*, No. 149 (novembre 1963), pp. 61-62.

21. Fereydoun Hoyveda, "Le plus grand anneau," *Cahiers du Cinéma*, No. 95 (mai 1959), pp. 40-41.

22. Paul-Louis Martin, "D'un Tati l'autre," *Cahiers du Cinéma*, No. 199 (mars 1968), pp. 27-28.

23. Ibid., p. 27.

24. Jean Domarchi, "L'homme des cavernes," *Cahiers du Cinéma*, No. 149 (novembre 1963), pp. 65-66.

25. Pierre-Richard Bré, "Des photos fanées," *Cahiers du Cinéma*, No. 152 (février 1964), p. 69.

26. Michel Mourlet, *Sur un art ignoré* (Paris: La Table Ronde, 1965), p. 55; also in *Cahiers du Cinéma*, No. 107 (mai 1960).

27. Ibid., pp. 55-56.

28. Ibid., p. 73.

29. Jacques Serguine, "Education du spectateur, ou L'Ecole du MacMahon," *Cahiers du Cinéma*, No. 111 (septembre 1960), pp. 41-42.

30. Jacques Rivette, "Notes sur une révolution," *Cahiers du Cinéma*, No. 54 (Noël 1955), pp. 17-21.

31. Serge Daney, "La dé-faite," *Cahiers du Cinéma*, No. 196 (décembre 1967), p. 63.

32. Roland Barthes and Bernard Dort, "Brecht 'traduit,'" *Théâtre Populaire*, No. 23 (mars 1957), p. 1.

Chapter 4

1. Bernard Dort, "Brecht en France," *Les Temps Modernes*, XV (juin 1960), pp. 1855-57.

2. Roland Barthes, *Critical Essays*, trans. Richard Howard (Evanston, Ill.: Northwestern University Press, 1972), p. 38; also in *Théâtre Populaire*, No. 11 (janvier-février 1955).

3. Bernard Dort, "Brecht en France," p. 1858.

4. Ibid., p. 1859.

5. Ibid., p. 1873-74.

6. *Cahiers du Cinéma*, No. 129 (mars 1962).

7. Louis Marcorelles, "L'impossible gageure," *Cahiers du Cinéma*, No. 77 (décembre 1957), p. 52.

8. Bernard Dort, "Pour une critique brechtienne du cinéma," *Cahiers du Cinéma*, No. 114 (décembre 1960), p. 34.

9. Roland Barthes, "Diderot, Brecht, Eisenstein," trans. Stephen Heath, *Screen*, XV (Summer, 1974), pp. 33-39.

10. Ibid., p. 34.

11. Denis Diderot, quoted and translated in David Funt, *"Diderot and the Aesthetics of the Enlightenment,"* *Diderot Studies*, XI (Geneva: Librairie Droz S.A., 1968), p. 172.

12. Felix Vexler, *Studies in Diderot's Esthetic Naturalism* (New York: Columbia University, 1922), pp. 19-25.

13. Ibid., pp. 44-45.

14. Denis Diderot, *The Paradox of Acting*, trans. Walter Herries Pollock, introduction by Lee Strasberg (New York: Hill and Wang, Inc., 1957), p. 21.

15. Roland Barthes, "Diderot, Brecht, Eisenstein," p. 34.

16. Felix Vexler, *Studies in Diderot's Esthetic Naturalism*, p. 49.

17. Ibid., p. 56.

18. Denis Diderot, *The Paradox of Acting*, p. 15.

19. Jacques Rivette, quoted in Peter Graham, ed., *The New Wave*, pp. 125-26.

20. Jacques Rivette, "En attendant les Godons," *Cahiers du Cinéma*, No. 73 (juillet 1957), pp. 38-40.

21. Jacques Rivette, "Petit journal du cinéma: Revoir Verdoux," *Cahiers du Cinéma*, No. 146 (août 1963), pp. 42-43.

22. Ibid.

23. Ibid.

24. Eric Bentley, "MONSIEUR VERDOUX and the Theater," in *In Search of Theater* (New York: Alfred A. Knopf, 1953), pp. 161-73.

25. André Bazin, *What Is Cinema?* ed. and trans. Hugh Gray (Berkeley and Los Angeles: University of California Press, 1967), pp. 35-36.

26. Amédée Ayfre, "Néo-réalisme et phénoménologie," p. 6.

27. Jacques Rivette, "L'essentiel," *Cahiers du Cinéma,* No. 32 (février 1954), p. 44.

28. Jacques Serguine, "Education du spectateur, ou L'Ecole du MacMahon," p. 40.

29. Michel Mourlet, "Beauté de la connaissance," in *Sur un art ignoré,* pp. 125-26; also in *Cahiers du Cinéma,* No. 111 (septembre 1960).

30. François Weyergans, "Lola au Pays des Hommes," *Cahiers du Cinéma,* No. 117 (mars 1961), pp. 25-31.

31. Jean-Louis Comolli, "Secrète Agente," *Cahiers du Cinéma,* No. 164 (mars 1965), p. 84.

32. "Entretien avec Joseph Losey," *Théâtre Populaire,* No. 53 (1964), pp. 3-14.

Chapter 5

1. "Editorial," *Cahiers du Cinéma,* No. 114 (décembre 1960), p. 2.

2. Ibid.

3. Joseph Losey, "L'oeil du maître," *Cahiers du Cinéma,* No. 114 (décembre 1960), pp. 21-32.

4. Ibid., p. 29.

5. Ibid., p. 31.

6. Bernard Dort, "Pour une critique brechtienne du cinéma," p. 34.

7. Ibid., p. 38.

8. Ibid., pp. 38-43.

9. Louis Marcorelles, "D'un art moderne," *Cahiers du Cinéma,* No. 114 (décembre 1960), pp. 44-52.

10. Ibid., p. 53.

11. Peter Mathers, "Brecht in Britain: From Theatre to Television," *Screen,* XVI (Winter 1975-76), p. 81.

12. Louis Marcorelles, "Elia Kazan et l'Actors' Studio," *Cahiers du Cinéma,* No. 66 (Noël 1956), p. 43.

13. Louis Marcorelles, "L'impossible gageure," pp. 52-54.

14. Ibid., p. 55.

15. Louis Marcorelles, "Strip tease polonais," *Cahiers du Cinéma,* No. 102 (décembre 1959), p. 55.

16. Louis Marcorelles, "A l'école de la 'dramaturgie,'" *Cahiers du Cinéma,* No. 106 (avril 1960), pp. 57-59.

17. Louis Marcorelles, "Au pied du mur," *Cahiers du Cinéma,* No. 116 (février 1961), pp. 51-52.

18. Ibid., p. 53.

19. Ibid., pp. 52-53.

20. Louis Marcorelles, "Gehalt und Gestalt," *Cahiers du Cinéma*, No. 127 (janvier 1962), p. 58.

21. Ibid., p. 60.

22. Fereydoun Hoyveda, "L'eau et le miroir," *Cahiers du Cinéma*, No. 137 (novembre 1962), p. 36.

23. Ibid.

24. Ibid., p. 40.

25. André S. Labarthe, "Le plus pur regard," *Cahiers du Cinéma*, No. 108 (juin 1960), p. 48.

26. Ibid., p. 49.

27. Ibid., p. 50.

28. Jean-André Fieschi, "Si nos brechtiens...," *Cahiers du Cinéma*, No. 143 (mai 1963), p. 58.

29. The film, about the famous Bluebeard of the early part of this century, takes for its same subject that of the Chaplin MONSIEUR VERDOUX, already mentioned more than once in this study. It is indeed entirely likely that Chabrol was inspired not only by the historical character but also by Chaplin.

30. Jean-André Fieschi, "Si nos brechtiens...," pp. 60-62.

31. Ibid., p. 62.

32. Luc Moullet, "France alienée et France consciente," *Cahiers du Cinéma*, No. 182 (septembre 1966), pp. 72-73.

33. Ibid., p. 73.

34. Jean-Luc Godard, quoted in Jacques Pétat, "Bertolt Brecht et le cinéma," *Cinéma 75*, No. 203 (novembre 1975), p. 70.

35. Paul Vechialli, "La guerre tout court," *Cahiers du Cinéma*, No. 145 (juillet 1963), p. 52.

36. Ibid., pp. 53-54.

37. Ibid., p. 55.

38. Jean-Louis Comolli, "Contrariwise," *Cahiers du Cinéma in English*, No. 3 (1966), p. 57; also in *Cahiers du Cinéma*, No. 168 (juillet 1965).

39. Ibid., p. 58.

40. Michel Delahaye, "La règle de Rouch," *Cahiers du Cinéma*, No. 121 (juin 1961), p. 2.

41. Fereydoun Hoyveda, "Cinéma Vérité ou Réalisme Fantastique," *Cahiers du Cinéma*, No. 125 (novembre 1961), p. 34.

42. Jacques Joly, "Un nouveau réalisme," *Cahiers du Cinéma*, No. 131 (mai 1962), p. 12.

43. Jacques Doniol-Valcroze, "Un buisson de questions," *Cahiers du Cinéma*, No. 152 (février 1964), p. 64.

44. Michel Mardore, "La douce-amère," *Cahiers du Cinéma*, No. 149 (novembre 1963), pp. 64-65.

45. Jean-Louis Comolli, "L'esprit d'aventure," *Cahiers du Cinéma*, No. 154 (avril 1964), pp. 11-14.

46. Michel Mardore, "Age of Gold (Buñuel), Age of Iron (Rossellini)," *Cahiers du Cinéma in English*, No. 3 (1966), p. 49; also in *Cahiers du Cinéma*, No. 175 (février 1966).

47. Ibid., p. 49.

48. Ibid., pp. 49-50.

49. Ibid., p. 50.

50. Ibid.

51. Jean-Louis Comolli, "Notes on the New Spectator," *Cahiers du Cinéma in English*, No. 7 (January, 1967), p. 61; also in *Cahiers du Cinéma*, No. 177 (avril 1966).

52. Ibid.

53. Ibid.

Chapter 6

1. Considered here are *Positif, Ecran, La Revue du Cinéma, Cinéthique, Cinéma,* and of course *Cahiers du Cinéma*. Ironically, the magazine most seen as leftist during the 1950's, *Positif,* is now regarded by some as relatively right wing.

2. "Vingt ans après," *Cahiers du Cinéma*, No. 172 (novembre 1965), pp. 18-31.

3. Jean-Louis Comolli, "Les miettes de l'existence," *Cahiers du Cinéma*, No. 166-67 (juin 1965), p. 128.

4. Roland Barthes, "Rhétorique de l'image," *Communications*, No. 4 (1964), p. 48.

5. Jean-Louis Comolli, "Le point sur l'image," *Cahiers du Cinéma*, No. 194 (octobre 1967), pp. 29-30.

6. Noël Burch, *Theory of Film Practice* (New York: Praeger Publishers, 1973), p. 15.

7. Pascal Bonitzer, "Hors-champ (un espace en défaut)," *Cahiers du Cinéma*, No. 234-35 (décembre 1971-janvier 1972), p. 20.

8. Noël Burch, *Theory of Film Practice*, p. xix.

9. "Film et roman: Problèmes de récit," *Cahiers du Cinéma*, No. 185 (décembre 1966).

10. Louis Althusser, *For Marx*, trans. Ben Brewster (New York: Pantheon Books, 1969).

11. Roland Barthes, *Critical Essays*, pp. 74-75.

12. Sylvia Harvey, *May '68 and Film Culture;* Maureen Turim, "The Aesthetic Becomes Political: A History of Film Criticism in *Cahiers du Cinéma*"; Thomas Elsaesser, "French Film Culture and Critical Theory: *Cinéthique,*" *Monogram*, No. 2 (Summer, 1971), pp. 31-37.

13. Maureen Turim, "The Aesthetic Becomes Political: A History of Film Criticism in *Cahiers du Cinéma*," p. 15.

14. Thomas Elsaesser, "French Film Culture and Critical Theory: *Cinéthique,*" p. 32.

15. Jean-Louis Comolli and Jean Narboni, "Cinéma/idéologie/critique," *Cahiers du Cinéma*, No. 216 (octobre 1969), p. 12.

16.   Ibid., p. 13.

17.   Ibid., pp. 12-14.

18.   Jean-Louis Comolli and Jean Narboni, "Cinéma/idéologie/critique (2): D'une critique à son point critique," *Cahiers du Cinéma*, No. 217 (novembre 1969), pp. 8-9.

19.   Jean-Louis Comolli, "Dernier acte, encore," *Cahiers du Cinéma*, No. 215 (septembre 1969), pp. 55-59.

20.   "Le 'groupe Dziga-Vertov,' " *Cahiers du Cinéma*, No. 240 (juillet-août 1972), p. 5.

21.   Ibid.

22.   Ibid.

23.   Ibid., pp. 5-6.

24.   Ibid., p. 6.

25.   Ibid., p. 8.

26.   "Editorial," *Cahiers du Cinéma*, No. 244 (février-mars 1973), p. 5.

27.   Jacques Aumont, "Groupe 3: Les acquis théoriques—premier bilan du groupe," *Cahiers du Cinéma*, No. 244 (février-mars 1973), pp. 42-43.

28.   Serge Daney, "Fonction critique," *Cahiers du Cinéma*, No. 248 (1973), p. 39.

29.   Ibid., p. 40.

30.   Serge Daney, "Anti-rétro (suite); Fonction critique (fin)," *Cahiers du Cinéma*, No 253 (octobre-novembre 1974), pp. 30-36.

31.   Ibid., p. 34.

Chapter 7

1.   Another (and very good) English language summary of many of the issues covered in this chapter is James Spellerberg, "Technology and Ideology in the Cinema," *Quarterly Review of Film Studies*, II (August, 1977), pp. 288-301.

2.   Jean-Louis Baudry, "Ideological Effects of the Basic Cinematographic Apparatus," *Film Quarterly*, XXVIII (Winter, 1974-75), pp. 39-47; also in *Cinéthique*, No. 7-8 (1970).

3.   Pascal Bonitzer, " 'Réalité' de la dénotation," *Cahiers du Cinéma*, No. 229 (mai 1971), p. 41.

4.   Pascal Bonitzer, "Fétichisme de la technique: La notion de plan," *Cahiers du Cinéma*, No. 233 (novembre 1971), pp. 4-7.

5.   Ibid., pp. 8-10.

6.   Pascal Bonitzer, "Hors-champ (un espace en défaut)," *Cahiers du Cinéma*, No. 234-35 (décembre 1971-janvier 1972), p. 15.

7.   Ibid.

8.   Ibid., p. 16.

9.   Ibid., pp. 16-18.

10.   Ibid., p. 21.

11. Ibid., pp. 24-26.

12. Ibid., p. 26.

13. Pascal Bonitzer and Serge Daney, "L'écran du fantasme," *Cahiers du Cinéma*, No. 236-37 (mars-avril 1972), pp. 31-40.

14. Pascal Bonitzer, "L'espace politique," *Cahiers du Cinéma*, No. 249 (février-mars 1974), p. 42.

15. Ibid.

16. Pascal Bonitzer, *Le regard et la voix* (Paris: 10/18, 1976).

17. Pascal Bonitzer, "Voici," *Cahiers du Cinéma*, No. 273 (janvier-février 1977), pp. 5-8.

18. Ibid., pp. 8-18.

19. Pascal Bonitzer, "Les deux regards," *Cahiers du Cinéma*, No. 275 (avril 1977), pp. 40-46.

20. Pascal Bonitzer, "Les dieux et les quarks," *Cahiers du Cinéma*, No. 295 (décembre 1978), pp. 5-7.

21. Ibid., pp. 7-8.

22. Some other major theatrical pieces by Bonitzer have been: "La surimage," *Cahiers du Cinéma*, No. 270 (septembre-octobre 1976), pp. 29-34; "Décadrages," *Cahiers du Cinéma*, No. 284 (janvier 1978), pp. 7-15; "La vision partielle," *Cahiers du Cinéma*, No. 301 (juin 1979), pp. 35-41. The latter is also in English as "Partial Vision" in *Wide Angle*, IV, 4 (1981), pp. 56-63.

23. André Bazin, *What Is Cinema?* I, pp. 9-22.

24. Jean-Louis Comolli, "Technique et idéologie: Caméra, perspectif, profondeur de champ," *Cahiers du Cinéma*, No. 229 (mai 1971), pp. 4-16; also in English as "Technique and Ideology: Camera, Perspective, Depth of Field," *Film Reader*, 2 (1977), pp. 128-40.

25. Ibid., p. 18.

26. Ibid., pp. 19-21.

27. Jean-Louis Comolli, "Technique et idéologie (2): Caméra, perspectif, profondeur de champ," *Cahiers du Cinéma*, No. 230 (juillet 1971), pp. 51-57.

28. Jean-Louis Comolli, "Technique et idéologie (3): Caméra, perspectif, profondeur de champ," *Cahiers du Cinéma*, No. 231 (août-septembre 1971), pp. 42-49.

29. Jean-Louis Comolli, "LA CECILIA" *Cahiers du Cinéma*, No. 262-63 (janvier 1976), pp. 69-78.

30. Jean-Louis Comolli and François Géré, "Deux fictions de la haine," *Cahiers du Cinéma*, No. 286 (mars 1978), pp. 31-47; No. 288 (mai 1978), pp. 5-15; No. 290-91 (juillet-août 1978), pp. 89-98.

31. Jean-Louis Comolli and François Géré, "Deux fictions de la haine (1)," *Cahiers du Cinéma*, No. 286 (mars 1978), p. 33.

32. Jean-Louis Comolli, and François Géré, "La real-fiction du pouvoir," *Cahiers du Cinéma*, No. 293 (octobre 1978), pp. 24-27.

33. Jean Narboni, Sylvie Pierre, Jacques Rivette, "Montage," *Cahiers du Cinéma*, No. 210 (mars 1969), p. 25.

34. Ibid., p. 27.

35. Ibid.

36. Ibid., pp. 29-31.

37. Ibid., p. 28.

38. Ibid., p. 29.

39. Jean-Louis Comolli, "Le détour par le direct," *Cahiers du Cinéma,* No. 209 (février 1969), pp. 48-53; the article is also available in English in Christopher Williams, ed., *Realism and the Cinema* (London: Routledge and Kegan Paul, 1980), pp. 225-243.

40. Ibid., p. 50.

41. Ibid., pp. 50-51.

42. Ibid., p. 52.

43. Ibid.

44. Jean-Louis Comolli, "Le détour par le direct (2)," *Cahiers du Cinéma,* No. 211 (avril 1969), pp. 41-43.

45. Ibid., p. 44.

46. Ibid.

47. See Louis Marcorelles, with the collaboration of Nicole Rouzet-Albagli, *Living Cinema,* trans. Isabel Quigly (London: George Allen & Unwin Ltd., 1973), p. 149. *Cahiers'* continuing interest in *cinéma direct* can be seen in "Reportage en images, cinéma direct: L'expérience du terrain," *Cahiers du Cinéma,* No. 315 (septembre 1980), pp. 43-48; and in Serge Daney and Serge Le Péron, "Le direct en dix images," *Cahiers du Cinéma,* No. 323-24 (mai 1981), pp. 20-22. It is also evident in the magazine's praise for the films of Maurice Pialat; see in particular, Louis Skorecki, "Un mélodrame de notre temps," *Cahiers du Cinéma,* No. 303 (septembre 1979), p. 65; Jean Narboni, "Le mal est fait," and Thérèse Giraud, "Note sur PASSE TON BAC D'ABORD," *Cahiers du Cinéma,* No. 304 (octobre 1979); Pascal Bonitzer, "LOU-LOU," *Cahiers du Cinéma,* No. 316 (octobre 1980), pp. 45-47; Nathalie Heinich and Pascal Bonitzer, "A propos de LOULOU," *Cahiers du Cinéma,* No. 318 (décembre 1980), pp. 41-43; Pascal Bonitzer, "Le rayonnement-Pialat," *Cahiers du Cinéma,* No. 323-24 (mai 1981), pp. 66-67.

48. Louis Marcorelles, *Living Cinema,* p. 123.

49. Michel Ciment, "France," in Peter Cowie, ed., *International Film Guide 1975* (London: The Tantivy Press; New York: A.S. Barnes & Co., 1975), pp. 181-83.

50. Pascal Kané, "Encore sur le naturalisme," *Cahiers du Cinéma,* No. 249 (février-mars 1974), p. 36.

51. Ibid., p. 38.

52. Serge Daney, Pascal Kané, Jean-Pierre Oudart and Serge Toubiana, "Une certain tendance du cinéma française," *Cahiers du Cinéma,* No. 257 (mai-juin 1975), pp. 5-6. (The original Truffaut article by the same name is in *Cahiers du Cinéma,* No. 31 [janvier 1954], pp. 15-29.)

53. Ibid., pp. 7-8.

54. Ibid., pp. 8-11.

55. Ibid., p. 13.

56. Daniel Dayan, "The Tutor-Code of Classical Cinema," *Film Quarterly*, XXVIII (Fall, 1974), pp. 22-31.

57. Jean-Louis Baudry, "Ideological Effects of the Basic Cinematographic Apparatus," p. 45.

58. Ibid., pp. 41-42.

59. Jean-Louis Schéfer, "Sur le Déluge universel," *Cahiers du Cinéma*, No. 236-37 (mars-avril 1972), pp. 42-65.

60. Jean-Pierre Oudart, "L'effet de réel," *Cahiers du Cinéma*, No. 228 (mars-avril 1971), pp. 19-27; "Notes pour une théorie de la représentation," *Cahiers du Cinéma*, No. 229 (mai 1971), pp. 39-41; No. 230 (juillet 1971), pp. 43-45.

61. Daniel Dayan, "The Tutor-Code of Classical Cinema," p. 27.

62. Jean-Louis Baudry, "Ideological Effects of the Basic Cinematographic Apparatus," pp. 45-46.

63. Jean-Pierre Oudart, "La suture," *Cahiers du Cinéma*, No. 211 (avril 1969), pp. 36-39; No. 212 (mai 1969), pp. 50-55.

64. Ibid.

65. Jean-Pierre Oudart, "Un discours en défaut," *Cahiers du Cinéma*, No. 237 (octobre 1971), pp. 5-12.

66. Serge Daney and Jean-Pierre Oudart, "Le nom-de-l'auteur," *Cahiers du Cinéma*, No. 234-35 (décembre 1971-janvier-février 1972), pp. 80-92.

Chapter 8

1. Pascal Bonitzer, "Film/politique," *Cahiers du Cinéma*, No. 222 (juillet 1970), pp. 33-35.

2. Ibid., p. 35.

3. Ibid., pp. 36-37.

4. Jacques Aumont, "Cinéma française, police et critique," *Cahiers du Cinéma*, No. 233 (novembre 1971), pp. 19-21.

5. Ibid., pp. 21-22.

6. Ibid., p. 22

7. Pascal Kané, "Sur deux films progressistes," *Cahiers du Cinéma*, No. 241 (septembre-octobre 1972), pp. 25-28.

8. Ibid., p. 30.

9. Serge Toubiana, "Notes sur la place du spectateur dans la fiction de gauche," *Cahiers du Cinéma*, No. 275 (avril 1977), pp. 47-48.

10. Ibid., pp. 48-51.

11. Serge Toubiana, "Notes sur la place du spectateur (suite)," *Cahiers du Cinéma*, No. 276 (mai 1977), pp. 16-17.

12. Ibid., p. 20.

13. Ibid., p. 19.

14. "Russie années vingt," *Cahiers du Cinéma*, Numéro spécial 220-21 (mai-juin 1970).

15. Bertolt Brecht, "Extraits du journal de travail (inédit)," *Cahiers du Cinéma*, No. 254-55 (décembre 1974-janvier 1975), pp. 84-94; No. 256 (février-mars 1975), pp. 52-57.

16. Jean-Marie Straub, "Férore," *Cahiers du Cinéma*, No. 207 (décembre 1968), p. 35.

17. Jean-Louis Comolli, "Rhétorique de la terreur," *Cahiers du Cinéma*, No. 207 (décembre 1968), pp. 42-44.

18. Jean-Louis Comolli, "LES PAGES DU LIVRE DE SATAN," *Cahiers du Cinéma*, No. 207 (décembre 1968), pp. 66-67.

19. Pascal Bonitzer, Jean-Louis Comolli, Serge Daney, Jean Narboni, and Jean-Pierre Oudart, "LA VIE EST A NOUS, film militant," *Cahiers du Cinéma*, No. 218 (mars 1970), pp. 45-51.

20. William Guynn, "The Political Program of *Cahiers du Cinéma*, 1969-1977," pp. 32-33.

21. Pascal Bonitzer, Jean-Louis Comolli, Serge Daney, Jean Narboni, and Jean-Pierre Oudart, "LA VIE EST A NOUS, film militant," pp. 45-47.

22. Ibid., p. 47.

23. Ibid., p. 48.

24. Ibid., p. 49.

25. Ibid.

26. "John Ford's YOUNG MR. LINCOLN," *Screen*, XIII (Autumn, 1972), pp. 5-7; also in *Cahiers du Cinéma*, No. 223 (août 1970).

27. Ibid., p. 8.

28. Ibid., p. 14.

29. Ibid., pp. 15-19.

30. "MOROCCO de Josef von Sternberg," *Cahiers du Cinéma*, No. 225 (novembre-décembre 1970), pp. 5-13.

31. Pascal Kané, "Relecture du cinéma hollywoodien: SYLVIA SCARLETT," *Cahiers du Cinéma*, No. 238-39 (mai-juin 1972), pp. 84-90; also in English in *Sub-Stance*, No. 9 (1974).

32. Jacques Aumont, "Comment on écrit l'histoire," *Cahiers du Cinéma*, No. 238-39 (mai-juin 1972), p. 64.

33. Ibid.

34. Ibid., p. 65.

35. Roland Barthes, *Critical Essays*, pp. 41-50.

36. Jacques Aumont, "Comment on écrit l'histoire," p. 66.

37. Ibid., p. 68.

38. Ibid., p. 70.

39. Ibid., p. 70-71.

40. François Regnault, "LES CAMISARDS et le film d'histoire," *Cahiers du Cinéma*, No. 238-39 (mai-juin 1972), pp. 71-72.

41. Ibid., p. 74.

42. Pascal Kané, "Cinéma et Histoire: L'effet d'étrangeté," *Cahiers du Cinéma*, No. 254-55 (décembre 1974-janvier 1975), pp. 77-79.

43. Ibid., pp. 80-81.

44. Ibid., p. 81.

45. Ibid., p. 82.

46. Ibid., pp. 82-83.

47. Ibid., p. 83.

48. Ibid.

49. Bernard Sichère, "La bête et le militant," *Cahiers du Cinéma*, No. 251-52 (juillet-août 1974), p. 19.

50. Ibid., pp. 19-20.

51. Ibid., pp. 20-23.

52. Ibid., pp. 23-24.

53. Ibid., pp. 24-26.

54. Ibid., pp. 27-28. Pascal Bonitzer develops similar ideas in his reviews of LACOMBE LUCIEN (1974) and THE NIGHT PORTER. See *Le regard et la voix*, pp. 87-117.

55. Jean-Loup Rivière, "La race qua.," *Cahiers du Cinéma*, No. 274 (mars 1977), p. 26.

56. Ibid., pp. 26-27.

57. *Cahiers du Cinéma* discusses HOLOCAUST at great length in several articles in its June 1979 issue (No. 301).

58. Louis Skorecki, "L'amour n'est pas plus fort que l'argent," *Cahiers du Cinéma*, No. 322 (avril 1981), pp. 11-14.

59. Serge Daney, "L'état-Syberberg"; Pascal Bonitzer, "Les dieux et les quarks"; Jean-Louis Comolli and François Géré, "La real-fiction du pouvoir."

60. Jean-Pierre Oudart, "Notes de mémoire sur HITLER, de Syberberg," *Cahiers du Cinéma*, No. 294 (novembre 1978), p. 5.

61. Ibid., pp. 7-9.

62. Ibid., p. 13.

63. Ibid., p. 15.

Chapter 9

1. Jean Narboni, "Le Pirée pour un homme," *Cahiers du Cinéma*, No. 210 (mars 1969), p. 54.

2. Ibid., pp. 54-55.

3. Ibid., p. 55.

4. Ibid.

5. Jean-Louis Comolli, "Film/politique (2); L'AVEAU: 15 propositions," *Cahiers du Cinéma,* No. 224 (octobre 1970), p. 48.

6. Ibid.

7. Ibid.

8. Ibid.

9. Ibid.

10. Ibid., p. 49.

11. Ibid.

12. Ibid.

13. Ibid.

14. Ibid.

15. Ibid.

16. Ibid.

17. Ibid., p. 50.

18. Ibid., p. 50-51.

19. Ibid., p. 51.

20. Ibid.

21. Pascal Bonitzer and Serge Toubiana, "ETAT DE SIEGE," *Cahiers du Cinéma,* No. 245-46 (avril-mai-juin 1973), p. 49.

22. Ibid., p. 50.

23. Ibid.

24. Ibid., p. 52.

25. Ibid., pp. 52-53.

26. Ibid., pp. 53-54.

27. Serge Toubiana, "... Mais qui raisonne," *Cahiers du Cinéma,* No. 258-59 (juillet-août 1975), pp. 43-46.

28. See in particular, Robert Benayoun, "Les enfants du paradigme," *Positif,* No. 122 (décembre 1970), p. 22.

29. Jean Narboni, "La vicariance du pouvoir," *Cahiers du Cinéma,* No. 224 (octobre 1970), pp. 43-44.

30. Ibid., p. 45.

31. Ibid.

32. Ibid.

33. Ibid., p. 46.

34. Narboni considers this a rejection of the notion found in *Cinéthique* that direct sound is only another branch of cinematic illusionism; the existence of random, natural, and artificial

noises on the sound track (particularly the latter, which have no existence apart from the world of the microphone) reemphasizes the man-made nature of the spectacle.

35. Jean Narboni, "La vicariance du pouvoir," pp. 46-47.

36. See Serge Daney, "Un tombeau pour l'oeil," *Cahiers du Cinéma*, No. 258-259 (juillet-août 1975), pp. 28-35; Serge Daney, "Le plan straubien," *Cahiers du Cinéma*, No. 305 (novembre 1979), pp. 5-7; Pascal Bonitzer, "J.-M.S. et J.-L. G.," *Cahiers du Cinéma*, No. 264 (février 1976), pp. 5-10. An interesting connection between the early *Cahiers du Cinéma* and Jean-Marie Straub can be seen in Jacques Doniol-Valcroze, "Straub, vingt-quatre ans après Antonioni," *Pariscop*, No. 599 (14 novembre 1979), p. 6.

37. Jean Narboni, "Là," *Cahiers du Cinéma*, No. 275 (avril 1977), p. 11.

38. Jacques Aumont, Pascal Bonitzer, Jean-Louis Comolli, Jean-André Fieschi, Jean Narboni, and Sylvie Pierre, "Débat," *Cahiers du Cinéma*, No. 225 (novembre-décembre 1970), pp. 17-27.

39. Ibid., p. 18.

40. Ibid., p. 23.

41. Ibid., p. 19.

42. Ibid., pp. 19-20.

43. Ibid., p. 20.

44. Ibid., p. 24.

45. "MILESTONES et nous," *Cahiers du Cinéma*, No. 258-59 (juillet-août 1975), p. 61.

46. Serge Toubiana, "Robert Kramer," *Cahiers du Cinéma*, No. 295 (décembre 1978), pp. 17-18.

47. "MILESTONES et nous," *Cahiers du Cinéma*, No. 258-59 (juillet-août 1975), p. 73.

48. Ibid., pp. 73-74.

49. Ibid., p. 74.

50. Serge Daney, "L'aquarium," *Cahiers du Cinéma*, No. 264 (février 1976), pp. 55-59; Jean-Pierre Oudart, "A propos d'ORANGE MECANIQUE, Kubrick, Kramer et quelques autres," *Cahiers du Cinéma*, No. 293 (octobre 1978), pp. 55-58.

51. Groupe Lou Sin d'intervention idéologique, "Les luttes de classe en France; Deux films: COUP POUR COUP, TOUT VA BIEN," *Cahiers du Cinéma*, No. 238-39 (mai-juin 1972), p. 5.

52. Ibid., p. 8.

53. Ibid., pp. 8-9.

54. Ibid., p. 9.

55. Ibid., pp. 10-11.

56. Ibid., p. 11.

57. Ibid., p. 13.

58. Ibid., p. 14.

59. Ibid., p. 15.

60. Ibid., pp. 16-17.

61. Ibid., p. 18.

62. Ibid.

63. Ibid., p. 20.

64. Ibid.

65. Ibid.

66. Ibid., pp. 20-21.

67. Ibid., pp. 21-22.

68. Ibid., pp. 22-23.

69. Ibid., pp. 23-24.

70. Pascal Bonitzer, "Film/politique," pp. 33-35.

71. Pierre Baudry, "La critique et TOUT VA BIEN," *Cahiers du Cinéma,* No. 240 (juillet-août 1972), pp. 10-18.

72. Serge Daney, "Fonction critique (2)," *Cahiers du Cinéma,* No. 249 (février-mars 1974), pp. 26-27.

73. Ibid., p. 28.

74. Ibid., p. 29.

Chapter 10

1. "Editorial," *Cahiers du Cinéma,* No. 285 (février 1978); "Chronologie (sélective)," *Cahiers du Cinéma,* No. 323-24 (mai 1981), pp. 23-25.

2. "Editorial," *Cahiers du Cinéma,* No. 285 (février 1978).

3. Sylvie Pierre, "Des douleurs des uns et du bonheur des autres (A propos de BYE BYE BRASIL)," *Cahiers du Cinéma,* No. 319 (janvier 1981), p. 44.

4. Pascal Bonitzer, "Juste une image," *Cahiers du Cinéma,* No. 323-24 (mai 1981), p. 17.

5. Louis Skorecki, "Contre la nouvelle cinéphilie," *Cahiers du Cinéma,* No. 293 (octobre 1978), pp. 31-50.

6. Ibid., pp. 45-52.

7. Pascal Kané, "Reponse a 'C.N.C.'," *Cahiers du Cinéma,* No. 293 (octobre 1978), pp. 52-54.

8. Bernard Boland, "Sur PASSE-MONTAGNE, film français," *Cahiers du Cinéma,* No. 298 (mars 1979), pp. 39-41.

9. Ibid., pp. 41-44.

10. Ibid., p. 45.

11. Jean-Pierre Oudart, "A propos d'ORANGE MECANIQUE, Kubrick, Kramer et quelques autres," *Cahiers du Cinéma,* No. 293 (octobre 1978), pp. 55-58.

12. Ibid., pp. 57-58.

13. Serge Daney, in a 1977 interview, lists the American filmmakers who currently interest him: "Kramer, Cassavetes, Paul Newman (why is he no longer doing anything?), Dwoskin, Hellman, etc." See T.L. French, ed., *Cahiers du Cinéma* (New York: The Thousand Eyes, 1977), pp. 30-31. In listing the most important films from the 1970's, four out of eight *Cahiers du Cinéma* critics mentioned a film by either Newman or Cassavetes or both. See "Les films marquants de la décennie (1970-1980), *Cahiers du Cinéma*, No. 308 (février 1980), pp. 44-47. In a similar set of lists for the best films of 1981, several of *Cahiers'* critics mention Cassavetes' GLORIA. See "Les 10 meilleurs films de l'année 1981," *Cahiers du Cinéma*, No. 332 (février 1982), pp. 48-49. About Cassavetes, see also Yann Lardeau,"LE BAL DES VAURIENS," *Cahiers du Cinéma*, No. 289 (juin 1978), pp. 41-45; and Louis Skorecki, "Sans famille," *Cahiers du Cinéma*, No. 320 (février 1981), pp. 45-48.

14. Bernard Boland, "Sur PASSE-MONTAGNE, film français," p. 42.

15. François Regnault, "Plaidoyer pro Niro," *Cahiers du Cinéma*, No. 286 (mars 1978), p. 51.

16. Ibid., p. 51.

17. Serge Le Péron, "Ici ou ailleurs," *Cahiers du Cinéma*, No. 273 (janvier-février 1977), p. 47.

18. Jean-Louis Comolli, "Un corps en trop," *Cahiers du Cinéma*, No. 278 (juillet 1977), pp. 6-8.

19. Ibid., pp. 8-16.

20. "Les Acteurs," *Cahiers du Cinéma*, No. 323-24 (mai 1981), p. 97.

21. *Cahiers du Cinéma*, No. 334-335 (avril 1982).

22. Jacques Doniol-Valcroze, "Les titres auxquels vous avez échappé," *Cahiers du Cinéma*, No. 323-24 (mai 1981), pp. 5-6.

23. Pascal Bonitzer and Serge Daney, "Entretien avec Eric Rohmer," *Cahiers du Cinéma*, No. 323-24 (mai 1981), pp. 28-41; Serge Daney and Jean Narboni, "Entretien avec Jacques Rivette," *Cahiers du Cinéma*, No. 323-24 (mai 1981), pp. 42-51; Jean-Claude Biette, "Claude Chabrol; l'homme centre," *Cahiers du Cinéma*, No. 323-24 (mai 1981), p. 93.

24. Serge Daney, "Le cru et le cuit," *Cahiers du Cinéma*, No. 323-24 (mai 1981), pp. 10-14.

25. Pascal Bonitzer, "Juste une image," p. 15.

26. Ibid., p. 18.

27. "Les 10 meilleurs films de l'année 1981," *Cahiers du Cinéma*, No. 332 (février 1982), pp. 48-49.

28. Pascal Bonitzer, "LA CHAMBRE VERTE," *Cahiers du Cinéma*, No. 288 (mai 1978), pp. 40-42.

29. Bernard Boland, "L'image et le corps," *Cahiers du Cinéma*, No. 279-80 (août-septembre 1977), pp. 52-54; Bernard Boland and Serge Daney, "L'AMOUR EN FUITE," *Cahiers du Cinéma*, No. 298 (mars 1979), pp. 55-57. See also Yann Lardeau, "Une nuit au théâtre," *Cahiers du Cinéma*, No. 315 (septembre 1980), pp. 19-20; and Pascal Kané, "Qui y a-t-il sous les jupes des femmes?" *Cahiers du Cinéma*, No. 329 (novembre 1981), pp. 51-52.

30. Serge Toubiana, "Truffaut ou le juste milieu comme expérience limite," *Cahiers du Cinéma*, No. 315 (septembre 1980), pp. 5-6.

31. Ibid.

32. Pascal Bonitzer, "Glorieuses bassesses," *Cahiers du Cinéma*, No. 272 (décembre 1976), pp. 26-30.

33. François Géré, "Poor and Lonesome," *Cahiers du Cinéma*, No. 297 (avril 1979), pp. 44-46.

34. Pascal Bonitzer, "La carte cachée ou les absents ont toujours raison," *Cahiers du Cinéma*, No. 322 (avril 1981), pp. 5-8.

35. See, on Dreyer—Jean-Pierre Oudart, "Une peur active," *Cahiers du Cinéma*, No. 292 (septembre 1978), pp. 61-62; on Mizoguchi—Pascal Bonitzer, "Violence et latêralité," *Cahiers du Cinéma*, No. 319 (janvier 1981), pp. 27-34; on Fuller—Serge Daney, "La fureur du récit," *Cahiers du Cinéma*, No. 311 (mai 1980), pp. 13-14; on Tati—the collection of articles in No. 303 (septembre 1979); on Rossellini—Jean Narboni, "ALLEMAGNE ANNEE ZERO," *Cahiers du Cinéma*, No. 289 (juin 1978), p. 47.

36. T.L. French, "The Tinkerers," in T.L. French, ed., *Cahiers du Cinéma*, p. 15.

37. Jean-Claude Biette, "Allan Dwan ou le cinéma nature, *Cahiers du Cinéma*, No. 332 (février 1982), pp. 21-22. Biette is one of the more interesting critics to become prominent in *Cahiers du Cinéma* in the late 1970's. Biette's work as a critic has tended toward the analysis of revived films by older filmmakers, such as Jacques Tourneur, and he has been a film programmer for the Action-République revival house in Paris, as well as a filmmaker himself. One of Biette's most interesting pieces of criticism is his defense of Claude Autant-Lara's GLORIA (1977), a film very much ridiculed by the majority of French critics. Autant-Lara had been, of course, a main object of abuse by François Truffaut in his famous "A Certain Tendency in the French Cinema"; Biette praises Autant-Lara's adherence to traditional, old-fashioned, even "dino-sauric" modes of filmmaking, even while comparing GLORIA to Godard's NUMERO DEUX (1975). See Jean-Claude Biette, "Imaginez deux enfants . . . ," *Cahiers du Cinéma*, No. 282 (novembre 1977). pp. 33-37. As a filmmaker, Biette's work, including LE THEATRE DES MATIERES (1977) and LOIN DE MANHATTAN (1982) have been much admired by the *Cahiers du Cinéma* critics. See Serge Daney, "Eloge d'Emma Thiers (J.-C. Biette et le réalisme)," *Cahiers du Cinéma*, No. 285 (février 1978), pp. 31-35.

38. Jean-Claude Biette, "Le cinéma se rapproche de la terre," *Cahiers du Cinéma*, No. 332 (février 1982), p. 7.

39. Ibid.

40. Ibid., p. 8.

41. See Chapter 3.

Bibliography

Sources in *Cahiers du Cinéma*

While early issues of *Cahiers* are given volume numbers, this practice has been discontinued by the magazine in recent years. For the sake of consistency, therefore, all articles will be listed by the number of the individual issue and its date. Included below are also English translations of articles originally appearing in *Cahiers du Cinéma*.

Ayfre, Amédée. "Néo-réalisme et phénoménologie." No. 17 (novembre 1972), pp. 6-18.

Aumont, Jacques. "Cinéma française, police et critique." No. 233 (novembre 1971), pp. 19-23.

———. "Comment on écrit l'histoire," No. 238-39 (mai-juin 1972), pp. 64-71.

———. "Groupe 3: Les acquis théoriques—premier bilan du groupe." No. 244 (février-mars 1973), pp. 40-43.

Aumont, Jacques; Bonitzer, Pascal; Comolli, Jean-Louis; Fieschi, Jean-André; Narboni, Jean; and Pierre, Sylvie. "Débat." No. 225 (novembre-décembre 1970), pp. 17-27.

Baudry, Pierre. "La critique et TOUT VA BIEN." No. 240 (juillet-août 1972), pp. 10-18.

Biette, Jean-Claude. "Allan Dwan ou le cinéma nature." No. 332 (février 1982), pp. 21-22.

———. "Le cinéma se rapproache de la terre." No. 332 (février 1982), pp. 7-8.

———. "Claude Chabrol; l'homme centre." No. 323-24 (mai 1981), p. 93.

———. "Imaginez deux enfants..." No. 282 (novembre 1977), pp. 33-37.

Boland, Bernard. "L'image et le corps." No. 279-80 (août-septembre 1977), pp. 52-54.

———. "Sur PASSE-MONTAGNE, film français." No. 298 (mars 1979), pp. 39-45.

Boland, Bernard and Daney, Serge. "L'AMOUR EN FUITE." No. 298 (mars 1979), pp. 55-57.

Bonitzer, Pascal. "La carte cachée ou les absents ont toujours raison." No. 322 (avril 1981), pp. 5-8.

———. "LA CHAMBRE VERTE." No. 288 (mai 1978), pp. 40-42.

———. "Décadrages." No. 284 (janvier 1978), pp. 7-15.

———. "Les deux regards." No. 275 (avril 1977), pp. 40-46.

———. "Les dieux et les quarks." No. 295 (décembre 1978), pp. 5-7.

———. "L'espace politique." No. 249 (février-mars 1974), pp. 40-42.

———. "Fétichisme de la technique: La notion de plan." No. 233 (novembre 1971), pp. 4-10.

———. "Film/politique." No. 222 (juillet 1970), pp. 33-38.

———. "Glorieuses bassesses." No. 272 (décembre 1976), pp. 26-30.

———. "Hors-champ (un espace en défaut)." No. 234-35 (décembre 1971-janvier 1972), pp. 15-26.

———. "J.-M. S. et J.-L. G." No. 264 (février 1976), pp. 5-10.

———. "Juste une image." No. 323-24 (mai 1981), pp. 16-19.

———. "LOULOU." No. 316 (octobre 1980), pp. 45-47.

———. "Le rayonnement-Pialat." No. 323-24 (mai 1981), p. 66.

———. "'Réalité' de la dénotation." No. 229 (mai 1971), pp. 39-41.

———. *Le regard et la voix.* Paris: 10/18, 1976.

———. "La surimage." No. 270 (septembre-octobre 1976), pp. 29-34.

———. "Violence et latéralité." No. 319 (janvier 1981), pp. 27-34.

———. "La vision partielle." No. 301 (juin 1979), pp. 35-41. Also in English as "Partial Vision," in *Wide Angle,* IV, 4 (1981), pp. 56-63.

———. "Voici." No. 273 (janvier-février 1977), pp. 5-18.

Bonitzer, Pascal; Comolli, Jean-Louis; Daney, Serge; Narboni, Jean; and Oudart, Jean-Pierre. "LA VIE EST A NOUS, film militant." No. 218 (mars 1970), pp. 45-51.

Bonitzer, Pascal and Daney, Serge. "L'écran du fantasme." No. 236-37 (mars-avril 1972), pp. 31-40.

———. "Entretien avec Eric Rohmer," No. 323-24 (mai 1981), pp. 28-41.

Bonitzer, Pascal and Toubiana, Serge. "ETAT DE SIEGE." No. 245-46 (avril-mai-juin 1973), pp. 49-54.

Bré, Pierre-Richard. "Des photos fanées." No. 152 (février 1964), pp. 69-71.

Brecht, Bertolt. "Extraits du journal de travail (inédit)." No. 254-55 (décembre 1974-janvier 1975), pp. 84-94; No. 256 (février-mars 1975), pp. 52-57.

———. "Notes sur l'opéra *Grandeur et décadence de la ville de Mahagonny.*" No. 238-39 (mai-juin 1972), pp. 28-32.

———. "Sur le système cinématographique." No. 114 (décembre 1960), pp. 14-20.

Burch, Noël. *Theory of Film Practice.* Translated by Helen R. Lane. Introduction by Annette Michelson. New York, Washington: Praeger Publishers, 1973.

Comolli, Jean-Louis. "LA CECILIA." No. 262-63 (janvier 1976), pp. 69-78.

———. "Contrariwise." *Cahiers du Cinéma in English,* No. 3 (1966), pp. 57-58. Also in *Cahiers du Cinéma,* No. 168 (juillet 1965).

———. "Un corps en trop." No. 278 (juillet 1977), pp. 5-16.

———. "Dernier acte, encore." No. 215 (septembre 1969), pp. 55-59.

———. "Le détour par le direct." No. 209 (février 1969), pp. 48-53; No. 211 (avril 1969), pp. 40-45. Also in English in Williams, Christopher, ed. *Realism and the Cinema.* London and Henley: Routledge and Kegan Paul, 1980, pp. 225-43.

———. "L'esprit d'aventure." No. 154 (avril 1964), pp. 11-14.

———. "Film/politique (2): L'AVEAU: 15 propositions." No. 224 (octobre 1970), pp. 43-47.

———. "Les miettes de l'existence." No. 166-67 (mai-juin 1965), p. 128.

———. "Notes on the New Spectator." *Cahiers du Cinéma in English,* No. 7 (January, 1967), p. 61. Also in *Cahiers du Cinéma,* No. 177 (avril 1966).

———. "LES PAGES DU LIVRE DE SATAN." No. 207 (décembre 1968), pp. 66-67.

———. "Le point sur l'image." No. 194 (octobre 1967), pp. 29-30.

———. "Rhétorique de la terreur." No. 207 (décembre 1968), pp. 42-44.

———. "Secrète Agente." No. 164 (mars 1965), p. 84.

———. "Technique et idéologie: Caméra, perspectif, profondeur de champ." No. 229 (mai 1971), pp. 4-21; No. 230 (juillet 1971), pp. 51-57; No. 231 (août-septembre 1971), pp. 42-49; No. 233 (novembre 1971), pp. 39-45; No. 234-35 (décembre 1971-janvier-février 1972), pp. 94-100; No. 241 (septembre-octobre 1972), pp. 20-24. No. 229, pp. 4-15, also in English in *Film Reader 2* (1977), pp. 128-40.

———. "Vivre le film." No. 141 (mars 1963), pp. 14-29.

Comolli, Jean-Louis and Géré, François. "Deux fictions de la haine." No. 286 (mars 1978), pp. 31-47; No. 288 (mai 1978), pp. 5-15; No. 290-91 (juillet-août 1978), pp. 89-98.

———. "La real-fiction du pouvoir." No. 293 (octobre 1978), pp. 24-27.

Comolli, Jean-Louis and Narboni, Jean. "Cinéma/idéologie/critique." No. 216 (octobre 1969), pp. 11-15; No. 217 (novembre 1969), pp. 7-13.

Daney, Serge. "Anti-rétro (suite); Fonction critique (fin)." No. 253 (octobre-novembre 1974), pp. 30-36.

———. "L'aquarium." No. 264 (février 1976), pp. 55-59.

———. "Le cru et le cuit." No. 323-24 (mai 1981), pp. 10-14.

———. "La dé-faite." No. 196 (décembre 1967), pp. 63-64.

———. "Eloge d'Emma Thiers (J.-C. Biette et le réalisme)." No. 285 (février 1978), pp. 31-35.

———. "L'état-Syberberg." No. 292 (septembre 1978), pp. 5-7.

———. "Fonction critique." No. 248 (1973), pp. 39-40; No. 249 (février-mars 1974), pp. 26-29.

———. "La fureur du récit." No. 311 (mai 1980), pp. 13-14.

———. "Le plan straubien." No. 305 (novembre 1979), pp. 5-7.

———. "Un tombeau pour l'oeil." No. 258-259 (juillet-août 1975), pp. 28-35.

Daney, Serge; Kané, Pascal; Oudart, Jean-Pierre; and Toubiana, Serge. "Une certaine tendance du cinéma française." No. 257 (mai-juin 1975), pp. 5-13.

Daney, Serge and Le Péron, Serge. "Le direct en dix images." No. 323-24 (mai 1981), pp. 20-22.

Daney, Serge and Narboni, Jean. "Entretien avec Jacques Rivette." No. 323-24 (mai 1981), pp. 42-51.

Daney, Serge and Oudart, Jean-Pierre. "Le nom-de-l'auteur." No. 234-35 (décembre 1971-janvier-février 1972), pp. 80-92.

Delahaye, Michel. "La règle de Rouch." No. 121 (juin 1961), pp. 1-11.

Domarchi, Jean. "L'homme des cavernes." No. 149 (novembre 1963), pp. 65-66.

Doniol-Valcroze, Jacques. "Un buisson de questions." No. 152 (février 1964), pp. 64-66.

———. "Les titres auxquels vous avez echappé." No. 323-24 (mai 1981), pp. 5-6.

Dort, Bernard. "Pour une critique brechtienne du cinéma." No. 114 (décembre 1960), pp. 33-43.

Editors of *Cahiers du Cinéma.* "Les Acteurs." No. 323-24 (mai 1981), p. 97.

———. "Chronologie (sélective)." No. 323-24 (mai 1981), pp. 23-25.

———. "Les 10 meilleurs films de l'année 1981." No. 322 (février 1982), pp. 48-49.

———. "Débat." No. 225 (novembre-décembre 1970), pp. 17-27.

———. "Editorial." No. 114 (décembre 1960), p. 2.

———. "Editorial." No. 244 (février-mars 1973), p. 5.

———. "Editorial." No. 285 (février 1978).

———. "Les films marquants de la décennie (1970-1980)." No. 308 (février 1980), pp. 44-47.

———. "La 'groupe Dziga-Vertov.'" No. 240 (juillet-août 1972), pp. 4-9.

———. "John Ford's YOUNG MR. LINCOLN." *Screen,* XIII (Autumn, 1972), pp. 5-44. Also in *Cahiers du Cinéma,* No. 223 (août 1970).

———. "MILESTONES et nous." No. 258-59 (juillet-août 1975), pp. 60-74.

———. "MOROCCO de Josef von Sternberg." No. 225 (novembre-décembre 1970), pp. 5-13.

———. "Reportage en images, cinéma direct: L'expérience du terrain." No. 315 (septembre 1980), pp. 43-48.

Fieschi, Jean-André. "Si nos brechtiens..." No. 143 (mai 1963), p. 57-62.

"Film et roman: Problèmes de récit." Numéro spécial 185 (décembre 1966).

Géré, François. "Poor and Lonesome." No. 297 (avril 1979), pp. 44-46.

Giraud, Thérèse. "Note sur PASSE TON BAC D'ABORD." No. 304 (octobre 1979).

Godard, Jean-Luc. "Review of Astruc's UNE VIE." In *The New Wave,* pp. 81-83. Edited by Peter Graham. Garden City, N.Y.: Doubleday & Company Inc., 1968. Also in *Cahiers du Cinéma,* No. 89 (novembre 1958).

Groupe Lou Sin d'intervention idéologique. "Les luttes de classe en France; Deux films: COUP POUR COUP, TOUT VA BIEN." No. 238-39 (mai-juin 1972), pp. 5-24.

Heinich, Natalie and Bonitzer, Pascal. "A propos de LOULOU." No. 318 (décembre 1980), pp. 41-43.

Hoyveda, Fereydoun. "Cinéma Vérité ou Réalisme Fantastique." No. 125 (novembre 1961), pp. 33-41.

———. "L'eau et le miroir." No. 137 (novembre 1962), pp. 35-40.

———. "Le plus grand anneau." No. 95 (mai 1959), pp. 40-47.

Joly, Jacques. "Un nouveau réalisme." No. 131 (mai 1962), pp. 3-14.

Kané, Pascal. "Cinéma et Histoire: L'effet d'étrangeté." No. 254-55 (décembre 1974-janvier 1975), pp. 77-83.

———. "Encore sur le naturalisme." No. 249 (février-mars 1974), pp. 34-38.

———. "Point de vue." No. 301 (juin 1979), pp. 12-14.

———. "Qui y a-t-il sous les jupes des femmes?" No. 329 (novembre 1981), pp. 51-52.

———. "Relecture du cinéma hollywoodien: SYLVIA SCARLETT." No. 238-39 (mai-juin 1972), pp. 84-90. Also in English in *Sub-Stance*, No. 9 (1974).

———. "Réponse à 'C.N.C.'" No. 293 (octobre 1978), pp. 52-54.

———. "Sur deux films progressistes." No. 241 (septembre-octobre 1972), pp. 25-30.

Labarthe, André S. "Le plus pur regard." No. 108 (juin 1960), pp. 47-50.

Lardeau, Yann. "LE BAL DES VAURIENS." No. 289 (juin 1978), pp. 41-45.

———. "Une nuit au théâtre." No. 315 (septembre 1980), pp. 19-20.

Le Péron, Serge. "Ici ou ailleurs." No. 273 (janvier-février 1977), pp. 44-47.

Losey, Joseph. "L'oeil du maître." No. 114 (décembre 1960), pp. 21-32.

Marcorelles, Louis. "A l'école de la 'dramaturgie'." No. 106 (avril 1960), pp. 57-59.

———. "Au pied du mur." No. 116 (février 1961), pp. 51-53.

———. "D'un art moderne." No. 114 (décembre 1960), pp. 44-53.

———. "Elia Kazan et l'Actors' Studio." No. 66 (Noël 1956), pp. 42-44.

———. "Gehalt und Gestalt." No. 127 (janvier 1962), pp. 57-60.

———. "L'impossible gageure." No. 77 (décembre 1957), pp. 52-55.

———. "Strip tease polonais." No. 102 (décembre 1959), pp. 55-57.

Mardore, Michel. "Age of Gold (Buñuel), Age of Iron (Rossellini)." *Cahiers du Cinéma in English*, No. 3 (1966), pp. 47-50. Also in *Cahiers du Cinéma*, No. 175 (février 1966).

———. "La douce-amère." No. 149 (novembre 1963), pp. 63-65.

Martin, Paul-Louis. "D'un Tati l'autre." No. 199 (mars 1968), pp. 27-28.

Moullet, Luc. "France aliénée et France consciente." No. 182 (septembre 1966), pp. 72-73.

Mourlet, Michel. "Apologie de la violence." No. 107 (mai 1960), pp. 24-27.

———. "Beauté de la connaissance." No. 111 (septembre 1960), pp. 34-38.

Narboni, Jean. "ALLEMAGNE ANNEE ZERO." No. 289 (juin 1978), p. 47.

———. "Là." No. 275 (avril 1977), pp. 6-14.

———. "Le mal est fait." No. 304 (octobre 1979), pp. 5-6.

———. "Le Pirée pour un homme." No. 210 (mars 1969), pp. 54-55.

———. "La vicariance du pouvoir." No. 224 (octobre 1970), pp. 43-47.

Narboni, Jean; Pierre, Sylvie; and Rivette, Jacques. "Montage." No. 210 (mars 1969), pp. 17-34.

Oudart, Jean-Pierre. "A propos d'ORANGE MECANIQUE, Kubrick, Kramer et quelques autres." No. 293 (octobre 1978), pp. 55-58.

———. "Un discours en défaut." No. 237 (octobre 1971), pp. 5-12.

———. "L'effet de réel." No. 228 (mars-avril 1971), pp. 19-27.

———. "Notes de mémoire sur HITLER, de Syberberg." No. 294 (novembre 1978), pp. 5-15.

———. "Notes pour une théorie de la représentation (suite)." No. 229 (mai 1971), pp. 39-41; No. 230 (juillet 1971), pp. 43-45.

———. "Une peur active." No. 292 (septembre 1978), pp. 61-62.

———. "La suture." No. 211 (avril 1969), pp. 36-39; No. 212 (mai 1969), pp. 50-55.

Pierre, Sylvie. "Des douleurs des uns et du bonheur des autres (A propos de BYE BYE BRASIL)." No. 319 (janvier 1981), pp. 44-46.

Regnault, François. "LES CAMISARDS et le film d'histoire." No. 238-39 (mai-juin 1972), pp. 71-74.

_____. "Plaidoyer pro Niro." No. 286 (mars 1978), pp. 49-51.

Rivette, Jacques. "De l'abjection." No. 120 (juin 1961), pp. 54-55.

_____. "En attendant les Godons." No. 73 (juillet 1957), pp. 38-40.

_____. "L'essentiel." No. 32 (février 1954), pp. 42-45.

_____. "Lettre sur Rossellini." No. 46 (avril 1955), pp. 14-24.

_____. "Notes sur une révolution." No. 54 (Noël 1955), pp. 17-21.

_____. "Petit journal du cinéma: Revoir Verdoux." No. 146 (août 1963), pp. 42-43.

_____. "La recherche de l'absolu." No. 52 (novembre 1955), pp. 45-47.

Rivière, Jean-Loup. "La race qua." No. 274 (mars 1977), pp. 23-32.

Rohmer, Eric. "Le celluloïd et le marbre, I: Le Bandit Philosophe." No. 44 (février 1955), pp. 1-6.

_____. "Le celluloïd et le marbre, II: Le siècle des peintres." No. 49 (juillet 1955), pp. 10-15.

_____. "Le celluloïd et le marbre, III: De la métaphore." No. 51 (octobre 1955), pp. 2-9.

_____. "Le celluloïd et le marbre, IV: Beau comme la musique." No. 52 (novembre 1955), pp. 23-29.

_____. "L'hélice et l'idée." No. 93 (mars 1959), pp. 48-50.

"Russie années vingt." Numéro spécial 220-21 (mai-juin 1970).

Schéfer, Jean-Louis. "Sur le Déluge universel." No. 236-37 (mars-avril 1972), pp. 42-65.

Schérer, Maurice. "A qui la faute?" No. 39 (octobre 1954), pp. 6-10.

_____. "Vanité que la peinture." No. 3 (juin 1951), pp. 22-29.

Serguine, Jacques. "Education du spectateur, ou L'Ecole du MacMahon." No. 111 (septembre 1960), pp. 39-45.

Sichère, Bernard. "La bête et le militant." No. 251-52 (juillet-août 1974), pp. 18-28.

Skorecki, Louis. "L'amour n'est pas plus fort que l'argent." No. 322 (avril 1981), pp. 11-14.

_____. "Contre la nouvelle cinéphilie." No. 293 (octobre 1978), pp. 31-52.

_____. "Un mélodrame de notre temps." No. 303 (septembre 1979), p. 65.

_____. "Sans famille." No. 320 (février 1981), pp. 45-48.

Straub, Jean-Marie. "Férore." No. 207 (décembre 1968), p. 35.

Toubiana, Serge. "... Mais qui raisonne." No. 258-59 (juillet-août 1975), pp. 43-46.

_____. "Notes sur la place du spectateur dans la fiction de gauche." No. 275 (avril 1977), pp. 47-51; No. 276 (mai 1977), pp. 15-20.

_____. "Robert Kramer." No. 295 (décembre 1978), pp. 17-18.

_____. "Truffaut ou le juste milieu comme expérience limite." No. 315 (septembre 1980), pp. 5-6.

Truffaut, François. "Une certain tendance du cinéma française." No. 31 (janvier 1954), pp. 15-29. Also in English as "A Certain Tendency in the French Cinema," in Bill Nichols, ed. *Movies and Methods.* Berkeley, Los Angeles and London: University of California Press, 1976, pp. 224-36.

Vechialli, Paul. "La guerre tout court." No. 145 (juillet 1963), pp. 52-54.

Weyergans, François. "Lola au Pays des Hommes." No. 117 (mars 1961), pp. 25-31.

_____. "Le verbe treize." No. 149 (novembre 1963), pp. 61-62.

Other Sources

Althusser, Louis. *For Marx.* Translated by Ben Brewster. New York: Pantheon Books, 1969.

Barthes, Roland. *Critical Essays.* Translated from the French by Richard Howard. Evanston, Illinois: Northwestern University Press, 1972.

_____. "Diderot, Brecht, Eisenstein." *Screen,* XV (Summer, 1974), pp. 33-39.

_____. "Rhétorique de l'image." *Communications,* No. 4 (1964), pp. 40-51. Also in English in *Image-Music-Text.* New York: Hill and Wang, 1977, pp. 32-51.

Barthes, Roland and Dort, Bernard. "Brecht 'traduit'." *Théâtre Populaire,* No. 23 (mars 1957), pp. 1-8.

Baudry, Jean-Louis. "Ideological Effects of the Basic Cinematographic Apparatus." *Film Quarterly,* XXVIII (Winter, 1974-75), pp. 39-47. Also in *Cinéthique,* No. 7-8 (1970).

Bazin, André. *What is Cinema?* I. Edited and translated by Hugh Gray. Berkeley and Los Angeles: University of California Press, 1967.

Benayoun, Robert. "Les enfants du paradigme." *Positif,* No. 122 (décembre 1970), pp. 7-26.

Bentley, Eric. *In Search of Theater.* New York: Alfred A. Knopf, 1953.

Brecht, Bertolt. *Brecht on Theatre: The Development of an Aesthetic.* Edited and translated by John Willet. New York: Hill and Wang, 1964.

_____. *Ecrits sur la littérature et l'art I: Sur le cinéma.* Textes français de Jean-Louis Lebrave et Jean-Pierre Lefebvre. Paris: L'Arche, 1970.

Cowie, Peter, ed. *International Film Guide 1975.* London: The Tantivy Press; New York: A.S. Barnes & Co., 1975.

_____. *International Film Guide 1976.* London: The Tantivy Press; New York: A.S. Barnes & Co., 1976.

_____. *International Film Guide 1982.* London: The Tantivy Press; San Diego and New York: A.S. Barnes & Co., 1982.

Dayan, Daniel. "The Tutor Code of Classical Cinema." *Film Quarterly,* XXVIII (Fall, 1974), pp. 22-31.

Diderot, Denis. *The Paradox of Acting.* Translated by Walter Herries Pollock. Introduction by Lee Strasberg. New York: Hill and Wang, Inc., 1957.

Doniol-Valcroze, Jacques. "Straub, vingt-quatre ans après Antonioni," *Pariscop* No. 599 (14 novembre 1979), p. 6.

Dort, Bernard. "Brecht en France." *Les Temps Modernes,* XV (juin 1960), pp. 1855-74.

"Editorial." *Screen,* XVI (Winter, 1975-76), pp. 3-4.

Elsaesser, Thomas. "French Film Culture and Critical Theory: *Cinéthique.*" *Monogram,* No. 2 (Summer, 1971), pp. 31-37.

French, T.L., ed. *Cahiers du Cinéma.* New York: The Thousand Eyes, 1977.

Funt, David. *Diderot and the Aesthetics of the Enlightenment.* Vol. XI of *Diderot Studies.* Geneva: Librairie Droz S.A., 1968.

Graham, Peter, ed. *The New Wave.* Garden City, N.Y.: Doubleday & Company Inc., 1968.

Guynn, William. "The Political Program of *Cahiers du Cinéma,* 1969-1977." *Jump Cut,* No. 17 (1978), pp. 32-35.

Harvey, Sylvia. *May '68 and Film Culture.* London: British Film Institute, 1978.

_____. "Whose Brecht? Memories for the Eighties." *Screen,* XXIII (May-June, 1982), pp. 45-59.

Losey, Joseph. "Entretien avec Joseph Losey." *Théâtre Populaire,* No. 53 (1964), pp. 3-14.

Lovell, Alan. "Epic Theater and Counter-Cinema's Principles." *Jump Cut,* No. 27 (1982), pp. 64-68.

Marcorelles, Louis, with the collaboration of Nicole Rouzet-Albagli. *Living Cinema.* Translated by Isabel Quigly. London: George Allen & Unwin Ltd., 1973.

Mathers, Peter. "Brecht in Britain: From Theatre to Television." *Screen,* XVI (Winter, 1975-76), pp. 81-93.

Metz, Christian. *Film Language: A Semiotics of the Cinema.* Translated by Michael Taylor. New York: Oxford University Press, 1974.

Mourlet, Michel. *Sur un art ignoré.* Paris: La Table Ronde, 1965.

Pétat, Jacques. "Bertolt Brecht et le cinéma." *Cinéma '75,* No. 203 (novembre 1975), pp. 66-71.

Polan, Dana B. "Brecht and the Politics of Self-Reflexive Cinema." *Jump Cut,* No. 17 (1978), pp. 29-31.

Roud, Richard. "The French Line." *Sight and Sound,* XXIX (Autumn, 1960), pp. 167-71.

Spellerberg, James. "Technology and Ideology in the Cinema." *Quarterly Review of Film Studies,* II (August, 1977), pp. 288-301.

Turim, Maureen. "The Aesthetic Becomes Political: A History of Film Criticism in *Cahiers du Cinéma.*" *The Velvet Light Trap,* No. 9 (Summer, 1973), pp. 13-17.

Vexler, Felix. *Studies in Diderot's Esthetic Naturalism.* New York: Columbia University, 1922.

Walsh, Martin. *The Brechtian Aspect of Radical Cinema.* Edited by Keith M. Griffiths. London: British Film Institute, 1981.

Index